OXFORD WORLD'S CLASSICS

EPIGRAMS FROM THE GREEK ANTHOLOGY

EPIGRAMS are the most concise form of ancient Greek poetry. Originating as inscriptions on monuments, they became a popular mode of poetic self-expression in the Hellenistic age, and were still being written a thousand years later in Christian Byzantium. In these tiny poems, ordinary Greeks grappled with the defining issues of their lives—love and sex, grief and loss, faith and despair. Epigram attracted famous names as well. Its roll-call of poets and intellectuals includes Simonides, Callimachus, Posidippus, Theocritus, Philodemus, Meleager, Lucian, and Palladas; and its brevity appealed to figures from public life, including the emperors Trajan and Hadrian. The genre throws light not merely on personal lives and emotions but also on the political, religious, and military history of Rome itself, and of the New Rome that succeeded it in the East at Constantinople.

THE GREEK ANTHOLOGY is our principal source for literary epigram, and includes as well many epigrams from monuments, such as Simonides' famous epitaphs at Thermopylae ('Go tell the Spartans . . .'). Its prototype was a monumental anthology compiled in the tenth century by a Byzantine educator, Constantine Cephalas; he in turn drew on older collections including the *Garlands* of Meleager (first century BC) and Philip (first century AD) and the *Cycle* of Agathias (sixth century AD). In its present form it contains over 4,000 epigrams, and other material besides, arranged into sixteen books.

GIDEON NISBET is Reader in Classics at the University of Birmingham. He researches and teaches in ancient epigram and the reception of classical antiquity. His publications include *Greek Epigram in the Roman Empire: Martial's Forgotten Rivals* (2003), *Greek Epigram in Reception* (2013), and Martial's *Epigrams* for Oxford World's Classics.

OXFORD WORLD'S CLASSICS

*For over 100 years Oxford World's Classics have brought
readers closer to the world's great literature. Now with over 700
titles—from the 4,000-year-old myths of Mesopotamia to the
twentieth century's greatest novels—the series makes available
lesser-known as well as celebrated writing.*

*The pocket-sized hardbacks of the early years contained
introductions by Virginia Woolf, T. S. Eliot, Graham Greene,
and other literary figures which enriched the experience of reading.
Today the series is recognized for its fine scholarship and
reliability in texts that span world literature, drama and poetry,
religion, philosophy and politics. Each edition includes perceptive
commentary and essential background information to meet the
changing needs of readers.*

OXFORD WORLD'S CLASSICS

Epigrams from the Greek Anthology

Translated with an Introduction and Notes by
GIDEON NISBET

OXFORD
UNIVERSITY PRESS

OXFORD
UNIVERSITY PRESS

Great Clarendon Street, Oxford, OX2 6DP,
United Kingdom

Oxford University Press is a department of the University of Oxford.
It furthers the University's objective of excellence in research, scholarship,
and education by publishing worldwide. Oxford is a registered trade mark of
Oxford University Press in the UK and in certain other countries

Published in the United States of America by Oxford University Press
198 Madison Avenue, New York, NY 10016, United States of America

British Library Cataloguing in Publication Data
Data available

Library of Congress Control Number: 2020009714

ISBN 978-0-19-885465-4

Printed and bound in Great Britain by
Clays Ltd, Elcograf S.p.A.

CONTENTS

INTRODUCTION

THE GREEK ANTHOLOGY is an extraordinary monument of literature. It preserves over four thousand epigrams on every topic under the ancient sun. These poems tell on a millennium and more of history, from the Persian Wars to early medieval Byzantium. The Roman Empire rises and falls, a New Rome flowers in the East, and still the poets sing of love and death and human folly as if almost nothing had changed.

The influence of this collection has been every bit as extraordinary. From the Renaissance onward, and well into the modern age, its epigrams formed the basis of Humanistic training in Greek language. The Anthology became thereby a foundational text of the Republic of Letters—and then a battlefield where, in the late nineteenth and early twentieth centuries, activists and censors fought over visions of human sexuality. The British Empire meanwhile ran on gin and epigram: on Aegean islands or beside the Nile, colonial administrators unwound at day's end with Anthology favourites remembered from their schooldays. When at last the whole Anthology was opened up to non-specialists by the Loeb Classical Library translation in the 1910s, it inaugurated literary modernism: the Anthology was a revelation to Virginia Woolf and a touchstone to the inventors of Imagism, H.D. and Ezra Pound. Later it inspired Kenneth Rexroth, the so-called 'Father of the Beats'.

Each new encounter refreshes the original and changes the receiving culture. To take one famous example, Simonides' 'Go tell the Spartans' (7.249), an Edwardian favourite, became the unavoidable point of reference for poets struggling to memorialize the Allied dead of the First World War, or indeed to critique its mass production of slaughter, as did Kipling in his 'Common Form'—

> If any question why we died,
> Tell them, because our fathers lied.

—but this famous epitaph for the Spartans who died fighting Xerxes at Thermopylae was also Hermann Goering's choice as he abandoned the Sixth German Army to its fate at Stalingrad (it did not go down well with his audience). In the United States the same poem is today invoked by nostalgists for the Confederate 'Lost Cause' and by heavily armed zealots who take Leonidas' reply to the Persian envoy, '*molōn labe*' ('come and take them'), as a sermon-text for their consumerist gloss on the Second Amendment. Many of these latest fans of Simonides' epitaph will know it not from any anthology of poetry, but from Zack Snyder's film *300* (2006).

Each reader of the Anthology is also its rewriter: we all bring our own concerns to the text and come away with something different. It is such a diverse body of work, the product of centuries of compromise between who-knows-how-many authors and editors, and a record of astonishing cultural continuity as well as radical social change. We can have no idea what it will do to us next. 'There's many a slip 'twixt cup and lip'—and this saying, too, began life as a Greek epigram (10.32). The Anthology is a *living* text, and that is part of what makes it exciting to read and study.

The Origins of Greek Epigram

The study of inscriptions is called epigraphy, and the resemblance between that word and 'epigram' is no accident: Greek epigram began as inscriptions. The Greeks had been cutting texts into objects ever since they adopted the Phoenician alphabet, and these texts had always included compositions in verse: Nestor's Cup and the Dipylon Inscription (both eighth century BC) are among the famous early instances.

Inscription defined the qualities of Greek epigram. It is *formulaic*, because the occasions that call for public inscription are limited in kind and must convey the same sorts of information each time. An epitaph must report the identity of the deceased, and will normally tell us something about their family and achievements. Very similar strictures apply to a celebration of a victory on the wrestling ground or battlefield. These texts have a job to do; they tell the reader what they need to know. Epigram is also *concise*, because inscriptional contexts—the base of a statue, the face of a tomb—encourage brevity. An inscription must be cut in large-enough letters to be read easily by passers-by, and must compete with everything else in the environment to secure those readers' attention (one can well imagine, too, that ancient stonecutters charged by the line).

Literary epigram carried forward the formulaic concision of its inscriptional parent, and its readers continued to see actual inscribed epigrams around them in their daily lives. The centuries passed and pagan funerals were replaced by Christian ones, but the dead still needed epitaphs; the old Panhellenic athletic festivals were put down, but there were still victors to be hailed in the chariot-races that Byzantium adored. However, epigram had long ago expanded to include poems that were never genuinely meant to be inscribed, and many that did not even pretend at an inscriptional function.

The big change came in the third century BC, early in what we call the Hellenistic age. When Alexander the Great died, his generals (the Diadochi or 'Successors') carved up his empire and declared themselves kings, founding dynasties that fought terrible wars over land and resources. They tried to outshine each other in culture as well, finding what roots they could for their new world order in mythical bloodlines and ancient places. It was in this context of competition and conspicuous display of power that the first or second Ptolemy of Egypt founded the Museum of Alexandria (not a museum in the modern sense but the world's first research university) and the great Library that powered it, a repository that aimed at total knowledge—every book that had ever been written. Its scholars collated manuscripts, emended texts, and compiled learned commentaries, marshalling the cream of their literary heritage into a canon that was to underpin humane education for centuries. What we call 'Classics' was an invention of the Alexandrians. This concentration of resources also created new and unforeseen possibilities in expression and understanding. Here, for instance, a team of seventy bilingual Jewish scholars working independently in parallel first turned parts of the Hebrew Bible into Greek, the famous Septuagint (*septuaginta* is Latin for seventy); here Eratosthenes calculated the circumference of the Earth.

Here, too, epigram crossed over from inscription to literature. What we think happened is that, as part of their larger project of mining the famous past for cultural capital, Alexandrian scholars compiled collections of historic verse inscriptions from statues and monuments at the culturally important sites of the old Greek heartland—places such as Athens, Delphi, and Olympia, the incised texts of which had long ago fascinated Herodotus and were to attract the attention of visitors centuries later under Rome (notably Pausanias). Then, poets started writing short verses that emulated the style and content of these historic inscriptions.

The transition came naturally because in the early Hellenistic age, 'poet' and 'scholar' were often one and the same. Callimachus, for instance, innovated brilliantly and polemically across a range of literary genres *and* invented library cataloguing; Eratosthenes dominated geography and mathematics, but also investigated the history of the Olympics (the pull of the heartland again) *and* wrote epic and elegy, fragments of which survive. Literature and scholarship had not yet gone separate ways: Eratosthenes wrote an epigram to celebrate his solution of the doubling of the cube. This was the great age of didactic epics such as Aratus' great poem of astronomy and astrology, the *Phaenomena* (Callimachus' epitaph for Aratus is in this collection, 9.507).

Because it began as a playful simulation of inscribed texts, literary epigram always included many poems that were notionally suited to inscriptional contexts, notably epitaphs for tombs and offerings to deities in return for life's successes. The 'epitaphic' and 'anathematic' (dedicatory) books of the Anthology are accordingly among its biggest.

Once it had become a literary genre, though, epigram's range expanded. A recent discovery has shown that poets at Alexandria immediately began to respond creatively to the challenges inherent in arranging dozens or hundreds of little texts into a single book. This is the third- or second-century BC 'Milan Posidippus' papyrus (P. Mil. Vogl. VIII 309), recovered from the papier-mâché 'cartonnage' that packaged a second-century mummy, and first published in 2001 (a good translation of it can be found online). Posidippus of Pella, an exact contemporary of Callimachus, was lured to Egypt from Macedon by the recently opened Museum and the sponsorship of the Ptolemies, and the Milan papyrus is in all likelihood a nearly complete book of his epigrams, composed to be read *as a book*, from start to finish. Epigram's origin in catalogued inscription is reflected in the arrangement of its content into categories under thematic headings (this practice remained constant throughout Greek epigram's thousand-year-plus lifespan), but the contents of each section are artfully arranged, and the poet establishes sophisticated internal allusions ('intratextuality') between different parts of the book. The categories are still primarily driven by the idea of inscription, but inventively so. They include the old monumental favourites (epitaphs and dedications, celebrations of athletic victories, thank-offerings for cures from illness) but also types that play with the conventions of inscription:

epigrams on precious stones that are far too small to bear inscribed texts; epitaphs for shipwrecked sailors who leave no bodies to be buried. We already knew some of Posidippus' epigrams through the Anthology tradition (5.186; 7.170; 16.68; etc.), but the discovery of the Milan papyrus hints at the versatility and innovation of literary epigram's first flowering.

The Museum and its revolution in information technology were one context for epigram's sudden flourishing as an inventive literary form. The other likely context was very different, though many of the same people enjoyed it: the symposium, that after-dinner social ritual at which for centuries Greek men had drunk wine and affirmed their human brotherhood (11.46). The symposium was no mere drunken party, or was not supposed to be: there were rules, one of which was that each participant ('symposiast') should contribute to the evening's entertainment. Guests of a traditional bent could still recite ancient drinking-songs from the lyric repertoire, but epigram's accessibility quickly made it a favourite party turn. Its elegiac metre came readily to Greeks, including many who might not otherwise have thought of themselves as poets, and some of the Anthology's epigrams probably began as improvisations at symposia before being worked up for inclusion in a poetry book.

The symposium celebrated life's pleasures, all the more worth grasping because of life's brevity and uncertainty. Elegy thus became the metre of hedonism in the face of death; wine, flowers, the sex trade, the beauty of youth, the pains of age, and the importance of good friends entered epigram's repertoire of themes, as did jokes, puns (some of them smutty), and riddles. So too did the kōmos, a tipsy procession with friends through the streets to make a nuisance of oneself loitering and singing outside the house of a boy or girl one fancied (5.112; 11.41; 12.117–18; etc.). The ethos of the symposium was narrowly homosocial. Like the archaic and classical elegy and iambus sung by previous generations of symposiasts, epigram came to express a masculine value-set that sometimes shaded into misogyny.

Like inscription on stone, performance at symposia encouraged variations on a theme. Some of the symposiac tropes that entered the genre in the Hellenistic age proved remarkably durable, even after the ancient customs had otherwise vanished from memory: we find senior court officials in Christian Byzantium boasting of drunken passions and clandestine love-affairs as if they were pagan pleasure-seekers in

Alexandria a millennium before (notably in the long sequence begin-
ning at 5.219).

The Tradition of the Anthology

The very first books of epigrams, garnered from inscriptions, had
been anthologies of a kind, and literary epigram proved ideal material
for the anthologist's art. For it was considered an art: *anthologia* liter-
ally means flower-gathering, and the main reason to pick flowers was
to weave a garland. The anthologist needed more than an eye for indi-
vidual beauties; he had to be able to plan, and arrange his choices into
a harmonious, fragrant whole. The two great anthologies of the
Hellenistic and Roman periods, compiled respectively by Meleager
(first century BC) and Philip (first century AD), prolific poets in their
own right, both took *Garland* as their title. In their prefaces, pre-
served in the fourth book of the Greek Anthology, these early
anthologists boast of how their discriminating taste has delivered art-
ful compositions that are more than the sums of their parts. Meleager
demonstrates his credentials as a Hellenistic scholar-poet by weaving
amid his epigrams strands of the older lyric poets whose definitive
editions the Alexandrians had curated (e.g. Alcaeus at 7.1; Anyte at
6.123 and 153; 7.538), before presenting the whole thing as an extrava-
gant lover's gift to a beautiful young man:

> Dear Muse, for whom this richly-cropping tune?
> Who crafted, too, this wreath of minstrelsy?
> The work was Meleager's, and he wrought
> For glorious Diocles this souvenir,
> Plaiting much lily out of Anyte,
> Moero's as well; of Sappho just a few,
> But they are roses. Melanippides:
> His are narcissus, heady with clear song;
> And a fresh vine-twig of Simonides . . .
>
> (4.1; my translation of lines 1–8)

Epigrams were now flowers and, whether of flowers or epigrams, a gar-
land was the symposiast's accessory of choice; the bloom of a boy's or
girl's beauty was a flower too, and amorous symposiasts were keen to
suggest they take advantage of it before it swiftly and inevitably faded.

After Philip, epigram waited half a millennium for its next important
collector: Agathias 'Scholasticus', poet and historian under Justinian

I ('the Great') in the sixth century. Christians were no strangers to the genre—a collection of epigrams by St Gregory of Nazianzus ('the Theologian'), composed in the fourth century, ended up as the eighth book of the Greek Anthology—and epigram was still going strong in Justinian's sixth-century Constantinople. Agathias wrote many himself and his contemporaries Paul 'the Silentiary' ('the Usher') and Macedonius of Thessalonica, 'the Consul', were at least as prolific. Agathias' *Cycle* was much larger than the *Garlands* of Meleager and Philip, and ran to several books: he structured it by scaling up the traditional arrangement of poems into categories, so that each category now occupied a whole book. The other material difference was in the physical form of the books themselves. The papyrus book-rolls of classical times had given way to a new format, the codex, with its separate pages bound at the spine. From now on, readers of anthologies would be able to browse, bookmark, and cross-reference much more easily.

Agathias collected only contemporary poets; accordingly there is a serious gap in the Anthology's coverage, though Gregory (Book 8) and Palladas (Book 10) are well-represented exceptions. Aside from the minor collector Diogenianus or Diogenian, whose *Anthologion* is dated to the reign of Hadrian, we know of no one anthologizing Greek epigrammatists between the mid-first and sixth centuries AD.

Four centuries later, another Byzantine, Constantine Cephalas, gathered the best manuscripts he could find of all these predecessors and wove them together, adding in as well some separate collections in the form in which they came to him. He also combed classical prose authors, among them Herodotus and Pausanias, for the inscriptional epigrams they had seen in their travels ('Go tell the Spartans' is one such). This huge labour created the prototype of the Greek Anthology we read today. However, we know Cephalas' anthology only imperfectly, and in two different ways. The best record of it is a manuscript known as the *Palatine Anthology* (*Anthologia Palatina*, conventionally abbreviated to *AP*). This manuscript was made close to Cephalas' own time; it includes some additional material (the extent of which is contested) but is essentially faithful to his design. However, it was unknown for the better part of a millennium; though rediscovered at the start of the seventeenth century, it was only properly published at the beginning of the nineteenth. In the meantime, the Anthology could be read only in a censored and rearranged abridgement made in the thirteenth century from poor copies of Cephalas by Maximus Planudes, whose activities are memorably described by John Addington Symonds (below, pp. xxiii–xxiv). Planudes concealed his skulduggery and eclipsed his source, and for five hundred years, as far as the world knew, his anthology was the only 'Greek Anthology' there had ever been.

The Greek Anthology we read today comprises the fifteen books of the *Palatine Anthology*, together with what is called the 'Planudean Appendix'. This Appendix, sometimes numbered as 'Book 16', is a modern compilation of all the poems that are found in Planudes' inferior recension but that are missing from the otherwise much better Palatine manuscript. Most of them are on works of art, which tells us that the original Anthology of Cephalas contained a whole book of such poems that the scribes of the Palatine text were unable to include; but enough of them are *not* on works of art, to let us know that there must have been losses elsewhere as well. Even fresh from Cephalas' pen, the Anthology cannot have been an elegant text, and it has become scrappier and more ramshackle along the way. Victorian and Edwardian critics with a vested interest in denying its design (see below, p. xxiv) dismissed it as a random ruin: 'simply a vast reservoir'; 'a garden run to weeds, in which the weeds predominate'; 'the scrapheap of Greece'. But in essence it is a designed text, made for a definite purpose, and its messiness throws up surprises that make it all the more pleasurable to explore.

The World of the Poets

Epigram kept the Greeks in touch with their past. Even as a brand-new literary genre in the third century BC, it rooted itself in social and political institutions that had been the bedrock of Hellenic identity since time immemorial—athletic competition, religious cult, and the symposium—and the inscriptional poems were history in stone. Epigram never became part of an educational curriculum dominated by long and morally elevating texts (the Homeric epics, the Attic orators) but it presupposed a readership schooled in the traditional forms.

Tradition was all the more vital because Alexander's conquests had spread Greek culture thin, across a much bigger slice of the globe than ever before (and with the coming of the Library and Museum it was not long before the Greeks knew its size with fair accuracy).

'Alexandrias' dotted the map from Egypt to the Indus. He had always pushed forward, never stabilized or taken stock, and when he died heirless (323 BC) the whole thing splintered into regional fiefdoms held by his generals, each jealous and suspecting the rest. A fragile stalemate quickly turned to war. As noted above, the smarter and luckier Diadochi lived long enough to found dynasties that carried on wearing each other down for generations, fielding vast armies that relied heavily on mercenaries (6.9; 13.7).

The whole time, a new superpower was growing in the west. Rome gobbled up the Successor states one after another: first Alexander's old homeland of Macedon, which had allied with Rome's great maritime enemy Carthage; then Macedon's ally, the Empire of the Seleucids in western Asia. Some of the dynasties became Rome's partners. Attalus III of Pergamum, the last of his line, left his kingdom to Rome in his will; even so the transition was not entirely bloodless. At the other extreme, the sack of Corinth in 146 BC still evoked horror a century later (7.493). The last to go was Ptolemaic Egypt, ruled by Cleopatra, the seventh of that name in her line, who committed suicide in 30 BC, the year after Actium. The young aristocrat who won that battle, Octavian, would soon be hailed as 'Augustus' by the Roman Senate.

Rome now ruled the whole Mediterranean basin and places much further afield, and enjoyed the spoils of conquest. Poets and other intellectuals could fall under that heading: Parthenius of Nicaea, who brought refined Alexandrian poetics to Rome and taught Virgil his Greek, arrived as a prisoner of war (you can read his mock-epitaph at 7.377, in this selection). Others came voluntarily seeking patronage, as previously they had come to the courts of the Hellenistic dynasts. Epigrams were charming accompaniments to modest gifts, or were themselves the gifts, by which talented newcomers might attract the attention and earn the generosity of Rome's great men and women. An early example is Archias (5.59; 6.39; 7.214; etc.), the poet from Antioch whose franchise rights Cicero defended in the speech named after him in 62 BC, and who may (suggests Alan Cameron in his 1993 book on *The Greek Anthology*) have brought Meleager's *Garland* to Rome. On receiving Roman citizenship he added to 'Archias' a Roman first name (*praenomen*), Aulus, and a family name (*nomen*), Licinius, honouring by the latter his wealthy patron, L. Licinius Lucullus. The Piso family kept Archias' contemporary, the Epicurean Philodemus of Gadara, in high style at their villa in Herculaneum, where he organized their library and wrote trenchant literary criticism (parts of which were long ago brought to light by archaeologists and are now being transcribed, thanks to digital imaging technologies that can tell apart soot-based ink from burnt papyrus); he also wrote erotic epigrams (5.112, 121, 131–2, etc.), which Cicero improbably claimed to be records of Piso's own excesses as a lover and symposiast in high Hellenistic style (*Against Piso* 29.70).

The shift from Republic to Empire did not end literary patronage by any means, but poets naturally turned first to the ruling family and its close allies. Antipater of Thessalonica (5.3; 10.25; 11.184; etc.) especially cultivates the friendship of Lucius Calpurnius Piso, a trusted friend of Augustus and the son of the Piso who had hosted Philodemus. His gifts—a book (9.93), a travelling hat— are humble, to declare his poverty (though clearly he was expensively educated), but he has chosen them with care. Piso is on his way to Thrace to put down a revolt. He will need a good hat (6.335):

> I am a hat of felt. In former time
> The Macedonians found me versatile:
> In falling snow, a roof; in war, a helm.
> Thirsting, stout Piso, for your sweat I came,
> Emathian, to your Italian brow.
> Accept me as a friend: surely our wool,
> That long ago put Persian arms to flight,
> Will, when you wear it, smash the Thracians too.

Often the poets mark occasions of state. Crinagoras (6.229; 7.633; 16.61; etc.) hails the return of Augustus' heir Marcellus from war in Spain (6.161), though he also tells the unlikely anecdote of the parrot that taught its fellow jungle birds to sing 'Hail, Caesar!' (9.562). Antipater and Crinagoras became regular court poets, but they did not limit themselves to official commissions, and kept the traditional epigram types alive, notably the epitaph. Antipater mourns the death of a girl who died outside Rome, a long way from her Libyan home (7.185); Crinagoras gloats at the fine tomb of Eunicides, 'A worthless rag who rots beneath the dust' (7.380).

Imperial patronage continued after Augustus. Philip celebrates the long peace ushered in by Actium (6.236) and the success of the city Augustus founded to mark his victory there, Nicopolis (6.251; cf. 9.553).

The isopsephic poet Leonidas of Alexandria (9.106; 11.70, 213; etc.) sends birthday poems to Agrippina the Younger, great-grand-daughter of Augustus and mother of Nero (6.329), and to her son (6.321). The pickings could be slim: Lucillius, by his account penni-less and desperate to get by (6.164), counts himself lucky to get pocket change (9.572). In the late first century, an unknown Greek poet cele-brates the beast-hunts that helped mark the grand opening of the Colosseum under Vespasian and Titus (7.626); the Latin epigramma-tist Martial got his first break reporting on these same games. Sometimes Rome's aristocrats tried writing epigrams themselves. Cornelius Gallus, Augustus' first prefect of Egypt and the founder of Latin love elegy, wrote at least one erotic epigram in Greek (5.49). A 'Pompey the Younger' who could easily be Sextus Pompey, piratical rival to Augustus, writes an epitaph in fine Hellenistic style for a dead courtesan (7.219); the Emperor Trajan leaves us a joke about a man with a big nose (11.418). His successor, Hadrian, was an accomplished Greek poet who specialized in epigrams for inscription, two of which (6.332; 9.387) are in this selection.

Though Latin was the language of government, the cities of the former Hellenistic kingdoms continued to run their affairs in Greek. It was the lingua franca of civilized culture wherever one went, even Gaul (a jibe against a Gaulish celebrity rhetorician is included in this selection, 11.223), and by Hadrian's time most educated Romans were fluent in it. The local aristocracies of the Greek East had long been granted the rights and obligations of Roman citizenship, and mixed on familiar terms with Rome's political elite, to the advantage of their cities (see note on 15.7), but they insisted on maintaining the distinctiveness of their traditional culture and celebrating its past glories (which indeed were the cultural coin they had to spend in their dealings with Rome). Their orators and public intellectuals competed to recreate the pure diction and spirit of the great orators of fifth- and fourth-century Athens, a nostalgic cultural turn that we now term the 'Second Sophistic'. Their pursuit of linguistic 'Atticism' (Athens was the chief city of Attica) turned its back on contemporary realities: the spoken language of everyday life in the Eastern Roman Empire was a simplified Ionic Greek called *koinē*, literally the common tongue (this is the Greek in which the New Testament was written, precisely because everyone could understand it). Pronunciation as well as grammar had changed. It is as though today's media celebrities were competing to speak in perfect Chaucerian, without an autocue. Audiences flocked to hear these sophists, perhaps waiting for the inevitable moment when the mask crumbled.

Literature as well continued to be composed in the best approximation to classical Attic that the authors could achieve: the best at it of all was Lucian of Samosata, a Syrian from the Euphrates who is famous for his satirical essays and dialogues in prose (a selection of which have been translated for Oxford World's Classics by C. D. N. Costa) but who also wrote epigrams, some of which (6.17; 9.367; 10.26; 11.405) are included here. Epigrams lent themselves to displays of rhetorical cleverness in miniature (the Anthology's book of rhetorical set-pieces, Book 9, is its biggest) and to sarcastic point-scoring: the early centuries AD were the heyday of 'scoptic' or satirical epigram (Book 11).

As noted above, there is a huge hole in our transmitted sources for epigram between Philip in the first century and Agathias in the sixth. With the exception of Diogenian (second century), about whose *Anthologion* we know little except that it was probably Cephalas' source for much of Book 11, nobody seems to have been collecting the epigrammatists during these important centuries—at least, nobody whose work lasted long enough to reach Cephalas in Byzantium. Gregory and Palladas aside, we have no way of knowing what has been lost from this half-millennium. We do, however, find a few snapshots of epigrammatic activity at Oxyrhynchus, the modern Bahnasa, a regional capital in the desert of Graeco-Roman Egypt. This 'City of the Sharp-nosed Fish' was a Hellenistic foundation and was still running its private and public business in Greek long after the Western Empire fell, right up to the Arab conquest of the seventh century: a lifespan of a thousand years. Few traces of the ancient city remain, but excavations of its rubbish dumps at the turn of the twentieth century retrieved many thousands of fragments of papyrus bearing documents and literature that are still being deciphered at Oxford.

The literary papyri of Oxyrhynchus tend to reproduce the canonical classics that schoolboys were required to read to improve their style and prepare themselves for public life, primarily Homer and the Attic orators, but there are traces of epigram as well. From the papyri we know that Oxyrhynchites were reading epigrams by (at least) Theocritus, Asclepiades, Meleager, Philodemus, and Nicarchus, who himself was Egyptian; and we gain some new poems by Nicarchus, very rude ones. A list of incipits suggests that literary-minded individuals were picking and choosing epigrams from poetry books by multiple authors, with a view to concocting personal anthologies that reflected their own literary tastes (an incipit is the first line or part-line of a text, and was a standard way for readers to specify works of literature: one could interchangeably say 'Sing, goddess, the wrath' or 'Iliad'). The list identifies itself as the epigrams that are being 'sought for' (*epizētoumena*) in the different sources, presumably so they can be copied into a book-roll. One square scrap of papyrus has been found with a single poem by Nicarchus carefully centred on it. Perhaps it was on its way to be copied into a personal anthology—or to be read aloud at a symposium. This is the difficulty and delight of the papyri: they are isolated survivals that invite us to read into the silence that surrounds them, and that only survive because they were thrown away. The documentary papyri survive in greater numbers to fill us in on the bureaucracy that kept track of the population and made sure the fields were irrigated; without agricultural wealth there was no revenue, no culture of scribes and scholars, no city at all.

The only really unusual thing about Oxyrhynchus was that it was founded a long way from a river (its commercial artery was a canal), in a place that never gets rain. Thanks to this happy accident its waste paper survives to attest the remarkable continuities in Greek culture across the first six or so centuries AD. The city's wealthier citizens attended symposia and exercised at the gymnasium just as the ancient Athenians had done, though they also enjoyed the more Roman amenity of lavish bathhouses. They probably also had good libraries in which to read the classics; most cities did. Men of the wealthier families stood for the traditional magistracies and added to the honour of their family name by means of more or less mandatory contributions to public amenities, a system known as 'liturgy' (compare Agathias at 9.662, persuading the sixth century and himself that there is glory in gentrifying a public toilet). Men and women alike watched chariot-racing (the grand passion of Romans and Byzantines and the subject of many surviving epigrams), and attended dramatic revivals in the city's great theatre, estimated by an early excavator to have held 11,000 spectators. They sacrificed at the temples of their composite Graeco-Egyptian gods (6.190 and 231) and to Rome's Capitoline Jupiter—until the temples closed, and Christian Oxyrhynchus became famous instead for its great numbers of monks (local tradition said that Mary and Joseph had taken refuge there on the flight into Egypt). The new religious devotion did not radically alter daily life: the people of Oxyrhynchus still paid their taxes and read their Demosthenes, and some of them surely wrote epigrams that no Meleager or Philip was around to collect.

Palladas mourned the passing of the old faiths (10.82)—

> Are we not dead and only seem to live,
> We pagan men, fallen disastrously
> Into a dream we only think is life?
> Or do we live, and life itself has died?

—but he had perhaps had his eye on a lucrative priesthood, of the kind the aristocracy had traditionally coveted; the religious change did not much affect the lives of ordinary citizens, and Christianized local elites still connected passionately with their pagan literary heritage. They may have begun to sense its vulnerability. Julian, sixth-century Prefect of Egypt and author of a sweet fictional epitaph for Anacreon (7.32), mourns the death of a friend who had devoted himself to researching and commenting on classical authors, probably the archaic and early classical lyric poets (7.595):

> Theodore, dead; with him a multitude
> Of ancient bards now truly dead and gone.
> For while he breathed they breathed in him, and now
> The multitude is gone, as he is gone;
> And all lie buried in a single tomb.

The great centre of literature and scholarship was now the capital, Constantinople on the Bosporus, where critics such as Cometas (15.37) curated Greek literary classics of which the West would remain ignorant for centuries to come. Many of the poems in the Anthology's first book were composed to mark the restoration of figurative art to its richly decorated churches following a period of iconoclasm. The place names of the city's Christian epigrams reflect territorial interests primarily centred in the south-eastern Mediterranean and its hinterland, though there are exceptions (Malta, 1.98). The great military threat, too, was to the south and east: Sassanid Persia (7.747; 9.210, 641, and 810; 16.38), centred at Ctesiphon on the Tigris in modern-day Iraq and occupying roughly the same territory as its predecessor, Arsacid Parthia (6.332; 16.61). The city Constantine had founded as a New Rome (14.115) drew in talent from far afield, just as had the old Rome that it was now supplanting. Here are four friends celebrating success in their law exams. Three are from what is now western Turkey, one from Egypt:

> Aemilianus, come from Caria,
> And John, who came with him along the way;
> Rufinus too, of Alexandria;
> Agathias, of Asia.
>
> (1.35)

We know Agathias as the sixth-century poet who compiled a *Cycle* from his own epigrams and those of his prolific contemporaries: epigram was as lively now as it had ever been. A young man with political ambitions (for which law was considered the best education) might equally have gone to Berytus in the Lebanon, the modern Beirut, then a great centre for legal teaching and research. Natural disasters soon rocked this world to its foundations (9.425), and within a century much of the Byzantine Empire was to fall to the followers of Muhammad who for good measure ended the Sassanids as well. For now, though, sixth-century Berytus celebrated its champions as reincarnations of the Spartans and Athenians who had defied Xerxes at Thermopylae, Salamis, and Plataea, and whose valour and sacrifice Simonides had immortalized in epigram more than *one thousand years* earlier (6.50, 215; and 7.248–51):

> Not only by Eurotas warlike men,
> Nor by Ilissus mindful of the law:
> As on a Spartan, or a citizen
> Of Athens even, Triumph and the Right
> Looked on Synesius in wonderment.
>
> (16.38)

The Synesius of this poem was himself no professional soldier, but a classically educated scholar—and an author of epigrams (16.267).

The Anthology in Reception

Past ages may have known the Anthology only in Planudes' inferior recension, but they knew it intimately. The Planudean Anthology was one of the very first Greek classics to be printed, by Janus Lascaris in Florence in 1494, and it became a cornerstone of the revival of Greek learning in the Renaissance. With the return of Greek to Western classrooms, selections of epigrams from the Anthology proliferated as teaching texts. Schoolboys learned their Latin with the help of graded selections from the epigrams of Martial, and those who went on to study Greek found their lessons taking a familiar format.

Generations of pupils at upmarket schools thereby read Greek epigram—and wrote it too: verse and prose composition in, and translation into, the classical languages were familiar rites of passage. The established universities of England and Scotland and the Queen's Colleges founded in Ireland in the 1840s made competence in Greek obligatory for entry regardless of the course of study being undertaken. Oxford and Cambridge only got rid of the requirement in the years following the First World War, not without a fight, and Cambridge still awards annual medals for the best epigrams in Latin and Greek.

'We might do worse than a Greek epigram,' declares a cub editor outlining a new school magazine in H. G. Wells's *The New Machiavelli* (1910): 'One in each number. It—it impresses parents and keeps up our classical tradition. And the masters *can* help.' Wells's schoolboys are fictions drawn from life: many old boys carried the epigrammatic habit into adulthood. Some of them submitted their prettier versions to the quarterly magazines, notably *Blackwood's*, where an epigram in translation could be just the right size to fill an awkward page-corner. The first book-length selections from the Anthology into English, compiled by Robert Bland (1806, 1813) and John Merivale (1833), emerged from the *Blackwood's* set; the first notionally mass-market translation, by George Burges for Bohn's Classical Library (1852), was pasted together from cribs to the proprietary mini-anthologies of the leading public schools.

These early translations had limited appeal. Epigram did not capture the popular imagination until the 1870s, when John Addington Symonds, beloved author of *Renaissance in Italy*, made the story of the Anthology the climax of his new bestseller, *Studies of the Greek Poets* (1873):

The Anthology may from some points of view be regarded as the most valuable relic of antique literature which we possess . . . Many subjects of interest in Greek life, which would otherwise have had to be laboriously illustrated from the historians or the comic poets are here fully and melodiously set forth. If we might compare the study of Greek Literature to a journey in some splendid mountain region, then we might say with propriety that from the sparkling summits where Aeschylus and Sophocles and Pindar sit enthroned, we turn in our less strenuous moods to gather the meadow flowers of Meleager, Palladas, Callimachus. Placing them between the leaves of the book of our memory, we possess an everlasting treasure of sweet thoughts, which will serve in after-days to remind us of those scenes of Olympian majesty through which we travelled.

Epigram's moment had arrived. Symonds was an excellent classicist; his outspokenness had spoiled his chance of an academic career but he had risen to public attention as a travel writer, and his evocation of Greek literature as an Alpine beauty-spot was calculated to grab the attention of a British public that had fallen in love with Thomas Cook's tours to Switzerland and Italy. They had long since been primed to regard themselves as the direct spiritual heirs to ancient Greece (Rome in the meantime having been sullied by association with Revolutionary France), and now the Anthology promised to bring modern readers into intimate contact with its lived reality, which turned out to be ravishingly beautiful. Thanks to Symonds, everyday readers suddenly found out what they had been missing—and former public-schoolboys who thought they knew Greek epigram from the selections they had read in class, could now see the bigger picture of the Anthology's origin, development, and content.

   Nobody had told this story before, and Symonds told it brilliantly, like detective fiction:

Early in the fourteenth century a monk Planudes set to work upon a new edition. It appears that he contented himself with compiling and abridging from the collection of Cephalas. His principal object was to expurgate it from impurities and to supersede it by what he considered a more edifying text. Accordingly he amended, castrated, omitted, interpolated, altered, and remodelled it at his own sweet will . . . He succeeded . . . to the height of his desire; for copies ceased to be made of the Anthology of Cephalas; and when Europe in the fifteenth century awoke to the study of Greek literature, no other collection but that of Planudes was known. Fortunately for this most precious relic of antiquity, there did exist one exemplar of the Anthology of Cephalas. Having escaped the searches of Poggio, Aurispa, Filelfo, Poliziano, and of all the emissaries whom the Medici employed in ransacking the treasure-houses of Europe, this unique manuscript was at last discovered in 1606 by Claude de Saumaise, better known as Milton's antagonist Salmasius, in the Palatine Library at Heidelberg. A glance at this treasure assured the young scholar—for Saumaise was then aged only twenty-two—that he had made one of the most important discoveries which remained within the reach of modern students. He spent years in preparing a critical edition of its text; but all his work was thrown away ...

Symonds told the tale in full and accurately, amazingly so given the state of knowledge in his time. The Anthology's secrets were out, and studies of epigram now blossomed. Actually most of what followed was a concerted campaign to obliterate Symonds's subtext. Gay and straight desire are placed separately in the Anthology as we find it, but that was Cephalas' doing; the poets of Hellenistic Greece and Imperial Rome had rarely drawn any ethical distinction between the two kinds of love, and often wrote about them interchangeably. In his account of epigram Symonds capitalized on this ancient equivalence and cour- ageously insinuated to the public that homosexuality was neither a sin nor an illness. It had always been there in history, a natural human way of being, and the Greek experience proved it could even be a social ideal (compare 6.340 and note). Epigram did not immediately deliver liberation, and Symonds's mission was to make little headway for another century, but generations of socially conservative critics were kept busy straightening out the Anthology for the public record.

By far the most influential of these critics of the backlash was John William Mackail, whose selection of the Anthology's five hundred 'best' epigrams (1890) was widely acknowledged as authoritative. By discarding four-fifths of its poems, interpolating others that had never belonged there, and rearranging these mixed winnowings under newly coined headings such as 'Prayers and Dedications', 'The Family', and 'Nature', he reinvented the Anthology as an austere and strictly heterosexual celebration of duty to God and country, rather against the drift of the original text. At home and overseas, translators and scholars worshipped at his altar for the next thirty years, and common readers loved him too. Mackail's smart, compact, and robust little volumes delivered an Anthology ideally suited to the needs of Empire: across a map turned red, colonial administrators refreshed their Greek and worked up new translations beside the campfire after a hard day putting the world to rights. Back in the home country, their former schoolfellows turned to Mackail's bucolicized selection to dispel the ennui of their commuter lifestyles. (These epigrammatic habits had staying power: addressing the assembled Classical Association of England and Wales in 1961, Lord Hailsham, who had been First Lord of the Admiralty under Anthony Eden, declared that 'in the middle of the Suez crisis I found it the most comforting thing in the world to translate Catullus; the tedium of a railway journey I have often used to render an epigram from the Greek Anthology'.) Mackail was popular in America too, directly inspiring Edgar Masters's *Spoon River Anthology*.

Then came the Great War, and as the great conflict drew to a close, Mackail's Anthology was the obvious model for heroizing the dead of Britain and its Empire. His stripped-down vision had in the meantime inspired the Imagists, notably H.D., whose early poems Ezra Pound extolled to a potential publisher as 'Objective—no slither; direct—no excessive use of adjectives; no metaphors that won't permit examination. It's straight talk, straight as the Greek!' Pound himself translated Palladas, leaning on Mackail's version, and the Anthology's epitaphs for drowned mariners tumble beneath the tide of T. S. Eliot's *The Waste Land* ('Consider Phlebas . . .'). Meanwhile in the small presses, gay and bisexual translators tried their hands at romanticized or saucy versions of Strato's Boyish Muse, climaxing in Daryl Hine's *Puerilities* (2001).

Selection can spin the Anthology any number of ways, and mainstream readers of the decades between the wars knew it primarily as a bucolic idyll: the domain of Pan, whose goatish appetites inspired free adaptation and occasional outright reinvention as soft-core erotica (notably in *Pagan Pictures* by Wallace Rice, 1927). Traces of this pseudo-pagan machismo lingered into the 1950s and 1960s, when the Anthology came into vogue among American poets—Dudley Fitts, Kenneth Rexroth, Robin Skelton—as a source text for translation and loose imitation. Rexroth's version (1962) stands out from the pack as a magnificently eccentric amalgam of miscellaneous Greek and Latin sources (by no means all of them epigrams, or even ancient) and heroic narcissism; an obliging press and a devoted fan base keep it in print. There has been next to nothing since, with the honourable and peculiar exception of Peter Jay's *Greek Anthology* for Allen Lane (1973), which was not an original translation but an anthology of past versions chosen to illustrate the long history of the Anthology in English.

Writers are still turning to the Anthology for inspiration. Greg Delanty fills the pages of his witty and moving *The Greek Anthology, Book 17* (2013) with an invented roll-call of new ancient Greeks ('Dan the Younger', 'Dermoton of the Nightshift') who take the Anthology forward into the future, in dialogue with the poets of antiquity, postmodernity, and everywhere in between.

NOTE ON THE TEXT AND TRANSLATION

THE ANTHOLOGY has complex origins and a shady history, but its received text is what it is, and one modern edition of it is very like another. I used W. R. Paton's Loeb Classical Library edition, and recommend it as a resource (see Select Bibliography).

I worked from Paton's Greek text, and his English speeded my progress as a browser and translator. My notes sometimes quote from his own, notably for the help he offers with arithmetical puzzles (Book 14), but also occasionally elsewhere in appreciation of his talent for dry understatement.

Paton's version has some rough edges, unavoidably given the scale of his undertaking, but students of the Greek Anthology will always be in his debt; nobody had translated the whole of it before for English readers (to get full value out of the first edition those readers needed also to know some Latin, because Paton could not bear to put the sexually explicit poems into English, but this was quietly fixed by a later editor). It is unlikely his work will ever be replaced; that it was ever commissioned, and has been kept constantly in print, does credit to the Loeb Classical Library's commitment to the philanthropic vision of its founder. Students of epigram eagerly await the completion of the revision of Paton's volumes now being undertaken by Jon Steffen Bruss, a scholar of rare sensitivity to the nuances of the genre.

The important thing about Greek epigram in reception (see Introduction, pp. xxi–xxv) is not to trust people who use selections from the Anthology to sell stories about ancient Greece. With this translation I join their number. We are all liars, we translators, otherwise we would not make it past the first page: to translate is literally to carry across, between languages, places, and times, and things are bound to get lost and found along the way even if we could be dispassionate, which of course we cannot. The academic who becomes a translator is put in mind (well, *I* am) of the famous last words Suetonius ascribes to the Emperor Vespasian: *Vae, puto deus fio.* Vespasian was a career soldier who cleaned up the chaos at the end of the Year of Four Emperors (AD 69) and founded the Empire's second, Flavian dynasty.

'Good' emperors received posthumous cult, and Vespasian knew he had done enough, but he was a hard-nosed realist and could not resist making a joke about it at the end: 'Oops, I think I'm turning into a god.' Similarly for the classicist who has made a career teaching classical authors, more often than not in translation: Oops, I think I'm turning into a primary text.

I have played fair with my source as best I can. Unlike most of my predecessors (the last of whom on this kind of scale was ninety-plus years ago), I respect the traditional structure of the Anthology and the ordering of poems within its books. Every book of epigrams is represented here, and poems of every kind. Any such selection is a compromise, as all my predecessors knew, and my conscious motives for choosing poems—that they would interest a modern reader, throw light on ancient history and daily life, represent the variety of the Anthology's content, and illustrate the tradition-minded art of the epigrammatist—pulled in every direction at once. I wish there could be more women in it, speaking for themselves, but epigram came out of spaces of male homosociality (the gymnasium and symposium) and never really opened up. At least we have Nossis (9.332 and 605) and we know some women were composing inscriptional epigram as well, notably Julia Balbilla on the Colossus of Memnon in Egypt. I hope some readers will feel sufficiently short-changed to read beyond what I have presented; there are free resources (see Select Bibliography) to help you do so.

The world that made these epigrams achieved many wonderful things besides. It gave its citizens security and freedom of movement, precious hallmarks of civilization that Europe would not again know for nearly two thousand years. 'I am a citizen of all the world', declared Meleager, confidently multicultural (7.417, 419) and knowing he could enjoy the same rights wherever he chose to go. That did not stop it being dangerous: the causes of illness were not well understood, and death was much more present in daily life. Many of its attitudes, too, were dreadful by any decent modern standard. This was a world of extreme inequality of wealth; it kept slaves, treated women at least differently and often badly, and did not share our understanding of sexual consent (5.272 merits a trigger warning on this basis) or human rights generally. My decision to include a poem should not be taken as endorsing the values it expresses or the practices it reflects. It was important to me not to present a consciously sanitized picture of a past to which we still too often turn uncritically for validation.

My translation is into verse. I have never thought of myself as any kind of poet, and in translating Martial's epigrams for Oxford World's Classics (2013) I found prose a good match to his conversational style and vicious punchlines. As I eased back into the Anthology, though, and particularly into its most ancient types of poem, I kept finding that its formulaic and tradition-minded qualities encouraged a more formal touch, a nod to the rhythms of tradition in English occasional verse—which for me meant blank verse, as straightforward for a non-poet to write in English as elegiacs were for a Greek (or a Roman who knew Greek). The classic English epigrammatists (Alexander Pope, John Dryden) favoured the rhyming couplet, and occasionally my version rhymes, as a largely unconscious nod to this tradition; you should not take these instances as marking any special feature in the source text. Lacking any formal training in verse, I felt my way as many of the Anthology's minor poets must themselves have done, with uneven results, then as now. Martial's advice about turning lots of little poems into a big book has been some consolation:

You're reading good poems here, Avitus—and a few that are so-so, and a lot that are bad; a book doesn't happen any other way. (1.16)

I also took heart from contemporary poetic movements around the world that seek to reclaim poetry for the everyday, as a way to make our memories count. Funerary epigrams are formulaic, but so will our own tombstones be; so in the meantime are our Valentine's cards. 'From this day forward', 'in deepest sympathy'—at the emotional crunch-points in our lives the clichés come alive. Epigram was always a social medium, capturing moments in life and preserving them the way Greeks wanted them to last, by putting them in dialogue with tradition; and so this translation needed to feel a bit old-fashioned, though I have avoided egregious archaisms (yea, I ween) and old metrical conveniences ('neath, 'tween, e'er, o'er). If my lines sometimes carry a whiff of hung-over Housman, that is fitting, since Greek epigram set the tone for his own melancholy verses.

Ancient Greek personal names do not sit easily in English verse rhythms, and many older translations left them out or substituted entirely different ones; I have preferred honesty to elegance, and limit my own substitutions to the familiar 'Theodore' for Theodorus,

'John' for Johannes, and once or twice 'Arcady' for Arcadia. Older versions often exchanged the gods for their Roman equivalents (Venus, Mercury, Jupiter or 'Jove'), but here they keep their Greek names (Aphrodite, Hermes, Zeus). I do, however, give the names of famous personalities in the Latinized and/or anglicized forms under which readers in English are likely to know them already (Plato, not Platōn; Homer, not Homēros). If a name ends with an -e or -o(n), that final syllable is always pronounced long; I mark some others where I think readers may find it helpful.

A note on cult titles: because Aphrodite was said to have been born at Paphos on Cyprus, she is often called 'the Paphian', 'the Cyprian', or 'Cypris'. Some stories had her born on the island of Cythera instead, so you will also see her addressed as 'the Cytherean', or 'Cytherea'. Athena is sometimes addressed as 'Pallas', and Apollo as 'Phoebus', the shining one.

Most of the poems in the Anthology are preceded by a heading that identifies the author, though not always correctly. They are set here in capitals. I have reproduced these headings faithfully, except when a poem was headed simply as having THE SAME author as the poem(s) it followed and the selection did not make their identity clear. My own supplements are indicated in angle brackets, ⟨THUS⟩, and evidently false attributions are placed in quotation marks, 'THUS'. These include 'PLATO'. Numerous epigrams are thus ascribed, and many are doubtless by the same author, whose name may well have been Plato and to whose Elysian shade I apologize: I considered it important to avoid confusion with the famous philosopher with whom some predecessors saw fit to associate these poems, but who lived before epigrams began to be performed at symposia or composed for publication in books.

The brief descriptions that introduce some of the epigrams, and the headings that from time to time inaugurate blocks of poems, are original to the Anthology's text. They are set here in italics. Again, angle brackets identify anything I have added, ⟨thus⟩.

Epigrams pack a lot in, and can be hard to unpack: if you see an asterisk beside a poem number, you will find an explanatory note on that poem at the back of the book.

SELECT BIBLIOGRAPHY

A Note on the Source

The ideal tool for readers who are inspired to read further in Greek epigram is W. R. Paton's Loeb Classical Library edition in five volumes (1916–18). It is unavoidably expensive compared to a selection in paperback but is terrific value, like all that series. And you do not need to buy it! Like most of the older Loebs it is out of copyright, and you can download its PDF for free from the website Loebolus, current URL https://ryanfb.github.io/loebolus/.

Commentaries on the Greek Anthology in English

Gow, A. S. F., and Page, D. L., *The Greek Anthology: Hellenistic Epigrams* (Cambridge: Cambridge University Press, 1965).

Gow, A. S. F., and Page, D. L., *The Greek Anthology: The Garland of Philip and Some Contemporary Epigrams* (Cambridge: Cambridge University Press, 1968).

Page, Denys L., *Further Greek Epigrams: Epigrams before AD 50 from the Greek Anthology and other sources, not included in 'Hellenistic Epigrams' or 'The Garland of Philip'* (Cambridge: Cambridge University Press, 1981.

Introductions to Epigram and the Anthology

Cameron, A(lan), *The Greek Anthology from Meleager to Planudes* (Oxford: Clarendon Press, 1993).

Henriksén, C. (ed.), *A Companion to Ancient Epigram* (Hoboken, NJ: Wiley Blackwell, 2019).

Kanellou, M., Petrovic, I., and Carey, C. (eds), *Greek Epigram from the Hellenistic to the Early Byzantine Era* (Oxford: Oxford University Press, 2019).

Livingstone, N., and Nisbet, G., *Epigram* (Cambridge: Cambridge University Press, 2010).

Historical and Cultural Contexts

Bowersock, G. W., *Greek Sophists in the Roman Empire* (Oxford: Oxford University Press, 1969).

Bowersock, G. W., *Hellenism in Late Antiquity* (Ann Arbor: University of Michigan Press, 1990).

Brown, P., *The World of Late Antiquity, AD 150–750* (San Diego, CA: Harcourt Brace Jovanovich, 1971).

Cameron, A(lan), *The Last Pagans of Rome* (Oxford: Oxford University Press, 2011).

Cameron, A(veril), *The Later Roman Empire, AD 284–430* (Cambridge, MA: Harvard University Press, 1993).

Clark, G., *Women in Late Antiquity: Pagan and Christian Lifestyles* (Oxford: Oxford University Press, 1993).

Cribiore, R., *Gymnastics of the Mind: Greek Education in Hellenistic and Roman Egypt* (Princeton: Princeton University Press, 2001).

Davidson, J., *Courtesans and Fishcakes: The Consuming Passions of Classical Athens* (London: St Martin's Press, 1998).

Erskine, A. (ed.), *A Companion to the Hellenistic World* (Malden, MA: Blackwell, 2003).

Garland, L., *Byzantine Empresses: Women and Power in Byzantium, AD 527–1204* (London and New York: Routledge, 1999).

Garnsey, P., *Food and Society in Classical Antiquity* (Cambridge: Cambridge University Press, 1999).

Gigante, M., trans. Obbink, D., *Philodemus in Italy: The Books from Herculaneum* (Ann Arbor: University of Michigan Press, 2002).

Goldhill, S. (ed.), *Being Greek Under Rome: Cultural Identity, the Second Sophistic and the Development of Empire* (Cambridge: Cambridge University Press, 2001).

Green, P., *Alexander to Actium: The Historical Evolution of the Hellenistic Age* (Berkeley and Los Angeles: University of California Press, 1993).

Heather, P., *The Fall of the Roman Empire: A New History of Rome and the Barbarians* (New York: Oxford University Press, 2006).

Heather, P., *Rome Resurgent: War and Empire in the Age of Justinian* (New York: Oxford University Press, 2018).

Johnson, W. A., and Parker, H. N. (eds), *Ancient Literacies: The Culture of Reading in Greece and Rome* (New York: Oxford University Press, 2009).

Jones, A. H. M., *The Later Roman Empire, 284–602: A Social, Economic, and Administrative Survey*, 2 vols (Baltimore: Johns Hopkins University Press, 1964).

König, J., *Athletics and Literature in the Roman Empire* (Cambridge: Cambridge University Press, 2005).

Lane Fox, R., *Pagans and Christians* (Harmondsworth: Viking, 1986).

Masterson, M., Rabinowitz, N., and Robson, J. (eds), *Sex in Antiquity: Exploring Gender and Sexuality in the Ancient World* (Abingdon: Routledge, 2018).

Murray, O., *Sympotica: A Symposium on the Symposion* (Oxford: Clarendon Press, 1990).

Parsons, P. J., *City of the Sharp-Nosed Fish: Greek Lives in Roman Egypt* (London: Weidenfeld and Nicolson, 2007).

Reynolds, L. D., and Wilson, N. G., *Scribes and Scholars: A Guide to the Transmission of Greek and Latin Literature* (4th edn, Oxford: Oxford University Press, 2013).

Shipley, G., *The Greek World After Alexander, 323–30 BC* (London: Routledge, 2000).

Swain, S., *Hellenism and Empire: Language, Classicism, and Power in the Greek World, AD 50–250* (Oxford: Oxford University Press, 1996).

Walbank, F. W., *The Hellenistic World* (rev. edn, Cambridge, MA: Harvard University Press, 1993).

Wallace-Hadrill, A., *Rome's Cultural Revolution* (Cambridge: Cambridge University Press, 2008).

Whitmarsh, T., *The Second Sophistic* (Oxford: Oxford University Press, 2005).

Whittow, M., *The Making of Orthodox Byzantium, 600–1025* (London: Red Globe Press, 1996).

Wilkins, J., Harvey, D., and Dobson, M. (eds), *Food in Antiquity* (Exeter: Exeter University Press, 1995).

Wilkins, J., and Nadeau, R. (eds), *A Companion to Food in the Ancient World* (Malden, MA: Wiley Blackwell, 2015).

Hellenistic and Imperial Greek Epigram

Barbantani, S., *Three Burials (Ibycus, Stesichorus, Simonides): Facts and Fiction about Lyric Poets in Magna Graecia in the Epigrams of the Greek Anthology* (Alessandria: Edizioni dell'Orso, 2010).

Bing, P., and Bruss, J. (eds), *Brill's Companion to Hellenistic Epigram, Down to Philip* (Leiden: Brill, 2007).

Bowie, E., 'Doing Doric', in Evina Sistakou and Antonios Rengakos (eds), *Dialect, Diction, and Style in Greek Literary and Inscribed Epigram* (Berlin: Walter de Gruyter, 2016), 3–22.

Bruss, J. S., *Hidden Presences: Monuments, Gravesites, and Corpses in Greek Funerary Epigram* (Leuven: Peeters, 2000).

Cairns, F., *Hellenistic Epigram: Contexts of Exploration* (Cambridge: Cambridge University Press, 2016).

Cameron, A., *Callimachus and His Critics* (Princeton: Princeton University Press, 1995).

Fantuzzi, M., and Hunter, R., *Tradition and Innovation in Hellenistic Poetry* (Cambridge: Cambridge University Press, 2004).

Goldschmidt, H., and Graziosi, B., *Tombs of the Ancient Poets: Between Literary Reception and Material Culture* (Oxford: Oxford University Press, 2018).

Gutzwiller, K., *Poetic Garlands: Hellenistic Epigrams in Context* (Berkeley and Los Angeles: University of California Press, 1998).

Gutzwiller, K., *A Guide to Hellenistic Literature* (Oxford: Blackwell).

Harder, M. A., Regtuit, R. F., and Wakker, G. C. (eds), *Hellenistic Epigrams* (Leuven: Peeters, 2002).

Nisbet, G., *Greek Epigram in the Roman Empire: Martial's Forgotten Rivals* (Oxford: Oxford University Press, 2013).

Rosenmeyer, P. A., *The Language of Ruins: Greek and Latin Inscriptions on the Memnon Colossus* (New York: Oxford University Press, 2018).

Tarán, S. L., *The Art of Variation in the Hellenistic Epigram* (Leiden: Brill, 1979).

Tueller, M. A., *Look Who's Talking: Innovations in Voice and Identity in Hellenistic Epigram* (Leuven: Peeters, 2008).

Late Antique and Byzantine Epigram

Agosti, G., 'Greek Poetry', in S. F. Johnson (ed.), *The Oxford Handbook of Late Antiquity* (New York: Oxford University Press, 2012), 361–404.

Cameron, A(lan), *Porphyrius the Charioteer* (Oxford: Oxford University Press, 1973).

Cameron, A(veril), *Agathias* (Oxford: Oxford University Press, 1970).

Mulligan, B., 'Epigrams, Occasional Poetry, and Poetic Games', in S. McGill and E. J. Watts (eds), *A Companion to Late Antique Literature* (Hoboken, NJ: Wiley Blackwell, 2018), 241–58.

Smith, S. D., *Greek Epigram and Byzantine Culture: Gender, Desire, and Denial in the Age of Justinian* (Cambridge: Cambridge University Press, 2019).

A great many epigrams survive in the margins of Byzantine manuscripts, commenting on the texts therein; https://www.dbbe.ugent.be gathers them in and records their contexts.

Individual Poets

Acosta-Hughes, B., Kosmetatou, E., Cuypers, M., and Angiò, F. (trans.), *New Poems Attributed to Posidippus: An Electronic Text-in-progress*, https://chs.harvard.edu/CHS/article/display/1343.

Gutzwiller, K. (ed.), *The New Posidippus: A Hellenistic Poetry Book* (Oxford: Oxford University Press, 2005).

Page, D., *The Epigrams of Rufinus* (Cambridge: Cambridge University Press, 1978).

Sider, D., *The Epigrams of Philodemos* (New York: Oxford University Press, 1997).

Reception of Greek Epigram

Haynes, K., 'The Modern Reception of Greek Epigram', in Bing and Bruss (eds), *Brill's Companion to Hellenistic Epigram*, 565–83.

Hutton, J., *The Greek Anthology in Italy to the Year 1800* (Ithaca, NY: Cornell University Press, 1930).

Hutton, J., *The Greek Anthology in France and in the Latin Writers of the Netherlands to the Year 1800* (Ithaca, NY: Cornell University Press, 1935).

Nisbet, G., 'Flowers in the Wilderness: Greek Epigram in the Late Nineteenth and Early Twentieth Centuries', in Stephen Harrison and Christopher Stray (eds), *Expurgating the Classics: Editing Out in Greek and Latin* (London: Bristol Classical Press, 2012).

Nisbet, G., *Greek Epigram in Reception: J. A. Symonds, Oscar Wilde, and the Invention of Desire, 1805–1929* (Oxford: Oxford University Press, 2013).

Nisbet, G., 'Kenneth Rexroth, Greek Anthologist', in Sheila Murnaghan and Ralph M. Rosen (eds), *Hip Sublime: Beat Writers and the Classical Tradition* (Columbus: Ohio State University Press, 2018).

Vandiver, E., *Stand in the Trench, Achilles: Classical Receptions in British Poetry of the Great War* (Oxford: Oxford University Press, 2010).

Some Notable Translations and Imitations

Bland, R., with Merivale, J. H., *Translations Chiefly from the Greek Anthology; With Tales and Miscellaneous Poems* (London: Richard Phillips, 1806).

Bland, R., with Merivale, J. H., *Collections from the Greek Anthology and from the Pastoral, Elegiac, and Dramatic Poets of Greece* (London: Richard Phillips, 1813).

Burges, G., *The Greek Anthology, as Selected for the Use of Westminster, Eton and other Public Schools, Literally Translated into English Prose* (London: George Bell and Sons, 1852).

Delanty, G., *The Greek Anthology, Book XVII* (Manchester: Carcenet, 2013).

Fitts, D., *From the Greek Anthology: Poems in English Paraphrase* (London: Faber and Faber).

Harrison, T. (1984), *Palladas: Poems; A Selection in Versions* (London: Rex Collings).

Hine, D., *Puerilities: Erotic Epigrams of the Greek Anthology* (Princeton: Princeton University Press, 2001).

Jay, P., *The Greek Anthology and Other Ancient Greek Epigrams* (Harmondsworth: Penguin Books, 1981).

Lang, Andrew, *Grass of Parnassus* (London: Longmans, Green, 1888).

Leslie, S., *The Greek Anthology Selected and Translated with a Prolegomenon* (London: Ernest Benn, 1929).

Mackail, J. W., *Select Epigrams from the Greek Anthology: Edited with Revised Text, Translation, Introduction, and Notes* (London: Longmans, Green, 1890).

Mackail, J. W., *Select Epigrams from the Greek Anthology: Translated* (London: Longmans, Green, 1908).

Merivale, J. H. (ed.), *Collections from the Greek Anthology: A New Edition, Comprising the Fragments of Early Lyric Poetry, with Specimens of All the Poets Included in Meleager's Garland* (London: Longman and John Murray, 1830).

Paton, W. R., *The Greek Anthology*, 5 vols (London: William Heinemann; New York: G. P. Putnam's Sons, 1916–18).

Rexroth, K., *Poems from the Greek Anthology* (Ann Arbor: University of Michigan Press, 1962).

Rice, W., *Pagan Pictures* (Chicago: Boni and Liveright, 1927).

Rodd, J. R., *Love, Worship and Death: Some Renderings from the Greek Anthology* (London: Edward Arnold, 1916).

Further Reading in Oxford World's Classics

Greek Lyric Poetry, trans. M. L. West.

Achilles Tatius, *Leucippe and Clitophon*, trans. Tim Whitmarsh.

Catullus, *The Complete Poems*, trans. and ed. Guy Lee.

Herodotus, *The Histories*, trans. Robin Waterfield.

Longus, *Daphnis and Chloe*, trans. Donald McCail.

Lucian, *Selected Dialogues*, trans. C. D. N. Costa.

Martial, *Epigrams*, trans. Gideon Nisbet.

TIMELINE OF MAIN POETS AND ANTHOLOGISTS

6th to 5th century BC	Simonides
3rd century BC	Asclepiades
	Callimachus
	Dioscorides
	Hedylus
	Leonidas of Tarentum
	Mnasalcas
	Posidippus
	Theocritus
2nd century BC	Antipater of Sidon
1st century BC	Archias
	Antipater of Thessalonica
	Gaetulicus
	Meleager (*Garland*)
	Philodemus
1st century BC–1st century AD	Antipater of Thessalonica
	Crinagoras
	Marcus Argentarius
1st century AD	Leonidas of Alexandria
	Lucillius
	Nicarchus
	Philip (*Garland*)
	Rufinus?
	Strato
2nd century AD	Ammianus
	Diogenian (*Anthologion*)
	Lucian
4th century AD	Gregory of Nazianzus 'the Theologian'
	Palladas
6th century AD	Agathias (*Cycle*)
	Julian, Prefect of Egypt
	Macedonius the Consul
	Metrodorus (arithmetical puzzles)
	Paul the Silentiary
	The poet of the Cyzicene epigrams?

OUTLINE OF THE ANTHOLOGY

THE following account gives the transmitted title of each book, translates its editorial preface (if any), summarizes its content, and adds a little context.

Book 1: The Christian Epigrams

'Let the pious and godly epigrams of the Christians be placed first in our sequence, even if the pagans are displeased.'

This anonymous compilation, much of it inscriptional in origin, preserves valuable information on many lost Byzantine churches. Many of its poems are in hexameters rather than epigram's traditional elegiac couplets.

Book 2: Christodorus, Poet of Coptic Thebes

'Description of the statues of the public gymnasium known as Zeuxippus.'

A single hexameter poem of 416 lines by an Egyptian-born epic poet, composed on the occasion of a visit to Constantinople some time before AD 532 (the year the Zeuxippus Baths burned down). It does not contain epigrams.

Book 3: Epigrams at Cyzicus

'At Cyzicus, inside the Temple of Apollonis, mother of Attalus and Eumenes: epigrams which were inscribed on the tablets set into the columns. These tablets contained narrative scenes, carved in low relief, as is set out below.'

This short sequence of nineteen epigrams by an unknown author was written to accompany artistic representations of scenes from myth placed at regular intervals inside the temple, a kind of pagan Stations of the Cross. They are the only evidence for a temple to Apollonis.

She was the wife of Attalus I (second century BC), a member of the Attalid dynasty that ruled parts of Asia Minor in the later Hellenistic era. All the scenes illustrate filial piety; the sequence culminates in the myth of Romulus and Remus (the Attalids were Roman allies). The book was probably not part of Cephalas' anthology.

Book 4: The Prefaces of the Various Anthologies

This book contains the authors' elegiac prefaces to the *Garlands* of Meleager and Philip, Agathias' hexameter preface to his *Cycle*, and an additional elegiac poem that Agathias must have written to conclude it (Meleager had closed his *Garland* with at least two such epigrams, now found at 12.256–7). With this one Agathian exception, the book contains no epigrams. Cephalas perhaps placed all this material at the start of his Anthology by way of an introduction.

Book 5: Erotic Epigrams by Various Poets

Here we enter the Cephalan anthology proper, with elegiac epigrams on the frustration and fulfilment of heterosexual desire.

Book 6: Dedicatory Epigrams

These 'anathematic' epigrams are written as if to accompany dedications to gods. Many of them adopt the persona of a person hanging up their tools as a thank-offering at the end of a successful career: the book thus gives insight into ancient crafts and trades. Some of its epigrams are genuinely inscriptional and bear witness to significant historical events.

Book 7: Epitaphic Epigrams

Many of these poems are literary fictions that give their authors the last word on antiquity's great authors, philosophers, and heroes. There are numerous epitaphs for sailors and fishermen lost at sea, a type of epigram that we can now trace back to Posidippus (see Introduction, pp. x–xi).

Book 8: Epigrams of St Gregory the Theologian

All the poems in this book are by Gregory of Nazianzus, a fourth-century theologian who helped fix the Christian position on the Holy

Trinity and eventually became Archbishop of Constantinople. Gregory wrote sequences of epigrams mourning dead friends and family members, and protesting against the despoliation of tombs. His book is unlikely to have been part of the Anthology of Cephalas.

Book 9: Epideictic Epigrams

Paraphrased in the Loeb as 'declamatory and descriptive', the term 'epideictic' indicates that these epigrams are written primarily as demonstrations of rhetorical technique. Since every would-be poet was rhetorically educated, this makes for a very broad and loosely defined category, and the book is by far the Anthology's biggest, at over 800 poems.

Book 10: Advisory Epigrams

The 'protreptic' epigrams in this book give advice for or against courses of action. The book is much shorter than most, at not much more than 100 poems, and its content is much more of a mixed bag than the title suggests. Many of its poems are by Palladas (fourth century AD). It was not compiled by Cephalas.

Book 11: Scoptic and Sympotic Epigrams

Agathias had given each of these types its own book, but Cephalas combined them. It is a book of unequal halves: the sympotic content ends at epigram 64, in a book of well over 400 poems. The rest are 'scoptic' (roughly speaking, satirical) epigrams that mock human pretension and deviations from the social norm. The main poets of this book, Lucillius and Nicarchus, influenced Rome's master of epigram, Martial.

Book 12: Strato's Boyish Muse

'And who would I be if, having laid out for you the study of all that has been said, I concealed the *Boyish Muse* of Strato of Sardis? The author published it for his friends as a joke, finding his own delight in the diction of his epigrams rather than their meaning. So pay close attention to what follows, "For in dances," as the tragic poet says, "the sensible woman will not be led astray."'

This book of poems on the frustration and fulfilment of homosexual desire makes a pair with Book 5. The title *Boyish Muse* originally applied to a book composed wholly by Strato, as described in the editorial preface. The compiler of Book 12 then larded this Stratonian book with additional poems by other hands, foremost among them Meleager, whose *Garland* had made no distinction between homosexual and heterosexual loves (any more than did the poems of his Latin contemporary, Catullus). Strato himself wrote in the first or early second century AD; nineteenth-century critics preferred to place him as late as possible so as to preserve the purity of their vision of classical Greece.

Book 13: Epigrams in Assorted Metres

A very short book. Its point is to collect epigrams in many different metres, a feature that only the bravest of translators would attempt to reproduce. Since metrical variety was the criterion for inclusion, the content is thematically very varied, a kind of anthology-in-miniature. It was not compiled by Cephalas.

Book 14: Arithmetical Problems, Riddles, and Oracles

Puzzle-poems of various kinds, and riddling oracular pronouncements in hexameter, many of the latter excerpted from Herodotus. Very few poems here are assigned authors; the material was part of popular tradition. It was not compiled by Cephalas.

Book 15: Miscellaneous Epigrams

Miscellaneous descriptive poems along with the so-called *technopaegnia*, poems composed in lines of different lengths so that each forms, on the page, the shape of the object it describes: an altar, an axe, an egg, and so on. This book was perhaps added to Cephalas' Anthology by Constantine the Rhodian, some of whose poems it contains.

'Book 16': The Planudean Appendix

As described in the Introduction (p. xiv), this book assembles in order all the poems found in the Planudean Anthology but absent from the Palatine manuscript, mostly describing works of art.

EPIGRAMS FROM THE
GREEK ANTHOLOGY

BOOK 1
THE CHRISTIAN EPIGRAMS

I

On the lantern of Hagia Sophia

> The icons that the heretics pulled down
> Our pious lords did here set back in place.

2*

On the apse at Blachernae

> Sophia's husband Justin, man of God,
> Whom Christ ordained to settle all aright
> And granted glory on the battlefield,
> Seeing the Virgin Mother's house unsound,
> Redressed its flaws and wrought it sturdily.

3

On the same, in the same place

> The Elder Justin to God's Mother raised
> This beauteous shrine ablaze with loveliness;
> The Younger Justin, ruling after him,
> Granted it splendour greater than before.

4*

On the Church of the Forerunner [John the Baptist] in the district of Studius

> To Christ's great servant, John, did Studius build
> This splendid house; and found his labours here
> Swiftly repaid, taking the Consul's rods.

5*

On the Church of the Holy Apostle Thomas in the district of Amantius

> This house, Amantius, you built for God
> In midst of sea to fight the gyring wave.
> No wind from south or north shall ever shake
> Your holy home, protected by this shrine
> As God ordained. May you live many days
> For making Newborn Rome more glorious,
> Who have attacked and conquered ocean's deep.

6*

On the Church of St Theodore in the district of Sphoracius

> Escaping safe from fire, Sphoracius
> Constructed for the martyr this new shrine.

10*

On the Church of the Holy Martyr Polyeuctus

> The Empress Eudocia, bending speed
> To honour God, first built this temple here,
> But did not build so mighty or so great:
> Not that she counted cost, or lacked the means—
> In what are queens found lacking? No, she owned
> A soul prophetic that her progeny
> Would know to beautify it all the more.
> From her did Juliana, fourth in line,
> A darling child of blessed parentage,
> Derive her royal blood, nor did she dash
> Her forebear's hopes, whose excellence bred true:
> From humble state she raised it great and fine,
> And magnified her ancestors' renown
> Who wielded many sceptres. All they wrought,
> Those forebears, she rebuilt more loftily,
> Keeping true faith in eager love of Christ.
> Who does not know this Juliana's fame:
> How with unstinting deeds she glorified

Her parents too, mindful of piety?
All by herself, by sweat of righteous brow,
She built a dwelling, worthy of the saint,
For Polyeuctus who will never die.
She ever knew to offer blameless gifts
To all the champions of the Heavenly King.
Every land shouts, and every city too—
The mightier her deeds, the happier
She made her parents. Where can one *not* find
That Juliana has set high and grand
A temple to the saints? And, where not see
The traces of your pious handiwork,
Wrought single-handed? What place in the world
That has not come to know your eagerness,
Brimming with piety? Every nation's men
Sing of your labours that shall ever live
In memory. Pious deeds cannot be hid,
Nor can neglect erase the prizes claimed
By excellence in charitable toil.
How many houses in the cause of God
Your hand erects, not even *you* can tell;
The whole world wide, you single-handed built
Shrines beyond number in my reckoning,
And ever paying fearful reverence
To servants of the Lord in Heaven above.
Treading each step her parents walked before
In charitable giving, she secured
Immortal life for all her family
And walked in piety until the end.
Therefore, you servants of the Heavenly King,
All you who knew her generosity
And whom she housed in temples, take her in:
Embrace her fondly, and her son as well;
His daughters too; and let this dynasty
Of benefactors see their fame endure
As long as Sun drives fiery chariot.

⟨*a second inscription of thirty-five lines is also preserved here, from inside the entrance to the church*⟩

11*

On the Holy Anargyri in the district of Basiliscus

> Unto your servants I, your servant too,
> Sophia, make this gift. Accept your own,
> Christ, and repay Justinian my lord
> In victories piled upon victories
> Against the plagues and the barbarians.

12*

On St Euphemia of Olybrius

> I am the house of Holy Trinity.
> Three generations built me in a row:
> The first came safe through wars and foreign tribes
> To found me, and to offer me to God
> In thanks for His protection in her trials;
> She was Eudoxia, Theodosius' child.
> Placidia her daughter next contrived
> To make me lovely, with her husband's aid,
> Most blessed man; and if in any way
> My beauty failed to reach magnificence,
> Then Juliana, sparing no expense,
> Bestowed it in her parents' memory.
> She brought the highest glory to them both,
> And to her famous grandmother as well,
> By adding to my ornament of old.
> Thus was I made, and thus I came to be.

13

On the same church, inside the gallery

> Even aforetime, I was exquisite;
> But now I shine more splendid than before.

14

Another

> Like mother and like foremother before,
> My former skin did Juliana slough:
> The bloom now rises fresh upon my face.

15

Another

> Beauty then outdid beauty: for my work,
> Already sung in fame across the world,
> Attained a beauty higher than that boast,
> Rising with Juliana's to the stars.

16

Another

> The temple's patron martyr did inspire
> And aid our Juliana in her toils,
> Else she had never worked such and so great:
> A masterpiece, that Heaven's glory swells.

17

Another

> Marvel no more at tales of men of old.
> Their praise among the late-born will endure,
> But not for craft, as Juliana's fame:
> Ingenious worker, who surpassed the plans
> Of all her brilliant ancestors of old.

23

(MARINUS)

On the Lord Christ

> Of deathless Father co-eternal Son,
> Lord of all things, of earth and sea and sky:

Your servant, Marinus, who wrote this book,
Asks that you favour him with eloquence
And with the gift of clever argument.

25

CLAUDIANUS

On the same

Lord Christ, God's wisdom, and Creation's king,
Who shaped our mortal race in former time,
Grant I may run life's course in Your commands.

32

CLAUDIANUS

On the Archangel Michael

Here lies by God's command the remedy
For mortals pressed by woe of flesh or soul;
Creation's woe and grief flee at your name,
Your icon, or your dwelling, Michaël.

34*

AGATHIAS SCHOLASTICUS

On an icon of the Archangel on Platē

Prince of the Angels, whom we cannot see,
His form and essence incorporeal:
Daring indeed the wax that mimicked him.
Yet it does not lack grace: the mortal man
Who looks upon this icon guides his soul
Towards an Image mightier by far;
No longer does his worship vacillate,
But he engraves this likeness deep within,
And quakes as if the Archangel were there.
The eyes stir depths of soul, and art knows well
How colours may translate the spirit's plea.

35*

BY THE SAME

On the same in the Sosthenium

> Aemilianus, come from Caria,
> And John, who came with him along the way;
> Rufinus too, of Alexandria;
> Agathias, of Asia. They attained
> The fourth year in their study of the Law,
> And in your honour, blessed Archangel,
> Offered this painted image, praying too
> For a bright future. Make your presence felt
> And guide their hopes for life that is to come.

36*

BY THE SAME

On a picture of Theodore the Illustrious, who was twice consul, in which he is shown receiving his offices from the Archangel in Ephesus

> Look kindly on your portrait, Archangel;
> We cannot see your face, but these our gifts
> Are such as mortals make. Because of you
> Theodore wears the Magistrus' belt,
> And twice contends for the Proconsuls' throne.
> The painting witnesses his gratitude:
> He struck its coloured image in reply,
> To imitate the favour you have shown.

37

On the birth of Christ

> Trumpets and lightning, and the earth resounds;
> But to your Virgin Mother you came down
> And trod all silently upon your way.

38

On the same

> This manger was as Heaven, and was more;
> For Heaven is this newborn's handiwork.

39

On the shepherds and the angels

> One dance, one song for men and angels too,
> For man and God have now become as one.

47

On the baptism [of Christ]

> From deathless Father might Spirit came,
> At His Son's baptism in Jordan's stream.

49

On Lazarus

> 'Come here', said Christ, and Lazarus left Hell,
> His dusty nostrils once more drawing breath.

53

On Easter

> Christ spared the lamb the Law required, and made
> An offering for Eternity—Himself.
> He was both priest and chosen sacrifice.

56

On the Resurrection

> Christ, being God, dragged all the dead from Hell;
> Man-slaying Hades He left all forlorn.

62*

On the Ark when it crossed the Jordan

> The torrent yielded to the golden Ark.
> Look kindly, Christ: the Ark foreshadows You,
> For it is in this stream You were baptized.

80*

On John the Apostle

> John the Divine, high priest of Ephesus,
> At God's command first told 'the Word was God'.

88*

On St Dionysius

> You sang the ordered ranks of Heavenly Hosts;
> You drag to light the meaning that lay hid
> Beneath the surfaces of graven forms.
> You light the signal-fire that pleases God—
> The fire of holy sayings, wise of life.

94

⟨GREGORY OF NAZIANZUS⟩

On the death of the Holy Virgin

> By God's commands they came, exalted high,
> The radiant disciples, to her home:
> The Virgin, all immaculate. They called
> To one another coming, some from East,
> Some West, some South, some North, all to inter
> The body of the one who saved the world.

98*

⟨GREGORY OF NAZIANZUS⟩

In ⟨Melite⟩

> You see the Emperor Justin's famous work,
> Justinian's too, that mighty general,
> Glinting with precious metal beyond count.
> Famed Theodorus built it, raising up
> This city; for the third time shielding it,
> When a third time he held the Consulate.

101

⟨MENANDER PROTECTOR⟩

On a Persian magus who became a Christian and was martyred

> Before, I was a magus among Medes,
> I, Isbozētes, balancing my hopes
> On deadly lies. My city was in flames:
> I ran to help; so too a servant came
> Of Christ Almighty, and he quelled its force.
> Worsted, I won a Godlier victory.

103*

On the lintel of a house in Cyzicus, saved from a fire

> Momus the bloodthirsty, your bitter dart
> Slew your own self; for God delivered me
> From all your rage. I am a blessed home.

106*

In the Chrysotriclinus (Golden Banquet-hall) of Mazarinus

> Once more the ray of Truth has shone out bright,
> And dazed the liars; pious reverence
> Has multiplied, and error falls away.
> Faith blossoms and Grace spreads her foliage.

For see—Christ shines in images again
Atop the Empire's throne, and puts to rout
The gloomy shadow of the heresies.
Above the entrance, as at Heaven's gate,
The panel-painted Virgin stands her guard;
Our Emperor and Bishop close at hand
With their lieutenants are depicted there,
Dispelling error; in a circled band
Are all the sentries who defend this home:
Angels, disciples, martyrs, celebrants.
Therefore the Hall that bore a Golden name
We newly call the 'Banquet-hall of Christ',
Because it holds the throne of Christ the Lord;
His Mother's, also; icons of those men
Who bore Christ's message; and the portrait too
Of Michael, from whom holy wisdom springs.

109*

IGNATIUS, HEAD OF THE CHANCELLERY

On the Church of the Holy Mother at the spring

> The Virgin's tumbled shrine is now restored
> By Basil, Leo, and by Constantine.

110

In the same Church, in the dome, regarding the Ascension

> From earth ascending to your Father's throne,
> Saviour, your Mother's house you show to be
> A spring of thoughts tending to larger grace.

111

In the same Church, on the Crucifixion

> Hades has died, and vomits up its dead:
> Its purgative, the body of our Lord.

112*

In the same Church, on the Transfiguration

> Christ shines on Tabor brighter than the sun,
> And ends the shadow of the former Law.

113*

In the same Church, on the Presentation

> The infant we see now in elder's hands
> Was anciently the Architect of Time.

114

In the same Church, on the Salutation

> When our Lord greets the women, He declares
> The prelude to salvation of the world.

119*

The Argument: an eloquent defence. Homeric cento

The book of Patrick, a God-fearing priest, who wrought a great work, fashioning from the book of Homer a precious song of splendid lines, to declare the achievements of the invincible God:

- How He came to the society of men, how He took human form, and within the belly of a blameless maiden He lay hid, being little, He whom the boundless vault of heaven cannot contain;
- And how He latched upon the teat of the Virgin who bore God, sucking the stream of maiden milk it gushed;
- How wretched Herod slew the tender babes, seeking the doom of an Immortal God;
- How John washed Him in the river's flow;
- How He took twelve trusty mortals as his companions;
- How many people's limbs He made whole, as He banished foul diseases and made blind eyes see;
- And how He quelled the spurting flow of blood in the weeping woman who touched His robe;

- How many, conquered by the pitiless Fates, He led back to the light from the infernal Pit;
- And how He left us tokens of His holy Passion;
- And how at mortals' hands He languished in icy chains, of His own free will: for no earthly man could war against a God who rules on high, unless He Himself should bid it;
- How He died; how He burst the iron gates of Hell, and led from there to Heaven the souls of those obedient to God, in accordance with the immaculate commands of His Father, after He rose as the third dawn brought its light to mortals, scion of God the Father who has no beginning.

120*

In Blachernae. Iambs

> If upon earth you seek our God's dread throne,
> Marvel to look upon the Virgin's hall.
> She bears our God within her very arms
> And carries him unto this sacred place.
> Within, the fated rulers of this earth
> Have faith their sceptres share in victory;
> Within, the ever-watchful Patriarch
> Wards off the many crises of our world.
> When the barbarians invested us,
> They saw she was the general of our host
> And straight away bent unaccustomed necks.

END

BOOK 3
EPIGRAMS AT CYZICUS

At Cyzicus, inside the Temple of Apollonis, mother of Attalus and Eumenes: epigrams which were inscribed on the tablets set into the columns. These tablets contained narrative scenes, carved in low relief, as is set out below.

1*

On Dionysus, bringing his mother Semele up to heaven, with Hermes in the lead; and with Satyrs and Silens escorting them, bearing torches

> Slain in her labour-pains by Zeus's bolt,
> She was the fair-haired child of Harmony
> And Cadmus. From the depths of Acheron
> Her thyrsus-loving son leads her aloft,
> Avenging Pentheus' atheistic spite.

2*

The second pillar has Telephus when he has been recognized by his mother

> I left the lowland path of Arcady
> For mother Auge's sake, and so I came,
> I, Telephus, to this Teuthranian land,
> Being myself dear son of Heracles,
> To bring her back to the Arcadian plain.

3*

The third has Phoenix blinded by his father Amyntor, and Alcimede obstructing her husband

> Alcimede seeks to restrain her man,
> Amyntor, and to end the father's rage
> Against the son. Phoenix incurred that hate
> For his good mother's sake, and all because
> His father took a slave as concubine.

Slanderous whispers tricked him into wrath
Against the boy, and so he brought to bear
A filicidal torch against his eyes.

4*

The fourth has Polymēdes and Clytius, the sons of Phineus of Thrace, who butchered their father's Phrygian wife, because he brought her in as a second wife alongside their mother, Cleopatra

For sake of their own mother, Clytius
And Polymedes of famed intellect
Are murdering their Phrygian stepmother.
And Cleopatra now exults in pride,
For she has seen the bride of Phineus
Made subject, not to husband, but to law.

5

The fifth has Cresphontes killing Polyphontes, his father's murderer. Merope is there too, wielding a club and cooperating with her son in the man's demise.

Crephontes' father you did slay before:
You wanted, Polyphontes, to befoul
The bed of that man's lawful wedded wife.
Time passed, and then his son came after you,
Avenged his father's murder, for the sake
Of mother Merope. And this is why
His spear is in your back, and she assists,
Smiting about your brows with heavy club.

6*

The sixth has Python being killed by Apollo and Artemis, because it confronted Lēto and stopped her journeying to Delphi to take up her position as oracle

The earth-born Python—Leto turns her head,
Disgusted at its mass of scaly coils.
It means the prudent goddess harm: but see,

Apollo from his vantage aims his bow
And soaks the beast in blood. At Delphi soon
He will imbue the tripod with his power;
The monster hisses in its agony.

7*

*The seventh, on the north side ⟨of the temple⟩, has the story of Amphiōn
and Zethus tying Dirce to the bull because she was unduly harsh to their
mother, Antiope, on account of her seduction by ⟨Dirce's⟩ husband Lycus,
⟨after she had been betrayed⟩ by her own father, Nycteus*

Zethus and Amphion, twin cubs of Zeus:
You slay this Dirce, who did so maltreat
Antiope, your mother. Bound in chains
She kept her then, for her own jealous rage;
But now she sobs, entreating for her life.
Hitch her with double cord upon the bull,
That it may drag her body through this copse.

8

*On the eighth is Odysseus' oracular consultation with the dead: he is depicted
questioning his mother, Anticlea, about what is happening at home*

Clever Odysseus' mother, Anticlea,
You did not live to greet your son's return
To Ithaca; but see him now amazed
To meet you on the banks of Acheron,
And look upon the mother he holds dear.

9

*On the ninth have been carved Pelias and Nēleus, the sons of Poseidon,
rescuing their mother Tyro from her bonds. Her father, Salmoneus, had
lately bound her because she had been seduced, and her stepmother, Sidēro,
had inflicted tortures upon her.*

Let not Sidēro's bonds afflict you now;
Cower no longer, Tyro, at the feet
Of Salmoneus, your father. For no more

Shall he cage you a slave, now that he sees
Neleus and Pelias, come to stop his game.

10*

*On the western side, at the start of the tenth tablet ⟨sic⟩ are carved
Eunous and Thoas, whom Hypsipyle bore, at the moment when they are
recognized by their mother. They are showing her the golden grapevine
that was the token of their birth, and they are rescuing her from being
executed by Eurydice for the death of Archemorus.*

Thoas, show Bacchus' plant, and thereby save
Hypsipyle, your mother, now a slave.
For since the serpent slew Archemorus
She has endured spite from Eurydice.
And you go too, Eunous: leave behind
Asopis' girl, in order to convey
To lovely Lemnos her who gave you birth.

11

*On the eleventh, Polydectes, King of Seriphus, is being turned into stone by
Perseus using the Gorgon's head. He had sent Perseus to fetch the Gorgon's
head because he wanted to marry Perseus' mother, and by the providence of
Justice he himself suffered the very death that he had intended for another.*

You dared, rash Polydectes, to defile
Danäe's bed, taking the place of Zeus
In shameful union; and as consequence,
Perseus here unveiled the Gorgon's eyes,
And for his mother's joy turned you to stone.

12

*On the twelfth is Ixion, killing Phorbas and Polymēlus for the murder of
his mother Megara. For when she chose not to marry either of them, they
took offence and slew her.*

Here Ixion lays Phorbas on the ground,
And Polymēlus too, and takes revenge
For their own vengeance on his mother dear.

13*

The thirteenth has Heracles leading his mother, Alcmene, to the Elysian Field, and giving her in marriage to Rhadamanthus; and Heracles himself being admitted into the company of gods

> To Rhadamanthus did bold Heracles
> Offer as bride his mother Alcmene.

14*

On the fourteenth is Tityus being shot by Apollo and Artemis, because he dared assault their mother, Leto

> Lustful and folly-drunk, why did you try
> To force Zeus' bedmate's bed? As you deserved,
> He dyes you in your blood; food for the beasts
> And birds he leaves you, justly, on the ground.

15*

On the fifteenth, Bellerophon is being saved by his son Glaucus, after he had fallen from Pegasus onto the Aleian plain. He was about to be mur-dered by Megapenthes, son of Proetus.

> No longer could Bellerophon withstand
> The murderous son of Proetus, the death
>
> .   .   .   .
>
> Glaucus, in vain . . . shall he flee Iobates' . . .
> For thus the Fates' . . . thread span.
> And you drew near and spared your father death,
> And witnessed closely to the glorious tale.

16*

Opposite the temple doors as you approach are Aeolus and Boeotus, the sons of Poseidon, rescuing their mother Melanippe from the bonds that she was confined in by her father because she had been seduced

> Aeolus and Boeotus, when you saved
> Your mother's life, your labour was both wise

And filially loving: by which deed
You showed yourself to be the bravest men,
One from Aeolis, one Boeotian.

17*

On the seventeenth, Anapis and Amphinomus, who, when the volcanoes of Sicily were erupting, reached safety through the flames carrying nothing but their parents

Of fire and earth . . .

⟨*the rest of the epigram is lost*⟩

18

On the eighteenth are Cleobis and Biton. Their mother was the priestess of Hera at Argos; they put their own necks beneath the yoke (because the team of oxen was too slow) and so enabled her to perform the sacred rites. According to the story, she was so pleased by this that she prayed to the goddess that her sons should meet with whatever was finest among mortals; and after she had made this prayer, the boys died that same night.

This story of Cydippe and her sons,
And of their holy reverence, is not false;
Its truth is ample. For their toil was sweet,
And in due season for their manly youth:
For holy love of mother, they performed
A famous labour. In the world below
May you rejoice, men famed for piety,
And may your tale alone endure all time.

19*

On the nineteenth are Remus and Romulus, rescuing their mother, whose name was Servilia, from Amulius' chastisement: for Ares had seduced her and fathered children on her; and they were exposed, and a she-wolf nursed them. When they grew to manhood, therefore, they freed their mother from her bonds, and when they had founded Rome they restored Numitor to his kingship.

In secret you brought forth this brood of boys,
For Ares, twins: Remus, and Romulus.
A she-wolf was their wet-nurse; in a cave
The creature raised them up till they were men,
Who rescued you by force from hardened woe.

                                END

BOOK 5
EROTIC EPIGRAMS BY
VARIOUS POETS

I
⟨CEPHALAS' PROEM⟩

I set a fire in young men's hearts—a flame
Intense, yet erudite. I put Love first,
Making the god the master of my speech:
For He it is who makes their torches blaze.

2
ANONYMOUS

Sthenelais, city-burner, of steep price,
Whose utterance is gold to those who yearn—
My dream laid her beside me all the night
Until sweet daybreak, all without a fee.
No more I'll beg for favour from that girl
From overseas, nor weep at my own fate:
I'll sleep, and sleep will grant me my desire.

3*
ANTIPATER OF THESSALONICA

The dark before the day is over now,
Chrysilla, and the cockerel of dawn
has long since trumpeted to usher in
Envious daybreak. Damn you, jealous bird!
You drive me now from home, and on toward
The endless babble of the bachelors.
Surely, Tithonus, you are growing old:
Why else would you have driven from your bed
Your bedmate, Dawn, before the sun was up?

4
PHILODEMUS

The silent lamp, complicit partner in
The things we mustn't speak of carelessly:
Philaenis, make it drunk with drops of oil.
Then take your leave: for Love alone desires
No living witness; close the jointed door.
And *you*, dear Xantho—but the lover's bed
Well knows what Aphrodite has in store.

5
STATYLLIUS FLACCUS

A silver lamp am I, and Flaccus' gift
To faithless Nape, faithful witness to
Her night-time loves: I gutter by the bed
And watch the young girl's versatile disgrace.
Flaccus, these sore concerns keep you from sleep:
Though we are parted, we are both ablaze.

6*
CALLIMACHUS

Callignotus swore he never would prefer
Another to Ionis, boy or girl.
He swore; but they say truly, that the oaths
Of lovers cannot reach the listening dead.
Now he is heated by a young man's flame;
And as for his pathetic fiancée,
It's like they say of the Megarians:
'Never was in the running'—such a shame.

8
MELEAGER

You holy Night, you lamp: no celebrants
But you we chose, to witness to our vows.

His was to love me always, mine to leave
Him never; and the two of you were there.
But now he says those oaths are borne away
On water, void: and, lamp, you see him now
Enfolded by another—and by more.

12

RUFINUS

Let's take a bath, dear Prodica, and then
Let's crown our heads with garlands, and knock back
The unmixed wine; we'll grab the bigger cups.
The *dolce vita*'s short, and then old age
Will end our fun, and then *we* end, in death.

15*

THE SAME

Where now Praxiteles? Polyclitus' hands,
That graced with life the art of bygone days?
Who now shall carve Melite's fragrant hair,
Her blazing eyes, the brilliance of her neck?
Where are the shapers, cutting into stone?
If gods are due a statue, then a shrine
Is owing to a beauty such as she.

17*

GAETULICUS

You watcher of the surf along the beach,
I send you barley-cakes and offerings
A poor man gives: tomorrow I must sail
The wide Ionian, racing to the arms
Of my own Eidothea. Shine and smile
Upon my love, and on my mast as well,
Cypris, the queen who rules both bed and shore.

19*

RUFINUS

I'm not boy-crazy like I was before,
Upon a time; girl-crazed they call me now,
Discus exchanged for rattle; and instead
Of artless boy-flesh, shades of powder please,
And plastered bloom of rouge. It comes to this:
Dolphins shall graze in Erymanthus' groves,
Swift-running deer nip at the grey sea's swell.

21*

RUFINUS

Didn't I say to you, 'We're getting old'?
And didn't I foretell it, Prodica:
'The passion-killers will be coming soon'?
And here they are: the wrinkles, the grey hairs,
The body worn and chafed, the mouth that lacks
Its former charms. You think yourself so high,
But no one makes advances to you now,
Or pays you court, or supplicates in prayer:
We all walk past you, like a roadside tomb.

24

'PHILODEMUS' (PROBABLY MELEAGER)

My soul is telling me to get away
From Heliodora, source of my desire.
These jealous tears: it knows them from before.
It tells me, but I cannot find the strength
To go. The tramp herself tells me I should,
And as she tells me, she is kissing me.

27

RUFINUS

Where are your golden beauties, Melissa,
that everyone admired and talked about,

and dreamed of? Where your frown, your self-regard,
Your swan-neck, and the bracelets all of gold
that ringed your haughty ankles? Now your hair
Is lank and splitting; rags around your feet;
Lascivious mistresses meet ends like these.

35*

RUFINUS

I judged three arses, me, the owners' choice,
Flaunting the naked splendour of their limbs.
The first: a rounded, dimpled masterpiece—
Her buttocks' bloom was pale, soft to the touch.
The next was prominent, with snow-white flesh
That blushed more redly than a scarlet rose;
The third, a calm sea with a silent swell,
That billowed all untouched with luscious skin.
And if the judge of goddesses had seen
Such arses, he would not have wished to gaze
Again upon the ones he judged before.

38

NICARCHUS

A fine, big girl's for me, friend Simylus,
Whether she's at her peak, or past her prime.
If young, she'll clasp me in her arms; if old,
And wrinkled, Simylus, she'll suck me off.

40

BY THE SAME

Don't listen to your mum, Philoumene:
And if I've gone and stepped away from town,
Don't listen to their mocking. Mock them back,
And make a better fist of life than I.
Turn every stone, and keep yourself, and write
To tell me to what happy shore you've come.

Try to control your spending. Pay the rent;
Whatever's left can buy a coat for me.
And if you're pregnant, keep it—don't be scared:
The child will know its father once it's grown.

41

RUFINUS

Who tore your clothes, exposed you, threw you out?
Who has a heart of stone, and cannot see?
He found you with a lover, I suppose;
He came at a bad time: that's how it goes.
Everyone's at it, child—women, I mean.
Just next time, when a man's in, and he's not,
Wedge the door shut, and don't get caught again.

42*

RUFINUS

I hate an easy woman, and I hate
One who puts too much store by her good name;
The one's too quick to yield; the other, slow.

46

PHILODEMUS

Good day. *Good day to you.* And what's your name?
What's yours? No need for deeper questions yet.
The same to you. And don't you have a man?
I do—whoever wants me. How about
Dinner with me tomorrow? *If you like.*
Good! What's your rate? *You needn't pay up front.*
That's odd. *Just pay me what you think I'm worth,
After you've slept with me.* You're very fair.
What's your address? I'll send word. *Take this down.*
What time will you arrive? *The time you like.*
I'd like it right now. *Well then; lead the way.*

49*

GALLUS

Lyde am I, who quickly services
Three for the price of one. I take the first
Above the waist, the second down below,
The third, behind. I can accommodate
The pederast, the devotee of girls,
The oral addict—simultaneously.
You're pressed for time? I've two in; don't hold back.

51

ANONYMOUS

I fell in love, I kissed, I was in luck,
And did the deed, and she is fond of me;
But who I am, and who she is, and how,
The god of love alone deserves to know.

55*

DIOSCORIDES

Doris, the rosy-buttocked: on her bed
I stretched her out, and at her tender touch
Became immortal. For she straddled me,
And rode me, dominant, unswervingly,
Till Aphrodite's marathon was run,
Looking me in the eye all sleepily;
And like the leaves that flutter in the wind
She shook that scarlet bottom till we came,
And the white seed had made us both a mess,
And she was spread there twitching, all undone.

59*

ARCHIAS

You must escape from Love. It's labour lost:
I am a mere pedestrian, and Love
Has wings to fly. He closes on his prey.

74*

RUFINUS

This garland, Rhodoclea, do I send,
With pretty flowers that my own hands did weave.
There's lily, rose, dewy anemone,
Drooping narcissus, violet's dusky gleam.
Crowned with this garland, cease to be so proud;
It blooms, and fades, and dies, and so must you.

101

ANONYMOUS

Hello, young miss. *Hello back.* Who's your friend?
What's it to you? I have something in mind.
My mistress. Any chance . . . *What do you want?*
Tonight. *What's in it for her?* Golden coin.
Well, you're in luck. This much. *I take it back.*

104

MARCUS ARGENTARIUS

Cast off your fishnets; don't take so much care
To roll your hips as you go walking by,
Naughty Lysidice. Your gauzy dress
Hugs all your curves (such fashionable pleats);
So tight we see it all—but don't quite see.
Think you're so clever? Two can play that game:
I'll pitch a silk tent on this pole of mine.

112

PHILODEMUS

I've been in love. Who hasn't? I've processed
Drunkenly after dinner to her door.
Everyone's done it. I went crazy. Why?
The god's fault, right? It's time to let it go:
Already grey hair is replacing black,

To say I'm ageing into common sense.
When it was time to play, I played: but now
I'll end it, and embrace sobriety.

116

MARCUS ARGENTARIUS

God made the love of women best, for men
Whose attitude to partnership is sound.
And if your taste is more for boys, I know
A cure for that love-sickness. Pay a call
To fine-arsed Menophila. Turn her round,
And then you can imagine it's a boy
You hold in your embrace: 'Menophilus'.

121

PHILODEMUS

Philaenion is small and dark; her hair
Is curlier than parsley, though. Her skin,
More delicate than bird-down; and her voice
Has magic more than Aphrodite's charms.
She always lets me, anything I want;
Most times she asks for nothing in return.
Goddess of gold, may she keep just the same,
And may I keep on loving her . . . until
I come upon a girl more perfect still.

131*

PHILODEMUS

The way she plucks the strings; the way she talks;
The way her eye speaks volumes, and her song:
Xanthippe. Soul of mine, you're going to burn:
The fire is catching. I can't tell you why,
Or when, or how: but I can tell you this:
You're doomed. You're going to burn. It won't be quick.

132

PHILODEMUS

Those feet! Those legs! And yes, those thighs
To die for (it was worth it). And that bum!
That pussy, and those flanks! The shoulders, breasts,
The slender neck, those hands, and then the eyes
That drive me crazy; and the way she moves,
Like a machine. Kisses beyond compare;
Sweet nothings: dear madwoman. And if she's
Italian, and called Flora, and can't sing
The songs of Sappho? Perseus himself
Fell for an Indian girl: Andromeda.

139*

MELEAGER

By Pan of Arcady, sweet is the song
You finger from the lyre, Zenophila;
By Pan, you pluck it sweet. Where shall I go?
I can't escape: the Loves have fenced me in;
They will not even let me catch my breath.
Either your beauty shoots desire at me,
Or else the Muse, your charm . . . what can I say?
It's the whole arsenal; I'm put to flame.

144

MELEAGER

Already the white violet is in bloom,
Narcissus too, that loves the rain, and on
The mountainside the flowering lilies roam.
And, dear to lovers, flower among flowers,
Zenophila blooms too, luxuriant,
Persuasion's rose. You meadows laugh, but why?
Your blaze of coloured tresses is in vain:
This girl outdoes all garlands smelling sweet.

148

MELEAGER

I tell you, one day legends will be told
Of Heliodora and how sweet she speaks;
And in those tales, her graces will outdo
Those of the very goddesses of grace.

150

ASCLEPIADES

She swore to come at nightfall: Nico swore
By holy Demeter; but now the watch
Is finished, and she comes not. Did she mean
To swear me false? The lamp, boys; put it out.

155

MELEAGER

Sweet-talking Heliodora in my heart
Did the god Eros forge—my soul's own soul.

169

ASCLEPIADES

Sweet in the summer's heat to one who thirsts
A snow-chilled cup; and to the sailor sweet
At winter's end to see the breeze of spring
Blow westerly. But sweeter is the time
When one cloak covers two who are in love,
Consenting both in Aphrodite's praise.

172

MELEAGER

Shadow that heralds dawn, lovers' despair,
How slow you roll across the world, when now
Another warms himself beneath the wool

Of Damo's fine-spun cloak. But when I held
That slender girl in my own arms, how swift
You took us by surprise, and shot me down
With light that laughed at my unhappiness.

179*

MELEAGER

I swear by Aphrodite, I will burn
All of your toys, Desire—the bow, the clutch
Of arrows in your Scythian quiver. Yes,
I'll do it. Why the smirk, the hollow laugh,
The snort through turned-up nose? Trust me, you'll rue
Your laughter soon enough. I'll clip your wings,
The quills that aim Desire, and I'll bind
Brass fetters round your ankles. Then again,
Pyrrhic will be my triumph, if my bond
Yokes you with my own heart. You'll be the lynx
Among the pastured goats. Instead, just go!
I want no hellish victory; fly off
On these winged sandals (take them with the rest),
Spread your swift pinions, dive at other men.

186

POSIDIPPUS

Your tears are plausible. Don't think me fooled:
I know, Philaenis. You love no one more
Than me, forever—while you're by my side;
No longer. If another man was here,
you'd swear you loved him more than you'd loved me.

189*

ASCLEPIADES

Long night, and storm; the Pleiads halfway set;
And I pass by her doorway in the rain,
Pierced by desire for her who lied to me.

What Cypris shot at me, it was not love:
It was a poison arrow from the fire.

197*

MELEAGER

I swear by Timo's lush, lascivious curl;
By Demo's scented skin, that stole my sleep;
By Ilias' darling games; and by the lamp,
The wakeful witness to so many rites
When I walked drunken to a lover's door.
I swear to you, Desire, that my lips
Will soon draw their last breath. You want *that*, too?
Just say the word; I'll spit it out with scorn.

198*

MELEAGER

By Timo's locks, by Heliodora's shoe,
By little Demo's door, that dripped with scent;
By Anticleia's ox-eyes, and her smile
That promised me delight; and by the blooms,
Fresh-plucked, that garland Dorothea's head;
I swear, Desire: *No more*. Your quiver hides
No more winged bolts; they all are fixed in me.

199

HEDYLUS

The wine put Aglaönice to sleep—
The cups they raised until her vision swam;
Wine, and her sweet love for Nicagoras.
In Cypris' shrine she left these offerings,
Still moist with scent all over, bloody spoils
Of her desire when she was yet a maid:
Her sandals, the chemise that cupped her breasts,
Relics of sleep, and carnage that came next.

202*

ASCLEPIADES OR POSIDIPPUS

The scarlet riding crop, the jewelled reins
Are Plango's, set above the temple door
Of Cypris, Queen of Riders. She outraced
The veteran, Philaenis, when the colts
Of evening had their blood up for the course.
Dear Cypris, may her victory endure
In memory forever: grant this boon.

203

ASCLEPIADES

Lysidice to Cypris leaves this spur,
The golden goad from off that shapely foot
With which she rode and broke so many colts,
Leaving them on their backs. She rode so light
Her thigh was never chafed. She won the race
Without a touch of spur, so hangs it here,
A golden trophy at your middle gate.

205*

ANONYMOUS

The amulet of Nico, that can draw
A man from over sea, boys from their bed,
Carved of bright amethyst and set in gold,
Her heirloom, Cypris; offered now to you,
Tied in the middle of a scarlet thread
Of lambswool, gift of a Larissan witch.

219

PAUL THE SILENTIARY

Rhodope, let's steal kisses—steal the joys
Of Aphrodite's bouts. Sweet to evade

The eagle eye of sentries; sweeter still
The honey of a secret love-affair.

221

PAUL THE SILENTIARY

Our glances, full of fire, when no one sees;
How long must we keep stealing them? It's time:
Let's get it out in public, tell our pain.
And if they keep us from the silken bond
That sets us free, our union, then one cure
Will serve us both: the sword. We'll see it through,
Together, to the end, in life or death.

231

MACEDONIUS THE CONSUL

Your lips with charm, your cheeks with flowers bloom;
Your eyes with Aphrodite; and your hands
Bloom with the lyre. Your glances captivate,
Your song enslaves the ear: at every turn,
Huntress, you set a trap for poor young men.

232*

PAUL THE SILENTIARY

I kissed Hippomenes, but in my mind
I'd fixed upon Leander; kissing *him*,
I pictured Xanthus; wrapped in *his* embrace,
My heart pursued Hippomenes again.
Whoever's in my arms is not the One:
I keep on turning, clasping to the next,
Chasing a Love that guarantees return.
Offended? May *your* arms enfold just one,
Monogamous in Love's insolvency.

233

MACEDONIUS THE CONSUL

'See you tomorrow.' But it never comes;
Each time I'm put off longer: it's your way.
That's all I get for loving you; but *they*—
You pass your favours round, and lie to me.
'See you this evening.' What's that, to a girl?
Evening's old age, and wrinkles everywhere.

259

PAUL THE SILENTIARY

Your eyes are lidded, Chariclo, as though
You'd just got out of bed: they breathe desire;
Your hair is tangled, and your rosy cheeks
Are pale; your body, limp. And if this means
You've tussled in your bedroom all night through,
The man who held you in his arms is blessed
Above the rest; but if it's hot desire
That wastes you, may your wasting be for me.

261

AGATHIAS SCHOLASTICUS

I do not care for wine, but if you care
To see me drunk, I'll take the cup from you,
That you have tasted. Press it to your lips,
And I cannot stay sober, nor escape
A cupbearer so sweet. Because that cup
Ferries your kiss across the gulf between,
And tells me of the grace that it has seen.

264

PAUL THE SILENTIARY

Why turn your nose up at my hair gone grey
Before its time, my eyes awash with tears?

These tricks were played by my desire for you;
Desire unrequited left these cares,
These arrow-wounds, these long and sleepless nights.
My flanks are wrinkled long before their time;
The skin bags at my throat: whatever bloomed
In me with youthful fire, is now made old
By limb-devouring anguish of the mind.
Take pity, grant your favour, and once more
My skin will bloom afresh, my hair turn black.

267

AGATHIAS SCHOLASTICUS

Why are you sighing? *I'm in love.* With who?
A girl. A pretty one? *She is to me.*
Where did she catch your eye, then? *I went out*
To dinner; there she was, upon the couch
With all the others. Think your luck is in?
My friend, I do—but I'm not looking for
A steady girlfriend, just a secret fling.
You don't want to get married, then. *I know*
For certain she has nothing to her name.
'You know'? You're not in love: no love-touched soul
Can keep its books in order. You're a liar.

270

PAUL THE SILENTIARY

The rose does very well without the wreath,
And you, my lady, do amazing well
Without your gowns and hairnets set with gems.
Your skin outshines the pearl, your uncombed hair
Out-glistens gold; the Indian hyacinth
Matches your fiery grace, but in your eyes
It is outclassed. As for your dewy lips,
The honeyed concord of your breasts—from these
Was Aphrodite's girdle made. Each part
Subdues and captures me: only those eyes
Bewitch me: gentle Hope therein abides.

272

PAUL THE SILENTIARY

I hold her breasts, she kisses back, I feed
In lover's fury round her silver neck—
And still she won't go all the way. I work
To win her round, she still denies her bed.
To Aphrodite she has given half,
Athena keeps the rest; nothing for me:
I fall between them both, and waste away.

273

AGATHIAS SCHOLASTICUS

She was so haughty once. She shook her plaits,
The beauty: put on airs, and when I pined,
She bragged about it. And now wrinkled age
Has taken all of it: her breasts descend,
Her prideful brow is fallen, and her eyes
Are dull. She stammers, senile. And that grey
I call Desire's requital: they judge true
Who say grey hair comes quickest to the proud.

275

PAUL THE SILENTIARY

Napping at evening, fair Menecratis
Sprawled with her forearm curled across her brow.
I dared, mounted her bed, and was halfway
To happy ending in the path of love,
When the girl woke from sleep. With her white arms
She tried to pluck me bald, and gave a fight
The whole time I was finishing the deed.
And then she brimmed with tears, and said to me:
'Bastard! You've taken what you long desired,
What I refused to take your money for,
Plenty of it, and often. Now you'll go,
And wind another girl in your embrace;
You men are slaves to Cypris' gluttony.'

279

PAUL THE SILENTIARY

'Later', says Cleophantis. And the lamp,
Refilled three times now, gutters and is dry.
If only my heart's flame would also die,
That burns me long with sleepless fantasies.
She swore by Aphrodite she would come,
Tonight—but she has sworn that oath before:
Mortal, immortal, none escapes her scorn.

297

AGATHIAS SCHOLASTICUS

They do not have it so bad, the young men;
Not like us girls with vulnerable hearts.
Mobbed by their peers, they confidently tell
Stories of how it *hurts*, of how they *care*,
But they've distractions plenty, and the streets
To stroll in; pretty pictures turn their heads.
We're not supposed to see the light of day;
We skulk indoors, depressed and withering.

END

BOOK 6
DEDICATORY EPIGRAMS

I
'PLATO'

My haughty laughter rang through all of Greece;
Young lovers used to swarm outside my door.
I, Laïs, offer to the Paphian
My mirror: what I see in it today,
I hate; what I saw then, is gone away.

3
DIONYSIUS

Treader of stony Trachis, Oeta too,
Pholoë's woody headland: Heracles.
To you did Dionysius dedicate
This cudgel of wild olive; with his knife
Himself he cut it when the wood was green.

4
LEONIDAS

The curving hook, long rods, and horsehair line;
The baskets that hold fish; the wicker trap
Woven to catch them, that the netsmen found
To cage the wanderers beneath the sea;
Sharp trident, too, Poseidon's weaponry;
The pair of oars from off his little boat.
These Diophantus, fisherman, presents
As tribute to the patron of his trade,
The relics of the craft he used to ply.

9*

MNASALCAS

This arrow-pouring quiver, and this bow,
Phoebus, are hung as offerings to you
From Promachus. His feathered arrows, no:
Mortals hold those: they hold them in their hearts,
Murderous gifts to strangers in the fray.

12

JULIANUS, PREFECT OF EGYPT

Of brothers three and from a threefold hunt
Receive these nets, Pan. Pigres from the birds
Brings these; Damis, from beasts; and Cleitor, sea.
By air, land, water, grant them all good sport.

13

LEONIDAS

The brothers three have pledged to you their nets,
Countryman Pan, each from his proper sport:
These, Pigres, from the birds, and Damis these,
From beasts; and Cleitor third, from fish at sea.
Grant them good sport: the first across the sky,
The second in the woods, the third, at shore.

17*

LUCIAN

The hookers three have offered up to you,
Cypris the bless'd, each from her proper sport,
Their tricks of trade. These Euphro, from her bum;
Clio these next, but from the proper place;
And Atthis third, from higher. Grant them gain,
My queen: the first from anal, and the next
From pussy, and the third from what remains.

18*

JULIANUS, PREFECT OF EGYPT

Laïs' great beauty was used up by Time.
She hates a witness to her wrinkled age:
So this detested mirror, bitter proof,
She offered to the goddess of her past,
When she knew glory. 'Cythereia, please,
Receive this disc, the comrade of my youth,
Since your own beauty has no fear of Time.'

19

JULIANUS, PREFECT OF EGYPT

Beauty is in your gift; but creeping Time
Withers it, queen. Now since your gift has flown
And left me, Cythereia, lady, queen,
Take too this witness that it once was mine.

21*

ANONYMOUS

The fork that dug his moisture-loving plot;
The cabbage-cutting sickle; and his coat,
The rags that kept the rain from off his back;
His sturdy rawhide boots; the peg that dibbed
Young brassicas into the well-turned soil;
The bucket, that with water from the sluice
Refreshed the thirsty shoots through summer's heat:
Priapus, the allotment god, to you
Did Potamo erect these offerings.
Gardening made of him a wealthy man.

33*

MAECIUS

Haunter of shore, Priapus, for your aid
Along this coast the dragnet-men bequeathed,
When in the gleaming narrows they had penned

The whirl of tuna in their flaxen net
Of finely woven thread, this beechwood bowl;
This home-made stool of heather; and this cup,
For wine, and made of glass. So when you tire
From dancing, you may rest a weary limb
And take your ease, and drive away dry thirst.

35
LEONIDAS

To goat-hoofed Pan, goat-mounter, Teleso
Stretches this hide upon a forest plane;
The spiky cudgel with the twisted head,
With which he used to bash the ravening wolves;
The pails in which he curdled milk for cheese;
Choke-chain and collar from his tracker dogs.

39
ARCHIAS

Satyrē, Heracleia, and Euphro,
Of Xuthus and Melitē daughters three,
Samians all. The first her spindle gave,
The shuttling servant of the spider-thread,
Her distaff too; the next, her clacking comb,
That saw the cloth close-woven; and the third,
Her basket that loved wool. Athena, queen,
Accept these gifts from experts in your trade.

40
MACEDONIUS

My pair of oxen, that brought forth the corn:
Accept them in good spirit, Demeter,
Though these are dough; grant the real beasts may live.
My acres, fill with sheaves; give rich return,
Because your honest ploughman has endured
Eight decades, four years back. He never reaped

Harvests like those at Corinth, nor did taste
The bitter poverty that knows no corn.

44

ANONYMOUS, THOUGH SOME SAY
LEONIDAS OF TARENTUM

To Satyrs who drink wine when it is new,
And Bacchus who plants vines, does Hēronax
Make offering of these first-fruits: barrels three,
One for each vineyard, filled with new-made wine,
The fresh stuff. We will pour out what is due
For ruddy Bacchus' and his Satyrs' sake;
And then we'll drink, and more than Satyrs can.

45*

ANONYMOUS

Bristly with spines that gather up the grapes,
This hedgehog, terror of the drying-floor,
Cōmaulus hung alive as offering
To Bacchus, when he caught it rolling through.

49*

ANONYMOUS

Tripod of bronze am I, at Delphi placed.
Swift-foot Achilles offered me as prize,
Honouring Patroclus; and Tydeus' son,
Far-shouting Diomedes, set me here,
Who drove the fastest by wide Hellespont.

50*

SIMONIDES

This altar did the Hellenes once endow,
Who followed the bold urging of their souls

And drove the Persians out by strength of hand
In battle: fitting monument to Zeus
The Liberator, and Greek liberty.

51*

ANONYMOUS

Nursemaid of Phrygian lions, Mother Rhea,
My mother, whose initiates traverse
Mount Dindymus: Alexis the effete
Offered to you the stings that drove him mad,
Now he no longer madly clashes brass:
His strident cymbals, and the booming flute,
Shaped from a bullock's twisted double horn;
The drums that echoed, and the bloody swords;
The hair he tossed when it was blond and long.
Mistress, be kind: he raved when he was young;
Now he is old, let former wildness cease.

58*

ISIDORUS SCHOLASTICUS OF BOLBYTINE(?)

The bed he kept in vain, the coverlet
That saw no action: Moon, to you in shame
Your friend Endymion left them, for grey hair
Holds sway across his head, and not a trace
Is left him of that beauty that once shone.

62*

PHILIP OF THESSALONICA

The disc of lead, that marked the column's edge;
The penknife, notcher of his pointed reeds;
The guiding rule; dry pumice from the beach,
That porous sea-stone; these, Callimenes
Gives to the Muses. He has ceased from toil
Because his eye is clouded with old age.

66

PAUL THE SILENTIARY

Unwetted lead, that scribes the steadfast line
In which we root the letters' harmony;
The ruler, helmsman of that rolling lead;
The porous, spongy stone; the well for ink,
Stained black; the ink-tipped pens, precise of line;
The sea-born sponge, soft flower of the deep;
The knife, bronze carpenter of slender reeds:
These are the offerings of Callimenes
To laugher-loving Muses, since old age
Has spent in toil his eye and cunning hand.

69

MACEDONIUS THE CONSUL

Crantas the wanderer to Poseidon
Offered this ship, set firm in temple floor.
It minds no breeze now it has come to shore,
Safe harbour for a captain fast asleep.

71

PAUL THE SILENTIARY

Ten thousand petals torn from off the wreath;
The shattered cups, that brimmed with maddening wine;
Locks of his perfumed hair: all these your spoils
Taken from lovestruck Anaxagoras
Lie in the dust here, Laïs, at your feet.
Often he spent the night outside your door,
The wretch, with all his friends: from you no word,
No pleasing promise. All his honeyed hope
Could not provoke even a word of scorn.
Alas! He wastes away, and leaves these signs
To mark his vigils, casting all the blame
Upon a lovely woman's iron will.

73*

MACEDONIUS THE CONSUL

I, Daphnis, piper, tottering with age,
Offered this crook to country-loving Pan,
Hung by a weary hand that rests from toil
Now I am old and drive the flock no more.
I can still play, you see: my voice is firm,
Only the body that it lives in shakes—
But let no goatherd tell the ravening wolves
Upon the hills how age enfeebles me.

74

AGATHIAS SCHOLASTICUS

Eurynomē am I, who ran the crags
A Bacchant, once. I clawed the breasts of bulls;
Killed lions, bellowed out my victories;
Took heads of monsters as my toys. But now—
Forgive me, Dionysus—I have left
Your dances and prefer to run amok
In Cypris' rites instead. I leave to you
These cudgels, toss aside my ivy wreath:
Fetters I'll wear, in golden luxury.

76*

AGATHIAS SCHOLASTICUS

Your spouse Anchises, for whose sake before,
Cypris, you often rushed to Ida's shore—
Now he has cut a black hair from his head
And offered it, a relic of his prime,
Long since. That one black hair was hard to find.
Goddess, restore my youth: I know you can.
Or have me old; you had the younger man.

78

ERATOSTHENES SCHOLASTICUS

These fluted reeds, this fleece and shepherd's staff
Were Daphnis' offerings to his friend Pan.
Daphnis loves women: Pan, accept his gifts.
You both love song, but love unhappily.

80

AGATHIAS SCHOLASTICUS

I am Agathias' *Daphniad*, in nine books.
My author dedicated me to you,
Paphian: for the Muses love me less
Than Love does, since I treat of lovers' trysts;
So many longings. For his pains, my scribe
Asks *he* may fall in love with none—or fall
For one who grants her favour readily.

87

ANONYMOUS

This club, these fawnskins, Bacchus, your own Pan
Has left you, as he left behind your dance.
It was the Paphian's fault: he is in love
With Echo, and he roams distraught. But you—
Bacchus, forgive him: you have been there too.

89

MAECIUS QUINTUS

Priapus, lover of the sea-worn reefs
And rugged headland of this coastal isle:
Paris the fisherman hung up for you
The hard-shelled crayfish, that he caught alive
Within a cunning trap he wove from reeds.
Its flesh he ate himself, fresh from the grill,
A treat for crumbling teeth; the detritus,

He left for you, divine one. In return,
Give him—not much; but may his crafty net
Prevent his belly growling like a dog.

96*

ERYCIUS

Glauco and Corydon, Arcadians both
And oxherds on the hills, drew back the head
Of this horned heifer, sacrificing it
To Pan Cyllenian, lover of the hills.
Its span of horns, twelve palms across, they fixed
With a long nail upon the shady plane,
A lovely offering to the herdsmen's god.

100

CRINAGORAS

The holy torch for which the youths compete:
Quickly he bore it, like a memory
Of when Prometheus stole the fire for men;
A famous prize of victory. The son,
Antiphanes, who bore his father's name,
Left it to Hermes, blazing from his hand.

102

PHILIP

The pomegranate in its yellow shirt;
The figs, all wrinkled like old men; the grapes,
A reddening bunch torn bitter from the vine;
The fragrant quince, all fleeced in tender down;
The walnut, peeping out from its green husk;
A trailing, leafy cucumber, picked fresh;
A dusky olive in a gilded rind.
To you, Priapus, friend of wayfarers,
Lamo the gardener left these offerings,
Praying that he may thrive just like his trees.

113

SIMMIAS GRAMMATICUS

Garlanded in green leaves, I was a horn,
A trophy from a shaggy, bounding goat.
But now the bowsmith has adapted me
For Nicomachus, stringing end to end
Strong sinew from an ox with crumpled horns.

114*

PHILIP OF THESSALONICA

An ox's hide and massive horns, we hang
Above the doorway of Amphitryo's Son;
A royal gift: the horns, fourteen palms long.
Philip's sharp spear drove it beneath the ground,
That bull, when proud it faced him on the hills
Below Orbelus, where the cattle graze.
Rich is Emathia, ruled by such a lord.

123

ANYTE

Stand here at rest, man-slaying spear; no more
Drip from your brazen barb the horrid gore
Of enemies: but in Athena's hall
Built high of marble, tell the bravery
Of Echecratides, a man of Crete.

125

MNASALCAS

I rest now in this place, apart from war:
My lord's fair breast I often did defend
By turning my own back. And though I took
Far-shooting arrows, deadly stones from slings,
And spear-thrusts, I declare I never left
Clitus' long arm in burly blare of war.

129*

LEONIDAS ⟨OF TARENTUM⟩

Eight shields, eight helms, eight linen coats-of-mail,
As many blood-stained cleavers: all this gear
Hagnon, Euanthes' son, mighty in war,
Offers as spoil from the Lucanians,
Athena's now, at Coryphasium.

131

LEONIDAS ⟨OF TARENTUM⟩

These long shields taken from Lucanians,
This row of bridles, and the polished spears
Hung on each side, bereft of horse and man:
To Pallas. Man and horse, black death devours.

145

ANACREON

These altars were endowed by Sophocles
In honour of the gods. He took first place
In fame, composing for the tragic Muse.

146*

CALLIMACHUS

Goddess of childbirth, come: Lycaenis calls
Once more; and so bring balm for childbirth's pain.
And *this*, my Queen, she offers for a girl,
A first instalment; if she has a boy,
Expect a bonus at your scented shrine.

153

ANYTE

A cauldron big enough to fit an ox:
It was Cleobotus who set it here,

Eriaspis' son. His city is Tegea:
Streets broad enough to dance in. And his gift
Is for Athena. Aristoteles
Of Clitor made it, son with father's name.

161*

CRINAGORAS

Marcellus from the western war returned,
Bearing the spoils of victory to the shores
Of rugged Italy. His first act, to trim
His yellow beard: for so his country wished:
To send him out a boy; welcome a man.

164*

'LUCIAN' ⟨LUCILLIUS⟩

To Glaucus, Nereus, and Ino's son,
Melicertes; to Cronos' son as well,
That rules the deep, and Samothracian gods:
Rescued from shipwreck, I, Lucillius,
Have shorn these locks. I've nothing else to give.

174

ANTIPATER ⟨OF SIDON?⟩

To Pallas, women three, all of an age,
Accomplished like the spider in their craft
At weaving subtle warp, offered these gifts:
Demo, her wicker creel; Arsinoe,
The distaff that unrolled the slender skein;
The well-made comb, the spinsters' nightingale,
That parted singing threads for Bacchylis.
Know that each chose to live without reproach,
Earning her living by her handiwork.

190*

GAETULICUS

Most honoured Cytherea, please accept
These pauper's gifts from bard Leonidas:
A bunch of five good grapes; the juicy fig
I picked this morning from a leafy branch;
This leafless olive, swimming in its brine;
A little clutch of frugal barley-cakes;
The drop of wine that's poured as offering
At every sacrifice—at least, the dregs
Left in the bottom of my little cup.
When I was gravely ill, you cured me; so,
If you can ward off poverty as well,
I'll offer you a fattened billy-goat.

197*

SIMONIDES

General of the Greeks, I here destroyed
The Persian army, and to Phoebus raised
This monument. My name: Pausanias.

199*

ANTIPHILUS OF BYZANTIUM

Hecate of the Crossroads, at your shrine
Antiphilus hung up the hat he wore,
The traveller's trademark: for you heard his prayers,
You blessed his paths. Although the gift is small,
It is devout: so let no passing thief
Covet and take it. Stealing from a god,
Even a petty theft, courts consequence.

200*

LEONIDAS

Emerging safe from childbirth's bitter pain,
Ambrosia laid before your glorious feet

Her hairbands, Ilythyia, and her gown:
For in her tenth month, you helped bring to birth
Her swollen belly—the result was twins.

204

LEONIDAS OF TARENTUM

Thēris the master-craftsman dedicates
His cubit-rule; his humpback, tensioned saw;
His axe, his glinting plane, his twirling drill:
Gifts to Athena, now he rests from toil.

210

PHILETAS OF SAMOS

Fifty years old, and then some: Nicias,
Lady of pleasure, here in Cypris' shrine
Hangs up her sandals and her curling locks;
Mirror of bronze, that told the truth enough;
Her costly negligee, and all those things
That men can't mention. See the panoply
Of Cypris in her every variant.

214*

SIMONIDES

Gelo, and Hiero; Polyzēlus too,
I say, and Thrasybulus—all the sons
Of Dinomenes set this tripod here.
Six hundred *litrae*, fifty talents' weight
Of Damarete's gold, tithed from their tithe.

215

SIMONIDES

Taken at sea from Persian enemies,
These arms to Leto as memorials
Did Diodorus' seamen dedicate.

217*

'SIMONIDES'

The eunuch priest escaped the winter storm
Into a lonely cave; he wiped the sleet
From off his hair. And on his heels at once
Into the cavern came a ravenous lion—
But he stretched out his hand and beat his drum.
The whole cave echoed with its sharp retort.
The forest monster did not dare endure
Cybele's holy thunder, but it ran
Swift up the wooded mountain—for it feared
The ambisexual servant of the god,
Who in remembrance dedicates to Rhea
These robes of his, and these blond locks of hair.

220*

DIOSCORIDES

To Sardis bound from Phrygian Pessinus,
In ecstasy, his hair whipped in the wind,
Chaste Atys went, Cybele's handmaiden.
The wild excess of his possession waned
As twilight overtook him; down he went
Into a sloping cave, just off the road.
A lion followed quickly in his tracks—
A terror even to the heartiest,
And to a *gallus*, woe ineffable.
Speechless he stood in fear—but then inspired
By higher power, struck his booming drum.
At its deep bellow, quicker than a deer
Ran off that most stout-hearted of the beasts,
And would not stand and hear its baritone.
Atys cried out: 'Great Mother, by the banks
Of the Sangarias I dedicate,
In ransom for my life, my *thalamē*
And this loud thing that made the lion run.'

223*

ANTIPATER ⟨OF SIDON?⟩

This ragged remnant of an ocean beast,
The *scolopendra*, twice four fathoms long,
Tossed in the surf upon a sandy shore,
All mangled by the reef, Hermōnax found
When he with netsman's art was drawing in
His haul of sea-fish. What he found, he hung
As offering to Ino and her son,
Palaemon—a sea-monster, for sea-gods.

225*

NICAENETUS

You Libyan Heroines of this mountain chain,
Girded in goatskin with a tasselled fringe,
Daughters of gods, accept from Philetis
These consecrated sheaves and garlands green,
Woven of straw, tithe of his winnowing.
Hail, Libyan Heroines; mistresses, be glad.

228

ADDAEUS OF MACEDON

His working ox, broken by age and toil,
Alcon did not lead to the slaughterman,
In honour of its labours. Now that ox
In some rich pasture bellows and is glad:
It celebrates its freedom from the plough.

229

CRINAGORAS

This hook-billed eagle's quill, honed with a knife,
Enamelled purple—if some trace remains
When you have eaten, this tool has the knack
To gently prise it from between your teeth.

Crinagoras, who loves you, Lucius,
Sends you this party-gift, small, but sincere.

231*

PHILIP

Linen-robed goddess, fertile Egypt's queen,
Attend my pious sacrifice. For you
Upon the coals a crumbling cake is laid,
And two grey river-geese, and powdered nard
Packed round a grainy fig, and withered grapes,
And honey-scented frankincense. My queen,
As you saved Damo from the sea, please now
Save him from poverty as well: if so,
He'll sacrifice a deer with gilded horns.

235*

THALLUS

Delight of furthest West and furthest East,
Caesar, the scion of an ancient line
Traced back invincible to Romulus,
We sing your heavenly birthday, and around
The altars pour libations to the gods,
Rejoicing. May you tread in grandsire's path,
And stay with us for many years, we pray.

236*

PHILIP

The brazen beaks, well-travelled naval arms,
Hung as memorial of Actium—
See how they, hive-like, hold the honeycomb,
Encircled by the humming swarm of bees.
Virtue and grace attend Augustus' reign:
Weapons of foes at his example learn
To bear the fruits of peace instead of war.

239

APOLLONIDAS

Cutting me sweet from out the honeycomb,
The beekeeper, old Clito, offered me
As sacrifice in place of herded beast,
Milking much honey from the sweet spring wax,
Gift of a flock that, shepherdless, flies far.
Forever multiply his dancing swarm,
And fill the waxen cells with nectar sweet.

244*

CRINAGORAS

Hera of Marriage, mother of Ilythyia,
And Zeus, father to all who come to be:
Come kindly, pray, and grant Antonia
An easy childbirth: let Hēpione
Lend her soft hands. So make her husband glad,
Her mother, and her husband's mother too.
Her womb bears blood of mighty families.

251*

PHILIP

Phoebus, you dwell on Leucas' craggy height,
Landmark to sailors in the Ionian Sea.
Accept these cakes kneaded by seamen's hands;
The wine we pour, mixed in a little cup;
The flame of this poor lamp, the oil it drank
Through tipsy mouth from a begrudging flask.
For these, be kind, and send our sails a breeze
That speeds us to the shores of Actium.

261

CRINAGORAS

Bronze, I look just like silver—Indian work.
I am a flask, a gift for a best friend,

Today being your birthday, Simon's son.
Crinagoras sends me with happy heart.

266

HEGESIPPUS

Here at the crossroads, Hēgelochia
Set up this Artemis, herself a maid
Still in her father's house, Damaretus'.
The god herself appeared beside her loom,
Lighting the warp-threads like a flash of fire.

269*

SUPPOSEDLY SAPPHO

Children, though I lack voice I sharply speak,
If any asks, since at my feet is set
A tireless voice: 'Arista placed me here,
Daughter of Hermocles, Sauneus' son,
A gift to Lēto's Ethiopian girl;
She is your priestess, queen of womankind:
Rejoice in her, pour glory on our line.'

277*

DAMAGETUS

O Artemis, whose weapon is the bow
And mighty arrows, at your fragrant shrine
Arsinoē, daughter of Ptolemy,
Has left this lock of hair from her own head,
Cut from the tresses that provoke desire.

281*

LEONIDAS

On Dindyma you roam, Mother of All,
And on the headlands of Burnt Phrygia.
Raise Aristodice, Sīlēne's girl,

Till she is ripe for marriage and its song,
At girlhood's end. For which, before your shrine
And at your altar many times she danced,
And tossed from side to side her maiden hair.

307*

PHANIAS

This mirror, and the sheet that caught the hair;
The scrap of felt on which he wiped his blade;
His comb, made out of reeds: these, Eugathes,
Barber of Lapithē, cast out with scorn;
His blades as well, for he would shear no more,
Even the probe for cleaning under nails.
His scissors and his razor, and his chair—
Out they all went; he left his shop behind
For Epicurus, as a Gardener.
He listened to him there, much as an ass
Might listen to a lyre; and would have died
Of hunger, if he'd not come running back.

321*

ISOPSEPHA BY LEONIDAS OF ALEXANDRIA

Leonidas's Muse, sprung from the Nile,
Offers this poem as a birthday gift,
Caesar. For always, Calliope sends
A sacrifice that rises without smoke.
When next year comes around, and if it please,
She'll offer you a greater sacrifice.

329*

LEONIDAS OF ALEXANDRIA

Another will send crystal; silver, one;
Topazes, others. All such birthday gifts
Are marks of wealth. Myself, I am content
To offer Agrippina these few lines,

In which I make each couplet count alike.
This gift is proof against all jealousy.

332*

HADRIAN

Trajan, Aeneas' heir, to Casian Zeus
Set up this trophy: to the king of gods,
As he is king of men. A pair of cups,
Intricate work; and this, an aurochs' horn,
Mounted in gold that dazzles all around—
The pick of first spoils, when he tireless slew
The overbearing Getae with his spear.
But you, Stormclouded, put into his hand
The power to conclude this strife as well,
Against the Persians. Be twice happy so,
Seeing a pair of trophies raised to you:
For Getae first, and then for Arsacids.

335*

ANTIPATER ⟨OF THESSALONICA⟩

I am a hat of felt. In former time
The Macedonians found me versatile:
In falling snow, a roof; in war, a helm.
Thirsting, stout Piso, for your sweat I came,
Emathian, to your Italian brow.
Accept me as a friend: surely our wool,
That long ago put Persian arms to flight,
Will, when you wear it, smash the Thracians too.

337*

THEOCRITUS

Apollo, son of Paeēon, has come
To Miletus, to keep the company
Of Nicias, the healer of disease,
Who each day comes to him with sacrifice,

And had this fragrant cedar statue carved,
Binding himself to pay the highest price
So to employ Ēetiōn's subtle hand,
Who channelled all his craft into the deed.

340*

THEOCRITUS

Pandemic Aphrodite, this is not;
If you would please the goddess, call her then
Uranian. This statue is the gift
Of chaste Chrysogone, who in the house
Of Amphicles bore children and was wife.
Their partnership improved with every year,
And you began it, Lady. Profit comes
To those on earth who make the gods their care.

343*

ANONYMOUS

The sons of the Athenians laid low
By deeds in battle the Boeotian tribes,
And those of Chalcis, putting out their pride
And bringing them to grief in iron bonds.
They set their horses here, as Pallas' tithe.

END

BOOK 7
EPITAPHIC EPIGRAMS

1*

ALCAEUS OF MESSENE

The Muses tell that boys on Ios' isle
Vexed hero-singing HOMER when they wove
A riddle that ensnared him. And at sea,
The Nereids anointed him with balm,
And laid him dead beneath the rocky shore:
For he had honoured Thetis and her son,
The clashes of the other heroes too,
And deeds of Odysseus the Ithacan.
Most blessed of the islands in the sea
Is Ios, though so small, for she interred
That shining star of Muses and of Grace.

6

ANTIPATER OF SIDON

Herald of heroes' virtue, he translates
The will of gods, and as a second sun
Lights up the life of Greece. The Muses' flame:
HOMER, the ageless mouthpiece of the world.
Stranger, the sea-beat strand inters him here.

9*

DAMAGETUS

The tomb beside Olympus' Thracian flank
Holds ORPHEUS, son of Calliope,
The Muse: whom oaks obeyed, and lifeless rock
Once followed, and the herds of forest beasts;
Who once uncovered Bacchus' secret rites,
And wrought the line conjoined in epic feet;

Who even charmed dread Hades' solemn will,
And with his lyre bewitched his stubborn heart.

11*

ASCLEPIADES

This sweet work is ERINNA's—it is small,
For she was but a girl of nineteen years,
And yet it is more powerful than most.
If Hades had not come for me so soon,
What other might now own so great a name?

15*

ANTIPATER ⟨OF SIDON⟩

SAPPHO am I; in woman's song I rise
As high as Maeon's son among the men.

25

SIMONIDES

The praise-singer ANACREON, who lives
Forever in the Muses, rests within
This native Tean tomb: the man who set
Lyrics that breathed of Graces and of Loves
To sweet desire of youth. And he alone
In Acheron is saddened, not to leave
The light of day and reach these halls of Lethe,
But that he left Megisteus the fair
Among his peers, and left his passion too
For Smerdïes of Thrace. Yet he sings on,
Lovely as honey; even among the dead
He has not laid his lyre down to sleep.

28

ANONYMOUS

Stranger who passes by ANACREON's shrine,
Pour offering as you go; I like my wine.

32*

JULIAN, PREFECT OF EGYPT

Often I sang it; from my tomb I'll cry,
'Drink up: this dust will shroud you, by and by.'

36*

'ERYCIAS' ⟨ERYCIUS?⟩

Ever about your splendid sepulchre
May stage-struck ivy creep with tender feet,
Great SOPHOCLES. And may it be bedewed
By ox-born bees, that offer at your tomb
Hymettan honey: thus the shining wax
May ever flow upon your Attic slate;
Your flowing locks, ever a garland bear.

42*

ANONYMOUS

Great famous dream of wise CALLIMACHUS,
Truly you were of horn, not ivory:
Such things you showed of gods and demigods
That we on earth had never known before.
From Libya you raised him to the heights
Of Helicon, and bore him in the midst
Of all the Muses: as he told the tale
Of primal heroes' *Causes*, they in turn
Answered with *Causes* of the gods as well.

45

'THUCYDIDES'

EURIPIDES: all Hellas is his tomb,
Though Macedon, his death-place, holds his bones.
His home was Athens, very Greece of Greece:
His art delighted; many give him praise.

53*

ANONYMOUS

To Heliconian Muses, HESIOD
Set up this token, when at Chalcis he
Defeated godlike Homer with his song.

63

ANONYMOUS

Ferryman of the dead, make room for me,
DIOGENES the Cynic, who stripped bare
The sheer hypocrisy of daily life.

71*

GAETULICUS

This seaside tomb is of ARCHILOCHUS,
Who first dipped bitter Muse in viper's bile,
And spattered gentle Helicon in blood.
Lycambes knows: he weeps for his three girls,
Who hanged themselves. Go quietly, traveller,
As you pass by: take care you do not stir
The swarm of wasps that sleep upon this tomb.

80*

CALLIMACHUS

Word reached me, HERACLITUS: you are dead.
It made me cry. I called to mind the times
The two of us had put the sun to bed
As we lay talking. For a long while now,
Halicarnassian friend, I must suppose,
You have been dust: but not your nightingales.
Hades takes everything, but *they* survive,
And he can never steal your songs away.

96

DIOGENES LAERTIUS

Drink now in heaven, noble SOCRATES:
The god spoke true who said that you were wise;
And Wisdom is a goddess. All they poured
For you in Athens was the hemlock cup:
But though you sipped it, it was they that drank,
And drained that cup unto the bitter dregs.

116*

DIOGENES LAERTIUS

DIOGENES, what sent you Hades' way?
Do tell. 'It was a dog—a nasty bite.'

142

ANONYMOUS

ACHILLES' tomb is this, breaker of men,
That once Achaeans raised to fill with fear
The Trojan generations yet to come.
It slopes toward the shore, that sigh of wave
May homage pay to sea-born Thetis' son.

153*

HOMER, OR SOME SAY CLEOBULUS OF LINDUS

I am a girl of bronze, on MIDAS' tomb.
While water flows and trees come into leaf,
I will remain upon this tearful shrine
Telling the traveller who lies buried here.

⟨Here end the epitaphs on the famous dead⟩

155*

ANONYMOUS

On Philistion, the clown from Nicaea

> The life of men is filled with cries of woe,
> But I, Philistion, Nicaean-born,
> Mixed in some laughter. And now here I lie,
> The remnant of a life of many parts,
> Who often died, but never died like this.

160

ANACREON

> Here lies Timocritus, the strong in war:
> Ares spares only cowards, not the brave.

163

LEONIDAS ⟨OF TARENTUM⟩

> Who are you, lady, of what family,
> Beneath this Parian pillar? *Praxo, I;*
> *My father was Calliteles.* Your home?
> *I came from Samos.* And who laid you here?
> *Theocritus, the match they made for me.*
> What killed you? *Giving birth.* You were how old?
> *Just twenty-two.* So, childless? *Not at all:*
> *I left Calliteles, a boy of three.*
> I hope he lives, then, to a ripe old age.
> *I wish the same to you, good passer-by:*
> *May Fortune smile upon you all the way.*

165

ANTIPATER OF SIDON, OR SOME SAY ARCHIAS

> Who were you, lady? Tell me. *Praxo, I.*
> Your father's name? *Calliteles.* And land?
> *Samos.* And who erected this, your tomb?
> *Theocritus, who took me as his wife.*

How did you perish? *In my labour-pains.*
And how old were you? *Twice eleven years.*
And did you leave a child? *Calliteles,*
A little boy of three. I hope he sees
Life's journey through in company of men.
I hope Fate brings to you, my wayfarer,
Glad welcome at the end of that long road.

166

DIOSCORIDES, OR SOME SAY NICARCHUS

Lamisca breathed her last in labour-pangs,
Eupolis' daughter and Nicarete's,
A Samian by birth, of twenty years.
She lies here with her boys, beside the Nile,
Beneath a Libyan shore. Bring wedding-gifts,
You girls, and shed hot tears upon her tomb.

170

POSIDIPPUS, OR CALLIMACHUS

He played beside the well, Archianax,
A boy of three. His mute reflection called.
The mother pulled him soaking out, her son,
To see if any trace of life remained.
The child did not pollute the spring with death;
He slept upon her knee, and here sleeps sound.

173

DIOTIMUS, OR SOME SAY LEONIDAS

Unbidden came the cows at eventide
From hill into the fold, all white with snow;
Thērimachus, alas, sleeps the long sleep
Beside the oak, by heaven's fire laid low.

179*

ANONYMOUS

Even beneath the ground, I now remain
Faithful to you, my master, as before;
Remembering your kindness, how three times
You led me back to health when I was ill:
And you have laid me now in this fine nook.
Manes they call me, of the Persian race.
You did well by me: thus your other slaves
Will be the more attentive to your need.

185

ANTIPATER OF THESSALONICA

Italian earth holds me, a Libyan girl:
Beneath these sands near Rome I lie unwed.
Pompeia raised me like I was her own,
And set me free, and wept to lay me here.
She hoped to see my marriage-torch ablaze;
But she was thwarted, and my brand was lit
Not as we'd prayed, but by Persephone.

198

LEONIDAS OF TARENTUM

Little and low the stone may seem to you
That leans above my grave, wayfarer friend:
But think well of Philaenis. For two years
She loved her singing cricket, that before
Had crawled among the thorns; and cherished me,
Because I chirruped her a pretty tune.
Nor did she cast me out when I had died,
But raised this little monument for me
In honour of my treasury of song.

207

MELEAGER

A hare was I, long-eared and swift of foot.
When I was still a baby, I was snatched
From mother's teat, but sweet-skinned Phanion
Cuddled me to her breast and helped me grow,
Feeding me springtime flowers, and in time
I did not miss the one who gave me birth.
Instead I died of eating far too much,
Grown fat on many feasts. She laid me here
Right by her couch, that ever in her dreams
She may behold me buried at her side.

214*

ARCHIAS

No longer will you dart through seething deep
And startle shoals of fish, or kick up spray
Dancing, O dolphin, to the reed-pipe's tune
Beside the boats. Nor will you offer rides,
O bubbler, to Nereïds as before,
Bearing them on your back to Tethys' end.
For when the swell rose high as Malea's cape,
It cast you out upon the sandy shore.

219*

POMPEY THE YOUNGER

She bloomed so finely, was desired by all;
She gathered by herself the lily-blooms
Of all the Graces. LAÏS looks no more
Upon the Sun driving its golden team
Across the sky. She sleeps the destined sleep.
The young men nightly vying at her door,
The lovers' scratches, the confiding lamp:
All these she has renounced and put aside.

224

ANONYMOUS

My name was Callicratia. I bore
Full twenty children, and then had nine more,
And did not lose a single boy or girl.
I lived a hundred years and five besides
And never held a stick in shaking hand.

228

ANONYMOUS

Androtiōn erected me as tomb
For his own self, his children, and his wife.
I am not anybody's grave, not yet,
And hope I long remain thus unemployed:
But if need be, I hope I may receive
The ones who came before, before the rest.

230

ERYCIUS OF CYZICUS

When your own mother met you run from war,
Your hoplite gear all lost and thrown away,
At once herself she thrust the bloody spear
Right through your sturdy ribs, Demetrius:
'Die, and no blame to Sparta,' she declared;
'It was not she who erred, if I nursed slaves.'

240

ADDAEUS

They lie who say that ALEXANDER died,
If Phoebus speaks the truth: for Hades' hand
Can never sully the invincible.

248*

SIMONIDES

From Pelops' Isle four thousand battled here
Against three million in a bygone year.

249

SIMONIDES

Go tell the Spartans, friend, that here we lie:
We heard what they were telling, and comply.

251*

SIMONIDES

Their glory cannot dim. For country dear
They wrapped themselves in gloomy mist of death.
They died, but are not dead: from Hades' hall
Their courage raises them to height of fame.

253

SIMONIDES

If to die well is virtue's greatest part,
Then Fortune gave us honour above all:
We set ourselves to make all Hellas free,
And we lie here with ageless eulogy.

254A

SIMONIDES

I, Brotachus of Gortyn, man of Crete,
Came not to lie here; I just came to trade.

260

CARPHYLLIDES

Traveller, pass my tomb with no regret;
Even in death, I offer no complaint.

I was a grandfather; had one good wife,
With whom I reached old age; I had three sons,
And found them marriages, and many times
I lullabied their children in my arms,
And never wept for any of them sick
Or mourned them dead. They sent me on my way
With offered wine, and laid me in sweet sleep
Into that happy place where dwell the blest.

269

'PLATO'

Sailors, keep safe at sea and on the shore;
This tomb you pass is of a shipwrecked man.

273*

LEONIDAS ⟨OF TARENTUM⟩

The hard and hasty squall from out the East;
The dark of night; the swell Orion sent
As he descended darkly out of view:
These did for me, Callaeschrus. Off I slipped,
Dead as I cleaved across the Libyan main.
Spun in the sea as food for fish I roam;
'Here lies' is lies. Nobody is at home.

299

NICOMACHUS

This place—should I say place?—was once Plataea,
That once a tremor caught all unaware
And tumbled it right down. All that remained
Was small posterity, and we the dead
Lie covered in the city that we loved.

307

PAUL THE SILENTIARY

My name is—*Should I care?* And my homeland—
Can I be bothered? And my family
Was famous—*Would it matter, if they weren't?*
I lived respectably, and—*What's your point?*
And now I lie here—*Who were you again?*
Do you imagine someone's listening?

343*

ANONYMOUS

Clear-voiced and lovable Paterius
Rests here, the dear son of Miltiades
and sorrowing Atticia. Athens' child,
From famous line of Aeacids, he knew
The whole of Roman law and all things wise.
Of the four virtues he bore every jewel;
A lovely youth, borne off by Fate's command,
Much as a gale might snatch a gorgeous bloom,
Aged twenty-three. He left his parents dear
More tears and grief than they could ever bear.

345*

ANONYMOUS

I am PHILAENIS: all men know my name.
Here I was buried after long old age.
As you come round the headland, do not jeer,
You foolish mariner, nor jest in scorn:
I swear by Zeus and by the Lords Below
I was no slut, passed round from man to man.
Polycrates of Athens is to blame—
A sly dissembler, and a wicked tongue,
When he wrote . . . what he wrote. *I* do not know.

346

ANONYMOUS

This little stone a mighty friendship marks.
Always, my dear Sabinus, I will feel
The loss of you. And when you drink of Lethe,
If gods allow, forget me not as well.

349

ANONYMOUS

I hardly ate or drank, I suffered much,
Lived longer—but still died. So damn you all!

352*

ANONYMOUS, OR SOME SAY MELEAGER

By Hades' hand we swear, by the dark bed
Of the unnamable Persephone,
We were still virgins when we came below.
Archilochus was bitter, and gushed forth
A stream of slanders on our maidenhead:
A pretty form of words to ugly end,
Part of his war against all womankind.
Pierian maidens, why against young girls
Did you direct these iambs of contempt,
And pander to a disrespectful man?

368

ERYCIUS

Lady of Athens, I: that was my town.
From there Italians in deadly war
Carried me off as loot, so long ago,
Made me a Roman citizen; and now
The isle of Cyzicus enwraps my bones.
Farewell, the land that nursed me, and farewell,
The land that had me later; farewell too,
That took me to its bosom at the last.

377*

ERYCIUS

Though under earth he lies, still tar with pitch
Foul-mouthed PARTHENIUS for the bile he spewed
A thousand times on the Pierians,
And for his vile, polluted elegies.
His journey into madness went so far,
He said that Homer's *Odyssey* was 'mud';
The *Iliad*, 'a thorn-bush'. For which crimes
The gloomy Furies in mid-Cocytus
Have put him in a choke-chain, like a dog.

380

CRINAGORAS

Perhaps a marble slab adorns this tomb,
Cut smooth and straight along the mason's line;
But this man was not good. So judge him not,
Good sir, by this his stone: for it is deaf,
No matter how much noise the fellow made
Whom it enshrouds. Here lies Eunicides,
A worthless rag who rots beneath the dust.

403

MARCUS ARGENTARIUS

Psyllus, who ever sent to young men's feasts
The rented ladies that they so desired;
Who stalked and snared the vulnerable girls;
Who made a shameful living from mankind:
He lies within. Refrain, you wayfarer,
From throwing stones, or bidding others throw;
This tomb, if nothing else, he earned by right,
For he is dead. So let him well alone:
Not for his love of profit, but because
In keeping whores, at least he did not teach
Young men to sleep with other people's wives.

417*

MELEAGER

Tyre was my nurse, and Gadara my town,
An Attica among Assyrians.
Eucrates was my sire, and—Muses' boon—
In Menippean Graces first I ran.
And what surprise, good friend who passes by,
If MELEAGER is a Syrian?
For we are citizens of all the world;
It is one nation, and the same expanse
Gives birth to all of us. In later years
I jotted down these couplets for my tomb;
Old age, you see, is neighbour to the grave.
But wish me well, this garrulous old man.
May you grow old to ramble just the same.

419*

MELEAGER

Walk softly as you pass, friend wayfarer;
This old man rests among the pious dead,
Sleeping the destined sleep. Eucrates' son,
That MELEAGER who did intertwine
Sweet tearful Love; the Muses; happy Grace.
Heaven-born Tyre and sacred Gadara
Raised him to manhood; Meropean Cos,
Beloved island, nurtured his old age.
Salaam, I say, if you are Syrian;
And *Naidios*, if you Phoenician be;
If Greek, *Farewell*. Reply to me the same.

424

ANTIPATER OF SIDON

I want to know why Agis carved these signs,
Lysidice, upon your upright stone.
What do they mean? The reins; the muzzled bit;
The raptor, from Tanagra rich in birds,

That dives and stirs a battle—none of these
Can please or suit the women of the house,
Whose taste is more for distaffs and the loom.
The bird, an owl, will tell I early rose
To work my wool; the reins, how hard I drove
My household; and this muzzle from a horse
Will tell I was not fond of endless talk,
Or gossip; I was silent and serene.

434

DIOSCORIDES

Demainete sent eight sons to the fray,
And buried all beneath a single stone.
No tears of grief she shed; only this boast:
'Ha! Sparta, for your sake I gave them life.'

442*

'SIMONIDES'

Let us remember in the time to come
The men who forthright fought; this is their tomb.
They fell in the defence of rich Tegea,
Spearmen before their city, so that Greece
Might not strip freedom from their fallen head.

447*

CALLIMACHUS

The man was short; so will this poem be.
Thēris, a Cretan, Aristaeus' son.
That was a slog enough, it seemed to me.

455

LEONIDAS OF TARENTUM

Marōnis liked her wine; she sucked jars dry.
Dead in old age she lies within this tomb.

Atop is placed an Attic drinking-cup:
We all know what it means. Beneath the ground
She weeps, not for her children or her man,
Whom she left living and in poverty;
Her cup is empty: this alone she mourns.

465

HERACLITUS

The earth is freshly dug, and on the tomb
Rustle the leaves of half-green coronets;
Read its inscription, wayfarer, and see
Whose polished bones it claims to keep within.
Friend, I am Aretēmias. My land
Was Cnidus, and I went to Euphro's bed.
I knew my share of labour-pains: of twins,
I left the one to guide my husband's step,
When he is old; the other came with me,
Memento of the man I leave behind.

476

MELEAGER

Tears are my parting gift, my Heliodora:
All that is left of love, now you are gone
Beneath the ground. They sting my eyes to shed:
Upon your tear-stained tomb I offer them
In memory of affection and desire.
Pitiful Meleager wants you still,
Though you are dead and gone, and my lament
Is offered up to Acheron in vain.
Alas, where is the child that I desired?
Hades has snatched her, snatched her all away;
The dust defiled the flower as it bloomed.
I beg you, mother Earth, who nurtures all:
Take this poor creature gently to your breast.

487

PERSES OF MACEDONIA

Philaenion, you perished still unwed:
Your mother Pythias never led you forth
To bridegroom's bed at the appointed hour.
Instead she tore her cheeks in agony,
And buried here her girl of fourteen years.

493*

ANTIPATER OF THESSALONICA

Rhodope and her mother Boïsca
Lie here. We did not fall by spear of foe,
But when our city Corinth was in flames
In horrid war, we chose a hero's end.
My mother slew me with a butcher's blade,
Nor was she sparing of her own poor life,
But fixed herself a noose: to die still free
We much preferred than live in slavery.

497*

DAMAGETUS

Thymōdes too, one time, piled up this tomb;
Wept as he did so for the ruined hope
Of his son, Lycus. No one lies within:
Not even far away is he interred;
But some Bithynian shore or Pontic isle
Has claimed him. There unwept he bares his bones,
And naked lies upon a friendless shore.

506*

LEONIDAS OF TARENTUM

A tomb ashore *and* burial at sea:
Surely the Fates outdid themselves for me,
Tharsys, Charmides' son. Into the deep

I dove to shift a stubborn anchor-stone,
Down into the Ionian; fought it free,
But as I came back up from the abyss
And was already reaching out my hands
Toward my shipmates, I was gobbled up.
A monster of the deep attacked—so big!—
And gulped me from my belly-button down.
My shipmates pulled one-half of me aboard,
A chilly catch; the shark bit off the rest.
The sad remains of Tharsys they interred,
Good stranger, on this shore: I went not home.

507a

SIMONIDES

Good man, this is not Croesus' tomb you see.
The tomb is small: I lived in poverty.
And yet this tomb was tomb enough for me.

514

SIMONIDES

Beside Theaerus' bank, respect for self
Led Cleodemus to lamented death
When he engaged a force of Thracians;
There too the spearman son of Diphilus
Established glory for his father's name.

521

CALLIMACHUS

If you should ever come to Cyzicus,
You'll have no trouble finding Hippacus,
And Didyme: the family is well known.
You'll pass word on: it's sad, but all the same,
Tell them that here I hold their Critias.

525*

CALLIMACHUS

You who step by my tomb, know me to be
The son and father of Callimachus,
Man of Cyrene. You may know them well:
The one led for his fatherland in war;
The other sang to make the jealous weep.
And justly so: those men who are their friends,
The Muses who looked kindly on their youth
Never cast off when they are old and grey.

535

MELEAGER

No longer would I live with billy-goats;
No longer dwell among the mountain-tops.
Goat-footed Pan am I. What sweetness there,
What might I now desire among the hills?
Daphnis is gone, Daphnis who lit the fire
That burned my heart. I'll live now here in town;
Some other god can hunt the wilderness.
These things were Pan's delight, but never more.

536*

ALCAEUS ⟨OF MESSENE⟩

Even in death, the old man nurtured not
Clusters of juicy grapes from tender vine
Upon his tomb, but tangled blackberries,
And prickly pear that swells the traveller's lips
And chokes the throat with thirst. Let any man
Who passes by HIPPONAX' sepulchre
Pray the dead man sleeps soundly and in peace.

538*

ANYTE

In life, this man was Manes; in the grave,
He rivals the great Darius in power.

542*

⟨STATYLIUS⟩ FLACCUS

Hebrus, locked solid in the winter frosts:
The little boy was skating, and fell through.
But as the current carried him away,
A jagged chunk of the Bistonian stream
Severed his neck clean through. His headless trunk
Was tumbled in the flow; upon the ice
The head alone remained. The mother wept
To bury it, poor dear: 'My son, my son!
The pyre gives part of you its funeral;
The cruel water buried all the rest.'

543*

ANONYMOUS

Well might one pray to shun all voyaging,
Since you, Theogenes, did make your grave
At sea off Libya, when a deadly cloud
Of cranes innumerable took their rest,
Alighting on your laden merchantman.

553

DAMASCIUS THE PHILOSOPHER

Zōsime's body was the only part
That used to be a slave, and now in death
She has obtained its liberty as well.

564*

ANONYMOUS

Upon this spot the earth once opened wide
For Laodice, buried by no rite,
But welcomed as she fled a wanton foe.
Maximus made this monument stand tall,
When as the proconsul of Asia

He found it wasted by unreckoned time;
And when he noted in another place
Her brazen statue lying all unsung,
He set it high upon this tumulus.

565*

JULIAN, PREFECT OF EGYPT

Just as she was, Theodote herself,
The painter gave us: and I wish his art
Had fallen short of life, and had instead
Given forgetfulness to we who mourn.

590*

JULIAN, PREFECT OF EGYPT

This John was famous, then. *Call him 'a man'.*
An in-law to an empress. *All the same.*
The flower of Anastasius' family.
And Anastasius was just a man.
They die. He lived a just and righteous life.
That makes him more: not just another man.
Virtue is mighty, and it masters death.

593*

AGATHIAS SCHOLASTICUS

She blossomed once in beauty and in song;
She minded justice in its high renown;
The dust of earth now covers her entire.
Eugenia, on whose tomb they cut their hair:
The Muse, and Themis, and the Paphian.

595*

JULIAN, PREFECT OF EGYPT

Theodore, dead; with him a multitude
Of ancient bards now truly dead and gone.

For while he breathed they breathed in him, and now
The multitude is gone, as he is gone;
And all lie buried in a single tomb.

605

JULIAN, PREFECT OF EGYPT

This handsome urn of stone, this marble tomb:
Rhodo, for you your husband raised them up,
Sweet man, and offers alms to save your soul;
All for your kindness, since you went and died
So very soon and set your husband free.

626*

ANONYMOUS

You Nasamonian fringe of Libya,
You uplands that no longer must endure
The packs of savage beasts: still you shall clap
With echo of the lions' desert roar,
Resounding yet beyond the Nomad sands.
Caesar the Son has trapped that countless tribe,
Assembled it in chains to face his spears.
The mountain ridges, once the wild things' lairs,
Are cattle-pastures now for civil men.

633*

CRINAGORAS

Rising at eventide, the very Moon
Made her light dim and veiled her grief in night,
Seeing her pretty namesake set and sink
Lifeless in Hades' dark. For she had shared
With Selene the beauty of her light,
And merged her passing with her own eclipse.

647

SIMONIDES, OR SOME SAY SIMIAS

As Gorgo spoke her last to mother dear,
She wept and threw her arms around her neck:
'Please stay for father, bear another girl
With better fate, to tend your grey old age.'

657

LEONIDAS OF TARENTUM

You solitary herdsmen, you who range
Along this ridgeline, pasturing your sheep
And shaggy goats: please give Clītagoras
This little comfort, in the name of Earth
And for the sake of lost Persephone.
May the sheep bleat for me; on living rock
May shepherd pipe them gently as they graze;
And may the countryman in early spring
Pluck meadow-flowers to weave and crown my grave.
And may some fellow sprinkle it with milk
Pressed from a sheep that bears him many lambs,
Lifting its milky teat and watering
My lowly tomb. The dead make fair return
For favours granted even in the grave.

667

ANONYMOUS

In the Church of St Anastasia in Thessalonica

Why wail in vain, and linger by my tomb?
I am among the dead, and find no cause
For lamentation. Leave your wailing be:
End it, my husband. Children too, be glad,
And still remember Amazonia.

714

ANONYMOUS

Rhegium I sing, of shoal-girt Italy
The furthest headland, sipping at the sea
That leads to Sicily: for she interred
The man who loved the lyre and loved the boys,
My IBYCUS, beneath the leafy elm.
He tasted many pleasures; on his tomb
She spread abundant ivy and white flag.

733*

DIOTIMUS ⟨OF MILETUS⟩

We pair of ancient ladies, of an age,
Are Anaxo and Clēno, and are twins,
Epicrates' daughters. While we lived,
Clēno was priestess of the Graces three;
Anaxo served Demeter. Just nine days
And we would have been eighty: but the years

We loved our men and children, and, grown old,
Arrived at gentle death ahead of them.

737

ANONYMOUS

I lie within who, thrice-unfortunate,
Was violently slain: a robber's deed.
And there is none who knows to mourn for me.

741*

CRINAGORAS

Name Sparta's hero, great Othryades;
Name Cynegeirus, battler at sea;
Name exploits of all battles gone before.

The brave Italian soldier at the Rhine
Who lay half dead of wounds beside the stream,
And saw his legion's eagle snatched away,
Sprang from among the slain to kill the foe
Who bore it off, and saved it for his chiefs.
This man alone achieved unconquered death.

747*

LIBANIUS

JULIAN lies within, beyond the stream
Of rapid Tigris, good 'on both accounts:
A worthy king and mighty with the spear'.

END

BOOK 8
EPIGRAMS OF ST GREGORY
THE THEOLOGIAN

1*

Epitaph for John and Theodosius

> This tomb contains two godlike, splendid men:
> The godly John, and Theodosius,
> Godly indeed. The virtue of the pair
> Was bounteous: it rose to heaven's vault,
> And showed them partners in inviolate light.

2*

On the great Basil, Bishop of Caesarea in Cappadocia

> I sooner thought body could outlive soul
> Than I could live without you, Basil, friend,
> Christ's workman. Yet I bore it, and remained.
> So must we wait? Will you not take me up,
> And place me in the chorus of the Blessed,
> Where you are stationed? Do not leave me here;
> Do not, I beg: I swear upon your tomb,
> Never will I forget you and move on;
> I could not, if I wanted. *Gregory.*

11*

On the same

> Fond greeting, Basil, though you went away.
> This little epitaph is Gregory's;
> Mine was the talk you liked to listen to.
> My Basil, please accept from your friend's hand
> The gift I prayed never to have to give.
> My godly Basil, to your mortal dust
> I dedicate these dozen epigrams.

16*

On his father

'My son, may you outdo me in the rest,
But may you equal me in kindliness:
I do not think it right to pray for more.
And may you make it to a ripe old age,
Blessed to have met with such a guardian.'

22*

On the same

'I, Gregory, have placed my shepherd's pipe
Into your hands, my son. Interpret well,
And may you open wide the gates of life
To everyone, and in time's fullness come
To greet again your father in this tomb.'

25*

On his mother, who was taken up from the altar

The sacred altar never saw your back;
No vulgar language ever passed your lips;
No smile alighted on your tender cheeks,
Initiate of God. I will not speak,
Blessed woman, of the pains that you concealed:
All such was hid within; your outward face
Was seen by all, and shone. And for that cause
You left your body in the House of God.

39

On the same

Your prayers and heartfelt groans and sleepless nights,
The tears you shed upon the temple floor;
Nonna the godly, they have earned for you
The perfect ending to your mortal span:
Within the Church to meet Death's reckoning.

43

On the same

> My father was this altar's faithful slave;
> My mother passed in prayer at its feet.
> Gregory; Nonna. Mighty is their fame:
> I ask the Lord that such a life be mine,
> And that I too may meet with such an end.

76

His parents' prayer

> 'Happy at peace we lie beneath the soil,
> His parents, by the hand of Gregory
> Here laid to rest. Our son it was as well
> Who by his pains eased our old age, and now
> He honours us with rites. You best of sons,
> Take rest from tending us, good Gregory,
> Your old and pious parents, whom you laid
> Beside the martyrs. Know that your reward
> Was to become the great and loving sire
> Of spiritual, pious progeny.'

82

On himself

> Of Gregory and Nonna the dear child,
> Here lies that Gregory who made his cause
> The service of the Holy Trinity,
> Who came through cleverness to Wisdom true,
> Who even as a young man set no store
> Except the hope of wealth laid up in heaven.

91

On Caesarius ⟨his brother⟩

> Wisdom and everything it comprehends:
> Geometry, the stations of the stars,

The stratagems of the logician's art,
Grammar and history too, and speaker's force:
Caesarius alone of mortal men
With subtle mind and soaring intellect
Could grasp them all. Alas! Now like the rest
He is become a scattering of dust.

98

On the same

Gregory's handiwork. In sad regret
For best of brothers, I proclaim to men
That they should hate and scorn this mortal life.
Who was so fine as my Caesarius?
Who of all men could match him, or could claim
So great a name for wisdom? None that live;
But he has flown from life, gone suddenly,
As might a rose from all the other flowers,
As does the dew from off the leaves at dawn.

112*

On Martinianus

Be off with you, away! For you provoke
A wicked contest for a wicked prize,
Heaving aside the stones that make my tomb.
I am Martinianus. So, begone!
I helped the living; now that I am dead
And buried, I retain no little power.

123*

On Euphemius

Though he had only twenty years, no more,
Euphemius flew to every Muse of Greece
And each of Rome, as no man ever flew
To any one of either. He burned bright:

A flash of brilliance and character.
Then he was gone. Alas, too quick comes death
When it is coming to the wonderful.

124

On the same

A token relic of the Race of Gold:
That was Euphemius. Of noble mind
And noble character, a gentle boy,
And sweet of speech; the beauty of his form
Rivalled the Graces. Surely that is why
He did not mingle long with mortal men.

134*

On Amphilochus

Amphilochus is dead. With him is gone
Whatever had remained for mortal men
Of goodness, and of strength in rhetoric;
The Graces too, and with them every Muse.
Above all else, at home your city mourns:
God's Caesarea, the fatherland you loved.

161

On Emmelia, the mother of St Basil

Emmelia, dead. Who thought it? She who gave
So worthy and so vast a progeny
To be a light for man: daughters and sons,
Unwed and wed alike. Alone on earth
She mothered many children, *and all good.*
Three of her sons were priests of wide renown;
A daughter married one; and all the rest
Are like an army of the virtuous.

163

On Macrina, the sister of St Basil

> A shining maiden I the earth contain,
> If ever you heard tell of one: her name,
> Macrina, whom the great Emmelia bore
> First of her children. All the eyes of men
> She modestly avoided, but her boast
> Excels all others now on every tongue.

170*

On those who feast lavishly in the Churches of the Martyrs, and on tomb-robbers

> You have deserved to die a triple death:
> First, that you laid your filthy bodies down
> Amid the winners of the martyr's palm,
> Their tombs now hemmed by pagan celebrants;
> Second, that you unlawfully destroyed
> Some of those tombs, though you yourselves possess
> Tombs that are like them; other tombs you sold,
> And often three times over. And the third—
> You robbed the shrines of martyrs you revere.
> Fountains of Sodom's flame, your time is come!

221

On tomb-robbers

> I used to be a tomb; now I am stones,
> A tumbled pile of them, a tomb no more.
> The avaricious thieves enjoyed their work.
> What kind of conduct, this? What kind of right?

237

Likewise

You are a man with everything you need,
Because you are alive; while I have died,
Possessing nothing but these few dear stones.
Therefore refrain from ruining the dead.

END

BOOK 9
EPIDEICTIC EPIGRAMS

19*
ARCHIAS OF MITYLENE

Of thunder-footed steeds he blazed most bright:
EAGLE, about whose legs the garlands hung;
Whom Phoebus' oracle at Pytho crowned,
His victory as swift as flashing wing,
And Nemea, the cruel Lion's nurse,
And Pisa too, and Isthmus with two shores.
Now he is prisoner in yoke and bit,
And grinds Demeter's grain with gritted stone,
Fated like Heracles—so much did he
Achieve, then don the yoke of slavery.

24
LEONIDAS OF TARENTUM

Driving his chariot, the fiery Sun
Blotted the stars and holy orb of Moon;
And brandishing the Muses' brightest torch,
HOMER cast shade on all the bardic clan.

25
THE SAME

This is the book of learned ARATUS,
Who once with subtle intellect explained
The everlasting stars: those set in place,
And also they that in their restless gyre
Constrain the sky and make it legible.
Let him be praised for labouring to make
A masterpiece, in second place to Zeus—
The man who made the stars shine out more bright.

26

ANTIPATER OF THESSALONICA

Helicon raised these women up with song,
And made their tongues divine: Pieria too,
The Muses' rocky crag in Macedon.
PRAXILLA; MOERO; ANYTE, in voice
A female Homer; SAPPHO too, the pride
Of Lesbian women with their lovely hair;
ERINNA; TELESILLA, of great fame;
And you, CORINNA, who once danced and sang
Athena's war-shield; NOSSIS, woman-tongued;
Sweet-sounding MYRTO—all the workwomen
Of everliving pages. Muses nine
Did great Olympus bear, and Earth nine too,
Immortal merriment for all mankind.

28*

POMPEY, OR SOME SAY MARCUS THE YOUNGER

I lie here desolate beneath the dust:
Mycenae, less to see than any knoll.
And yet whoever looks on Ilium,
That famous town whose walls I trampled down,
And purged the house of Priam—they shall know
What strength I owned. If age has slighted me,
I am content in Homer's witnessing.

59*

ANTIPATER OF THESSALONICA

Four Victories lift up on outstretched wing
Upon their back as many deathless-born:
The first bears up Athena of Campaign;
The second, Aphrodite, and the next,
Alcides; and the fourth, the god of war.
So it is painted in your well-roofed hall:
They rise to heaven, Gaius, you who shield
Your fatherland of Rome. May Heracles

Keep you unbeaten, and the Cyprian,
Happy in marriage; Pallas, keep you wise;
And Ares keep you fearless in the fight.

62

EUENUS OF ASCALON

I, sacred Ilium, that storied town
Whose tower-studded walls were famed in song:
Stranger, the dust of time has eaten me.
In Homer, though, I rest inviolate,
Behind my gates of bronze. Achaean spears
That ruined Troy can never root me thence;
I shall reside upon the very lips
Of every single Hellene yet to come.

63*

ASCLEPIADES

LYDE am I, and Lydian my tribe.
Antimachus has won me more respect
Than all the girls who came of Codrus' line.
Who has not sung me? Who has not yet read
The *Lyde*, composition held in share
Between the Muses and Antimachus?

69*

PARMENION OF MACEDON

Constant the malice of a stepmother;
Even desire cannot assuage her hate.
I know what chaste Hippolytus endured.

71

ANTIPHILUS OF BYZANTIUM

High twigs of spreading oak, you canopy
For men escaping from the savage heat,

Lovely in leaf, a tighter roof than tile,
A home for collared doves and cicadas:
You noonday branches, keep me as I rest
Beneath your leaves, the sunbeams' refugee.

74

ANONYMOUS

I was the field of Achaemenides,
And now Menippus has me; by and by
From one man to another I shall go.
One thought me his, the other thinks so now,
But I am no man's property at all:
Only the god of Fortune holds a claim.

92

ANTIPATER OF THESSALONICA

The cicadas get drunk on dew alone,
But give them wine and they outsing the swan:
Likewise the poet knows to give return,
Repays his benefactors with a tune.
He does not ask for much. And so I pay
My first instalment; if the Fates allow,
Often shall you be found upon my page.

93

THE SAME

Antipater to Piso sends this book,
A birthday present. It is only small:
He fashioned it in just a single night.
But give it a kind welcome just the same,
And think well of its poet, if you can:
A little incense often sways great Zeus.

106*

LEONIDAS 'OF TARENTUM' ⟨OF ALEXANDRIA⟩

I was a ship: I was consumed by fire.
I burned, who many times traversed the sea,
On land they stripped of pine for building me.
The ocean kept me safe; ashore I died.
The land that gave me birth I found at last
More treacherous than ever was the deep.

155*

AGATHIAS SCHOLASTICUS

If you are of the Spartans, passer-by,
Then do not mock me: not for me alone
Has Fortune so decreed. But if you be
A man of Asia, then you must not grieve:
For every city nods obedience
To Trojan sceptres and Aeneas' line.
If the assault of jealous enemies
Has purged my holy temples and my walls,
And emptied me of people, still I reign:
I am once more a queen. And you, my child,
Intrepid Rome, go set upon the Greeks
The yoke and harness of your righteous law.

187

ANONYMOUS

The very bees bore honey to your lips
From off the meadow-flowers of every Muse;
The very Graces offered you their gifts,
And filled your plays with perfect dialogue.
MENANDER, you live now and for all time;
And it is thanks to you that Athens' fame
Lays hold upon the very clouds of heaven.

190*

ANONYMOUS

This is ERINNA's Lesbian honeycomb.
Though it is small, the whole of it is brimmed
With honey from the Muses; and its lines,
Only three hundred, equal Homer's own,
Though she was just a girl of nineteen years.
Toiling with distaff under mother's rage,
Or at the loom, she stood as handmaiden
To every Muse. Sappho in lyric verse
Outdid Erinna by no more than she
Exceeded Sappho in the epic line.

203*

PHOTIUS, OR SOME SAY LEO

A harsh and bitter love, and yet a life
That models chastity and self-control:
Clitophon's tale displays them vividly,
And his Leucippe's steadfast temperance
Amazes all: how, beaten and ill-used,
Her hair cut off, and—greatest thing of all—
Thrice undergoing death, she persevered.
My friend, if you will live so chaste as she,
Look past the book's mere incidental thrills,
And learn at once what moral it conveys:
It joins in marriage lovers who are wise.

205*

ARTEMIDORUS THE GRAMMARIAN

The herdsmen's Muses once were all astray;
Now they are penned into a single fold,
A single flock embracing all of them.

210*

ANONYMOUS

On Orbicius' ⟨sic⟩ *Book of Tactics*

Behold the book that births heroic deeds:
Hadrian had me with him in his wars,
In olden days. I fell into disuse;
The aeons passed; I neared oblivion.
But under our lord Anastasius,
The strong in battle, I came back to light,
That I might aid him in his marshalling.
For I can teach the arts of bloody war:
I know the way to help you beat the men
Who ring the western sea, and Persians too,
And Saracens whose doom is now secure,
And charging cavalry of frenzied Huns;
Isaurians too, who lurk on lofty crags.
And I will bring them all beneath the rule
Of Anastasius, whom the ages fetched
To outshine even Trajan's sceptred sway.

220*

THALLUS OF MILETUS

See how the verdant plane conceals the rites
Of lovers with its sacred canopy;
About its branches, joyous in their hour,
Hang tasty grapes in bunches on the vine.
So may you ever come in leaf in spring,
O plane, and may your greenery conceal
The close companions of the Paphian.

227

BIANOR

Beside the shore, beneath the limpid brine
A spearfisher beheld an octopus.
He pounced there as it swam, and greedily

He tossed it onto land, before his prey
Could bind its captor. Spinning like a top,
By happenstance it landed on a hare,
A nervous creature, lying half asleep
Amid the reeds. It squirmed itself about
And bound the hare. The fellow's catch at sea
Netted him quarry on dry land as well.

232

PHILIP OF THESSALONICA

I am an Adriatic wine-jar's neck.
I had a honeyed voice upon a time,
When Bacchic graces filled my belly: now,
My broken throat supplies a sturdy prop
For a new vine-shoot clambering upon
What once held pleasure. I serve Bacchus still:
When he is old, I am his faithful guard;
When he is young, I cultivate and wean.

233

ERYCIUS

As you were hacking out some dry old stumps,
A nesting spider wounded your left foot,
Attacking you, poor Mindon, from below.
Its bite spread black decay through living flesh
Throughout your ankle. And because of this
They cut your sturdy leg off at the knee;
A crutch of tall wild olive guides your way.

234

CRINAGORAS

How long, you wretch, borne up by empty hopes
To finger-distance from the chilly clouds,
Will you outline your endless dreams of wealth?
No profit comes to men spontaneously.

Make your pursuit instead the Muses' gifts;
Let fools indulge these murky fantasies.

235*

BY THE SAME

The world's great borderlands, that spate of Nile
Cuts off from dark-skinned Ethiopians,
You have united both your sovereigns
In marriage, and have made a single tribe
Of Egypt and of Libya. Once more
May these the children born to royal sires
Hold strong and steady sway across both lands.

239*

CRINAGORAS

The five sweet lyric books within this case
Bear labours of inimitable Grace:
[Anacreon's, that the Tean, sweet old man,
Wrote in his cups or swayed by the Desires.]
We are a present, come to celebrate
The sacred birthday of Antonia,
Who stands supreme in beauty and in mind.

241*

ANTIPATER OF THESSALONICA

You herded cows, Apollo; and a horse
You made yourself, Poseidon; Zeus, a swan;
Famed Ammon was a snake. Some to get girls,
And *you*, a boy—but all as ambuscade:
You did not bed by wooing, but compelled.
But our Euagoras is made of brass:
He needs no tricks to have the girls and boys
Just as himself, no metamorphoses.

252

ANONYMOUS

The wayfarer leapt swiftly from the bank
Into the depths of Nile: he saw the wolves,
A greedy pack. But they pursued him on,
Across the water. Each bit onto each,
Latching upon the tail of the next.
A bridge of wolves stretched far across the stream:
The self-taught tactic of the swimming beasts
Bloodily overtook the traveller.

285*

PHILIP OF THESSALONICA

No longer, tower-girt and phalanx-bred,
The elephant with its prodigious tusk
Charges unchecked and eagerly to fight.
He sets his stout neck fearful to the yoke,
And draws the car of Caesar deified.
Even a beast can see the fruits of peace:
He casts aside the gear of bloody war,
Escorts the father of good governance.

293

PHILIP OF THESSALONICA

Gazing upon the mighty, self-slain frame
Of LEONIDAS, Xerxes covered him
With purple mantle. Even from the dead
Did Sparta's mighty hero call to him:
I spurn the wealth that traitors take in fee;
A shield is the best honour for my tomb.
Begone with Persian pomp; I shall descend
To Hades as a man of Sparta still.

313

ANYTE THE LYRIC POET

Sit here beneath the laurel's bright young leaves,
And draw sweet water from the lovely spring:
So rest your panting limbs from summer toil,
Buffeted by the Zephyr's gentle breeze.

332*

NOSSIS ⟨OF LESBOS⟩

Let us go to the temple, girls, and view
Its wooden Aphrodite. You must see
How intricately worked it is with gold.
For Polyarchis set it there, who won
A fortune by the splendour of her form.

333

MNASALCAS

Let us stand by the flatland of the strait,
To view the shrine of Cypris of the Sea;
And see the fount beneath the poplar's shade
Where sip the beaks of darting kingfishers.

342*

PARMENION

I tell you that prolixity of line
Is counter to the Muse in epigram.
Do not set out to run a marathon
Upon the racetrack: round and round it goes,
But in the sprint the pitch of breath is keen.

363*

MELEAGER

Now winter's storms have cleared, the rosy hour
Of flowered spring has broken into smile;

The dark earth wreathes herself in grassy green,
And plants burst out with newborn foliage.
As blooms the rose, the meadows laugh to drink
The gentle dew of Dawn the Gardener.
The shepherd playing shrill upon his pipe
Is happy in the hills; the goatherd too
Rejoices in the kids that grace his flock.
Now mariners set out upon the main,
Filling their sail with Zephyr's harmless breeze;
Now they cry 'Evoe!' and wreathe their hair
With berried ivy-flowers, who revere
Dionysus, the Bringer of the Grapes.
The ox-born bees resume their cunning trade:
They perch upon the hive and fabricate
The pale new cells of neatly moulded wax.
And all around the tribes of birds sing clear:
By sea the kingfisher; about the home,
The swallow; by the river's bank, the swan;
And deep within the grove, the nightingale.
If greenery is glad, if Earth in bloom,
And shepherds pipe, and fleecy flocks take cheer,
If sailors venture, and the birds give song,
And Dionysus dances, and the bees
Regenerate their race, how may the bard
In midst of spring sing out no lovely tune?

366*

ANONYMOUS

Mottos of the Seven Sages

The Seven Sages—my exact account
Will tell you cities, names, and adages.
'Best to be moderate', quoth the Lindian,
CLEOBULUS; CHILO in Sparta's vale
Said 'Know yourself', while PERIANDER's line,
Of Corinth, was 'Be master of your rage'.
'Do nothing in excess', said PITTACUS,
From Mytilene; 'Look toward life's end',

SOLON instructs, of Athens' sacred town;
BIAS: 'The more you meet, the worse you'll find'.
He was Priēnian; from Miletus came
THALES, of 'Cash not credit, all the way'.

367

LUCIAN OF SAMOSATA

Thēro, Menippus' son, was prodigal
With his inheritance when he was young;
Euctēmo, though, who was his father's friend,
Observed him shrivelled up by poverty,
And wept, and raised him up, and for his wife
Gave him his own dear girl, and offered too
A mighty dowry. But this second wealth
Made Thēro lose all sense, and straight away
He ran up bills as costly as before:
Disgustingly indulged his belly-lust,
And lust that lay below the belt as well.
Thus did the rising tide of penury
Close over him again. Euctēmo wept,
Not now for Thēro, but his daughter's share;
The marriage he had made. And so he learned:
No man who wastes his fortune can deal fair
When trusted with the wealth of other men.

369*

CYRILLUS

Two lines is perfect for an epigram;
Go over three, it's epic you declaim,
No longer speaking epigram at all.

383*

THE EGYPTIAN MONTHS

First *Thoth*, who learned to lift the hook and cut
The bunches from the vine; *Phaōphi* brings
A varied catch for fishermen to spear,

While *Athyr* marks the date of Pleiads' rise.
Choiac denotes the sprout of scattered grain,
While *Tybi* flaunts the Consuls' purple gown.
Mecheir bids sailors ready for the sea;
Phamenōth drills the warriors in arms.
Pharmouthi is first herald of spring rose,
While *Pachon* guards the harvest's drying wheat.
Paÿni brings first news of fruitful yield;
Epēphi lifts the bunch and aids the vine;
Mesori brings the quickening flow of Nile.

387

THE EMPEROR HADRIAN, OR SOME SAY GERMANICUS

Hector of Ares' race, if down below
You somehow hear us: Greetings. Stay a while,
For sake of fatherland. Your Ilium lives—
A famous city, and a living town;
Its men are not your match, but still love war.
The Myrmidons are dust. Stand at his side
And tell Achilles that his Thessaly
Is the dominion of Aeneas' sons.

388–9

A soldier wrote a response under these lines. Some say it was Trajan:

Brave men, who need not view my helmet's face.

Then, when the Emperor expressed his approval and wrote 'Let me know who you are', the soldier inscribed the reply:

I am a warrior of armoured Mars,
And serve Apollo upon Helicon,
Elect in the first rank of infantry.

395*

PALLADAS

'What could be sweeter than one's fatherland?',
Odysseus said: for bound on Circe's isle

He ate no cheesecake. Had he only sensed
Its smoke arising, he would have declared
That ten Penelopes could go to hell.

400*

'PALLADAS'

I look on you and kneel in reverence,
And on your writings, when I see the sign
Of Virgo entering her starry House:
For your work touches heaven, HYPATIA,
You sacred ornament to literature,
Pure shining star of teaching that is wise.

425*

JOHN BARBOCALLUS

I am a city pitiful, undone:
I lie all tumbled with my civic dead,
Unluckiest by far in all the world.
Hephaestus took me from Poseidon's rout.
How beautiful I was, and now am dust.
You that pass by, bewail my sorry fate:
Cry for Berytus that has been destroyed.

444

ERATOSTHENES SCHOLASTICUS

The virgin owns a treasury sublime;
And yet, observed by all, virginity
Would end our race. So take a lawful wife,
And give the world a mortal in your stead;
But do not be unmanned by wantonness.

451*

ANONYMOUS

What Philomela might say to her sister, Procne

Your evil husband shut me in a cave,

Alone and hopeless; tore my maidenhead;
And marked that dreadful match with vile gifts:
Cut out my tongue, robbed me of civil speech.

455

ANONYMOUS

What Apollo might say about Homer

I sang it; godlike Homer wrote it down.

460*

ANONYMOUS

What Achilles might say when he saw the armour laid out for him

Mother, these arms you gift your battling son
Are glorious; no man has seen their kind:
I know now that Athena wards my hand
And readies it for Hector, stirring doom
And degradation for the men of Troy.

467

ANONYMOUS

What Peleus might say if he heard that Achilles was refusing to fight

You peaks of Pelion who raised him up,
Go tell my boy, whom Chiron taught to shine
In heat of battle—*cast aside your rage!*
His hatred is a plague upon the Greeks.

468

ANONYMOUS

What Hera might say when Heracles became a god

Your noble work is handsomely repaid;
Your father's doing, Heracles, since toil
Can furnish men a praise that never ends,
After interminable labouring.

471*

ANONYMOUS

What Nestor might say when he heard Odysseus had come home

That splendid man escaped the cruel sea,
And passed through hardship to his native land;
He surely is a better man than me:
Knows well the cities, tribes, and minds of men.

479

ANONYMOUS

What Perseus might say after he defeated the sea-monster, if Andromeda turned him down

The rock's cruel bonds have turned your heart to stone;
Medusa's gaze, your body, through and through.

483*

ANONYMOUS

Perseus from Persia fetched a deadly fruit
That caused the death of Theognōstus' child.

490*

HELIODORUS

Wear Fear-all, and fear not the fiery blast:
The Fates with ease deliver paradox.

502*

PALLADAS

I need *conditum*. Whence derives its name?
For it is alien to Grecian tongue.
If it is named in Roman, you must know,
For you are the most Roman of them all.
So make me some: my stomach is not right;
They tell me it's exactly what I need.

507

CALLIMACHUS

The rhythm and the tone are Hesiod's,
Who is not least among the poets; still,
I fear ARATUS has imprinted on
Only the sickly-sweetest of his lines.
Until next time, you flimsy turns of phrase,
You monument to his insomnia.

516*

CRINAGORAS

'Each to his trade': beneath the Alpine peaks
The shaggy bandits with their spiky hair
Pursue their larceny and still avoid
The dogs of their pursuers, by this means:
They take a kidney, rub it on themselves
Till every bit of fat is on their skin.
Its pungent odour fools the keen-nosed hounds.
You savants of Liguria, inclined
More to devise the wicked than the good.

528*

PALLADAS

On the House of Marina

Olympus' denizens here Christianized
Live free from harm. Them shall the smelting pot
Not render on the fire for ready change.

553

⟨ANTIPATER OF THESSALONICA?⟩

In place of Leucas Caesar set me here,
And for Ambracia of fertile soil;
For Thyrreum, for Anactorium,

Amphilochian Argos—all the towns
That war with maddened spear had ranged upon
And left in pieces all along the shore.
Nicopolis he founded, godlike town:
Lord Phoebus welcomes it as tribute due
For Caesar's victory at Actium.

556

ZONAS

Nymphs of the shore, Nereids, yesterday
Did you see Daphnis? How he rinsed the dust
That lay like down upon his sunburned skin,
And plunged into your pools? His apple-cheeks
Blushed just a little. Tell me, was he fine?—
Or, being but a he-goat, am I lame
Not only in the shank but in the soul?

562

CRINAGORAS

A parrot that could talk just like a man
Escaped its wicker cage, and flew away
Into the woods on Technicolor wing.
He always sang to greet our famous chief,
Nor did the mountains bring forgetfulness
Of Caesar's name. At once the birds began
To learn his song, competing one and all
To sing the first 'Hail, Caesar!' to our god.
Orpheus charmed the beasts upon the hills;
Without conductor, too, now all the birds
Gather in orchestra to sing your name.

572*

LUCILLIUS

'From Heliconian Muses we begin',
Wrote Hesiod, as the tale tells, shepherding.

'Sing me the wrath' and 'Of that man, O Muse',
Were Calliope's words through Homer's mouth.
It falls to me, as well, to write a blurb.
But what to write, as I submit to press
Book Two? 'Olympian Muses, sired by Zeus:
I never could have made it, were it not
That Nero Caesar fronted me some coin.'

599

THEOCRITUS

Look closely on this statue, passer-by,
And tell, on your return: 'ANACREON:
His portrait was on Teos. There I saw
The greatest singer of antiquity,
If any man be such.' And if you add
That he was very partial to young men,
You will have told the truth of him entire.

605

NOSSIS

The portrait is of Callo, like to life
In every detail: she commissioned it,
And hung it here in Aphrodite's hall.
How nice she looks, and lovely for her age!
Good luck to her throughout her blameless life.

606*

ANONYMOUS

On a bath

Whom Ares loved before, behold her here:
The Cytherean, who bathes in sparkling springs.
Look as she swims, and do not be afraid:
No maiden, no Athena meets your eye;
You will not be the next Tiresias.

607

ANONYMOUS

Another

This was the Graces' bath; and for their fee
They granted it the glamour of their limbs.

609

ANONYMOUS

Another

This pool is where the Graces come to play:
Graces alone may enter and disport.

609A*

ANONYMOUS

Another

This one is where the Graces *really* bathed:
It has no room for any more than three.

618

ANONYMOUS

On another bath, in Byzantium

The Lotus-eaters' ancient tale is true:
This bath is witness. If a man once wash
Amid its pure, clear waters, he forgets
All pain at loss of country or of kin.

620

PAUL THE SILENTIARY

On a twinned bathhouse, in which both women and men bathe

The hope of love is imminent, but still
One cannot catch the women unaware.

A door so small cannot accommodate
The mighty Paphian. And yet in this
I find some balm: for men of broken heart,
Hope is more honeyed than reality.

622

ANONYMOUS

On another bath

If gripped by sweet desire for wedded wife,
Bathe here, and she will find you handsomer.
But if your itch inclines to easy girls
Who work for money, they will take no fee;
They will pay *you*, who took your bath herein.

631*

AGATHIAS SCHOLASTICUS

On the Spa of Agamemnon at Smyrna

I am a place Danaans used to love:
When they had come to me, they clean forgot
The healing arts of Podalirius.
With battle done, they tended to their wounds
Amid my streams, and drove the venom out
That foreign spears had planted. For this cause
I was enlarged, was fitted with a roof,
And in exchange for heroes' high esteem
Took 'Agamemnon' as my epithet.

641*

AGATHIAS SCHOLASTICUS

On the bridge over the Sangarius

First came proud Italy, and tribes of Medes;
The whole barbarian horde. Now you as well,
Sangarius, are made our emperor's slave,

His mighty arches shackling your streams.
Impassable before; yet now you lie
Pinioned and tamed in manacles of stone.

648*

MACEDONIUS CONSUL

On an inn in Cibyra

My townsman is my friend, the stranger too:
I do not ask 'Who are you? From what town?
Who were your parents?' That is not the style
Of open-minded hospitality.

662

AGATHIAS SCHOLASTICUS

I was a place detestable to see,
A mud-brick warren. Here the strangers came,
And native folk and boorish countrymen,
To noisily excrete their bowel waste,
Until our city's father intervened.
Agathias transformed me: now I shine,
Who was so ignominious before.

669*

MARIANUS SCHOLASTICUS

On a suburban park in Amasia called Eros

Break from your journey for a little while,
And sprawl at ease beneath the bosky glade
To rest your limbs from weary voyaging,
Where water bubbles from the fountain-spouts
And runs spontaneous amid the planes.
Upon the gleaming furrow here in spring,
Soft violet twines with rosebuds. Come and see:
The sprawling ivy weaves the dewy lawn
An arbour of its ample foliage.

Here too the river's banks are overgrown,
Skirting the meadow of a magic dell.
This is Desire for sure: what other name
Befits a spot to which from every side
The lovely Graces have been gathered in?

713*

ANONYMOUS

On Myron's Cow

I'm Myron's little Cow, set on a drum.
Come goad me, herdsman; drive me to the fair.

717

EUENUS

On the same

Either this is a cow-skin made of bronze,
And there is a whole cow concealed within,
Or else the bronze itself possesses life.

719

LEONIDAS

On the same

He did not sculpt me; Myron told a lie:
He rustled me at pasture from the herd,
And clamped me here upon a base of stone.

725

UNKNOWN

On the same

Myron himself once had to find his Cow
Among a herd, and managed in the end
Only by shooing all the rest away.

727

ANONYMOUS

On the same

Though she is bronze, the horned Cow would have mooed,
Had Myron fashioned her with inner parts.

729

ANONYMOUS

On the same

If any yeoman wishes, let him set
The yoke upon my neck, and jointed plough:
And I will pull—such, Myron, was your art.

746*

KING POLEMON

On a ring

This little jasper seal bears seven cows,
And every one of seven seems alive.
They might have scattered—but their little herd
Is safely penned with a golden pale.

767*

AGATHIAS SCHOLASTICUS

On a dice-table

Sit at this pretty table worked in stone
And shake the dice to start a pleasant game.
If you should win, you must not put on airs,
Nor fuss and blame the throws when left behind.
Such details lift the veil on character:
The die declares one's depth of common sense.

780

ANONYMOUS

On a sundial

> A clever stone to compass heaven's vault:
> My little gnomon parses all the sun.

810*

ANONYMOUS

> Justin is here, Sophia at his side:
> They had it wrought in gold to celebrate
> Their triumph over the Assyrians.

827

AMMONIUS

On a Satyr standing by a well, and Love asleep

> I am the faithful servant of my god,
> Horned Dionysus. I pour offering
> With streams of silver Naiads, and I lull
> The little boy now dozing into sleep . . .

⟨*the text of the epigram, and of the book, breaks off*⟩

END

BOOK 10
ADVISORY EPIGRAMS

I

LEONIDAS

Time now to sail. The swallow has arrived
To gossip to us in the pleasant breeze
Of Zephyr, and the meadows are in bloom;
The sea, just now whipped high in jagged squall,
Has fallen silent. Weigh the anchors then,
Cast off, you mariner, and make all sail:
Priapus of the Anchorage so bids
The merchantman to venture on his way.

2*

ANTIPATER OF SIDON

This is the moment for the ship to race,
And dash to foam a sea no longer scored
By shivering billow as it surges by.
The swallow curls her nest beneath the eaves;
Fresh meadow-growth is smiling: so now coil
Your dripping lines, you mariners, and weigh
The anchors from their burrows in the hithes.
Bowse up fresh canvas on the forestay line.
Priapus of the Port, I so decree,
The son of Bromius the boisterous.

3

ANONYMOUS

Straight is the road to Hades, and the same
Whether you start from Athens, or arrive
A corpse from Meroe. So if you die

Far from your fatherland, pay little heed:
The wind that blows us all to Hades' land
Is full abaft from every compass-point.

10

ARCHIAS THE YOUNGER

Upon this naked cliff, a holy place,
The netsmen raised and set me: I am Pan,
The coastal Pan beneath whose watchful eye
They find safe port. I watch the traps, at times;
Or guard the dragnet-men along this strand.
Sail by me, stranger; and for your good deed
A south-west breeze will follow on your way.

18*

MARCUS ARGENTARIUS

Let Dionysus and the Cyprian
Delight you with the pleasures they enjoy,
Young Gōbrys, as with literary forms
The sweet Pierians. You have drunk your fill
Of learning; now enlist upon her loves;
Exuberantly quaff his cheering cups.

19*

APOLLONIDES

Today the first sweet harvest of your cheeks,
Gaius, you'll shear; the young curls from your chin.
Your father Lucius will clasp the beard
That he has prayed to see, from one who'll grow
For many days to come. Others give gold,
But I these happy lines in elegy:
The Muse is every bit as good as wealth.

20*

ADDAEUS

If you should spy a lovely looking boy,
Then take his business quickly into hand;
Tell him exactly what you have in mind.
Really—get both your hands around his balls.
But if you say, 'I'll treat you with respect,
Just like a brother', then your sense of shame
Will stop you ever scoring in the game.

25*

ANTIPATER ⟨OF THESSANONICA⟩

Apollo who looks out across the port
Of Cephallenia from Panormus' strand,
Across from rugged Ithaca, I pray:
Grant me a favouring sea for Asia;
The wake of Piso's flagship summons me.
And help my mighty emperor be kind
Both to my patron and to songs of mine.

26

LUCIAN

Enjoy the good things life has given you,
As if you were a man about to die;
But keep a careful count of what you own,
As if it had to last you for all time.
Wise is the man who ponders both, and finds
Limit to thrift *and* liberality.

28

BY THE SAME

For those who find success, a human life
Is all too short; for those whose fortunes fail,
A single night is an eternity.

32
'PALLADAS'

There's many a slip 'twixt cup and lip.

40
ANONYMOUS

Never abandon an established friend
And go to make another, paying heed
To empty words that lowborn cowards say.

43*
ANONYMOUS

Six hours more than suffice for daily toil:
Their sequels, when reduced to ABC,
Spell out to mortal men that they must LIVE.

44*
PALLADAS

A friend who gets a gift writes 'Brother, *Sir*',
To head the letter he sends right away;
But if no gift, 'Brother' and nothing more.
These words are up for sale. For my own part
I ask no 'Sir': no *sur*-plus can I share.

50
BY THE SAME

Circe, says Homer, changed her visitors
From men to pigs, or wolves. I disagree.
She was instead a wily courtesan,
Who led men on and left them penniless.
She robbed them of all trace of common sense;
When they were left with nothing of their own
She kept them on as pets, like witless beasts.

Odysseus had his wits about him, though:
With youth behind him, he had gained a charm
That warded off her spells; not Hermes' gift,
But rooted in his own intelligence.

55*

BY THE SAME

You brag you never listen to your wife
When she gives orders? What a pack of lies.
You are not 'carved from oak, or out of stone',
To quote the bard; you cannot help endure
The same as most of us—or really, all.
Your wife is boss of you. But if you say,
'At least she does not hit me with her shoe;
My marriage isn't yet a knocking-shop
That I must tolerate with tight-shut eyes',
I'd say your slavery is moderate,
As these things go, since she who purchased you
Is sensible enough and not too mean.

57

BY THE SAME

May god despise the belly and its fare:
They are the reason chastity decays.

58

BY THE SAME

Naked I came and naked shall depart;
Why toil in vain, seeing my naked end?

60

BY THE SAME

You have a lot of money. Now what comes?
Tow it along behind you as you go,

And as they bear your coffin to its tomb?
You stockpile money and you squander time:
You cannot set aside a bigger store
Of human life than any other man.

63

BY THE SAME

The pauper never lived, so does not die:
The wretch who seemed to live was like a corpse.
They who enjoy good fortune and much wealth
Experience death as life's calamity.

64*

AGATHIAS SCHOLASTICUS

Where is that haughtiness we used to know?
The countless hangers-on who flattered you:
Where have they gone at once? In exile now
You leave your city, banished far away;
'Those wretches', as you called them, Fortune chose
To sentence you. Fortune, you earn your praise:
We give you thanks, for, treating all the same,
You toy with all, and keep us entertained.

68

AGATHIAS

Aspire to be disgusted by the thought
Of any sex; but in necessity,
Never give in to thoughts of sex with men.
To go with women is the lesser crime,
For Lady Nature gave them lovers' songs.
Look at the animals: not one of them
Sullies the norms of mating; to each male
Is joined a female—but we dreadful men
Embark upon outlandish union.

72

PALLADAS

All life is but a stage, a children's game,
So set your zeal aside and learn to play;
Or else be earnest, and feel all its pain.

79

BY THE SAME

Night ends, and we are born again each day,
Retaining nothing of our former life;
Estranged from all our doings yesterday,
Each day we start afresh what life remains.
So do not say, old man, that you have lived
A longer span than most: upon this day,
You have no share in all that have gone by.

82*

BY THE SAME

Are we not dead and only seem to live,
We pagan men, fallen disastrously
Into a dream we only think is life?
Or do we live, and life itself has died?

85

BY THE SAME

Death is our herdsman, and he feeds us up
For random slaughter like a pack of swine.

88

BY THE SAME

Our bodies are diseases of our soul.
They are our Hades and our destiny,
Our burden, our compulsion, and our bonds;
Our torture sentence. Once the soul breaks free,
As if from Death's own chains, it flies to God.

EPIGRAMS

105

SIMONIDES

Some 'Theodorus' laughs that I am dead.
Another man will laugh at him the same:
We are all debts that death is calling in.

112

ANONYMOUS

Wine and hot baths and sexual excess
Send us to Hades by the express lane.

116

ANONYMOUS

'No married man who is not tempest-tossed':
All know the words, and know them to be true;
And still all men get married anyway.

118

ANONYMOUS

How did I get here? Where did I come from?
Why did I come? Only to go away?
How can I learn, when I know nothing now?
Nothing at birth, I shall become again
What once I was. The race of man is null,
Inconsequential. Well then, never mind:
Serve me from Bacchus' pleasure-loving stream;
That is the antidote to ease our pain.

124

GLYCON

The world is laughter, dust, and nothingness;
Whatever happens is mere happenstance.

END

BOOK 11
SCOPTIC AND SYMPOTIC EPIGRAMS

8

ANONYMOUS

Don't crown stone columns with your flowered wreaths,
Or burn your incense on the altar-fire:
Your money is just going up in smoke.
Send them to me as presents, if you like.
Get ashes drunk, you end up making mud;
Corpses are not big drinkers anyway.

17

NICARCHUS

Stephanus used to beg and grow some greens,
but got his lucky break and made it big,
And right away he's 'Philostephanus',
Upgraded with new letters on the front.
Next moment he'll be 'Hippocrat-ippi-ades',
Or push the boat out: 'Dionysio-pegano-dorus'—
But down the market, he's still Stephanus.

19*

STRATO

Drink now with me and love, Damocrates:
We shall not always drink, nor be with boys.
Let us bind garlands to our heads as well,
And fragrance them with myrrh, for soon enough
Will men bear myrrh and garlands to our tombs.
Now let my bones be tipsy more than not;
Deucalion can drown my skeleton.

23*

ANTIPATER ⟨OF SIDON⟩

Stargazing men declare I shan't live long;
They're right, Seleucus, but I just don't care.
We all go down to Hades just the same,
And if my path is swifter, I shall see
Minos for judgement sooner than the rest.
So let us drink, for this is truth indeed:
Wine is a horse, and life the open road;
Pedestrians take the footpath to the grave.

29*

AUTOMEDON

Send and invite her: you have all in hand.—
But can you do the business if she comes?
Take measure of yourself, Automedon:
That thing that once stood forth so full of life
Is limper now than withered garden greens;
Its corpse lies buried underneath your thighs.
The laughter will ring out at your expense
If you put out to sea unseaworthy,
An oarsman with no paddle to your name.

36

PHILIP

Archestratus, you were so pretty then:
The young men fluttered round your wine-dark cheeks;
You singed their souls. I tried to be your friend;
You took no notice, played with other men,
And let your beauty wither like a rose.
Coarse hair is spreading: *now* you call me 'friend',
Who gave your summer harvest all away,
And saved for me the stubble of the field.

39*

MACEDONIUS OF THESSALONICA

A girl drank wine with me the other day—
She's in a story that is going round,
And not a nice one. Smash the wine-cups, boys.

41*

PHILODEMUS

Now thirty years and seven have been torn
From my life's book; already, Xanthippe,
The grey hairs spread to usher in an age
When I shall show more sense. But still I care
For revels and the chatter of the strings;
An ember smoulders in my greedy heart.
You mistress Muses, instantly inscribe
Xanthippe as THE END to this my rage.

43*

ZONAS

Pass me the cheering cup of earthenware;
From earth this human life of ours was made;
When I am dead, beneath this earth I'll lie.

44*

PHILODEMUS

Piso, my dear, your friend who loves the Muse
Insists you come tomorrow after nine,
To mark the twentieth, our special day.
Come to my simple hut, and if you miss
The udders and the toasts of snow-chilled wine,
At least you will see friends who never lie,
And what you hear will be more sweet by far
Than all Phaeacia. Piso, if your gaze
Should ever turn to me as to the rest,
Our twentieth shall be rich instead of poor.

46
AUTOMEDON OF CYZICUS

At evening in our cups, then we are men;
We are mankind. Come dawn, we rise as beasts,
And set about each other's throats again.

47
ANACREON

Wealth of Gyges, Sardis' king,
Is of no concern to me;
I am left unmoved by gold,
Do not care for tyranny.
I just want to douse my beard
In sweet oil, and on my head
Set a plaited crown of rose.
All I care for is *today*:
For tomorrow, no one knows.

51
ANONYMOUS

Enjoy your moment—you are in your prime:
All nature moves so swiftly past its peak;
One summer makes a kid a billy-goat.

56
ANONYMOUS

Drink up, and be as happy as you can:
For what tomorrow brings, or what will come,
No man can know. Ease off, and take your time;
As best you can afford, be generous;
Give equal share, and eat; think humanly.
The interval between alive and not
Is next to nothing. Life adds up to this:
A tilting of the scale, and nothing more.

If you are quick, then you can take it all,
But if you die, another does the same,
And you are left with nothing in the end.

⟨*in the manuscript, a row of asterisks after poem 64 marks the change from sympotic to scoptic poems*⟩

68

LUCILLIUS

Some lie, Nicylla, that you dye your hair,
That is as sable-black unto this day
As when you bought it in the marketplace.

70*

LEONIDAS OF ALEXANDRIA

Philinus wed a hag when he was young;
And now, grown old, he weds a girl of twelve.
His nuptials were always out of joint.
Childless he stayed, who sowed in barren land;
His present bride resorts to other men:
Thus neither marriage bears him progeny.

80*

LUCILLIUS

His fellow boxers set up Apis here;
He never did a fellow any harm.

84*

LUCILLIUS

None swifter than me in the wrestling . . . fell,
Nor any slower sprinted to the line;
At discus I was never even close;
In long-jump I could never get my legs
To leave the ground; and as for javelin,

A bowlegged cripple made a better throw.
I am the first pentathlete to be hailed
As penta-knocked-for-six at every turn.

102*

AMMIANUS, OR SOME SAY NICARCHUS

Diodorus was such a skinny runt,
One time he pulled a thorn out of his foot,
And poked his foot right through its sharpened spine.

108

ANONYMOUS

Cōnon is three feet tall, his wife is six.
In bed their feet lie all along a line;
Consider then where Cōnon's mouth must go.

121*

CALLICTER

When Agelaus began to operate
Upon his patient, Acestorides,
He promptly killed him. 'Well, if he had lived,
Poor fellow, he would surely have been lame.'

133*

LUCILLIUS

Eutychides the lyricist is dead!
You denizens of Underworld, now flee:
Eutychides is coming, with his songs.
He ordered twelve guitars upon his pyre,
And five-and-twenty cases of his tunes.
Now Charon has you in his grip indeed:
Where in the future might a person go,
When even in the kingdom of the dead
Eutychides is inescapable?

134*

THE SAME

Heliodorus, shall we now begin?
Shall we now banter verses back and forth?
Still keen? 'Come close, that swifter to death's door'—
You'll find in me so dense a bullshitter
That you will be out-Heliodorified.

135*

THE SAME

Marcus, enough—leave off about 'the boy';
Grieve not for him, but for your reader, *me*,
Whom you leave stone-cold dead—deader by far
Than your 'wee bairn'. So make *me* elegies,
You public hangman—sing for *me* your dirge,
Who lie a victim of your murderous line.
What I endure for sake of 'the deceased',
I wish upon whoever first devised
The book-rolls and the pens of authorship.

139*

THE SAME

Beardy Menander the grammarian
Has done a deal to teach Zenōnis' son,
As residential tutor—so she claims.
And all night long he drills her in her forms:
She studies to decline and to conjoin,
To master figures and to conjugate.

141*

THE SAME

I lost a little pig, a cow, one sheep:
For their sake, Menecles, you took your fee.
Othryades supplies no precedent;

I do not bring a charge of larceny
Against the heroes of Thermopylae.
My case is just against Eutychides,
So what is Xerxes doing on the stand,
And Spartans too? If only for form's sake,
Remember me, or I will loudly cry:
'Menecles, let the piglet testify.'

155*

THE SAME

That pillar of morality, the scold
Of all our vice, who never felt the cold,
The bearded sage—his game is up today.
What for? It is indecorous to say;
He was bad-mouthing and was caught that way.

162

NICARCHUS

A client brought his question to the seer,
Olympicus: 'Should I take ship for Rhodes,
And how can I ensure my safe return?'
The seer commanded: 'First you must ensure
The ship is newly fitted; next, set sail
In summer, not in winter. This achieved,
You will enjoy plain sailing, there and back—
Unless a pirate catches you at sea.'

163

LUCILLIUS

The seer Olympus had three visitors:
Onēsimus, Hylas, and Menecles,
Wrestler, pentathlete, sprinter. Each in turn
Wanted to know if he would win his game.
Olympus read the entrails, and declared:
'You all shall triumph! Only please ensure

That no one passes *you*, or tosses *you*,
Or leaves *you* in his dust. Then, victory!'

213

LEONIDAS OF ALEXANDRIA

When Mēnodotus had his portrait done,
The artist Diodorus caught the life,
The very image and the duplicate
Of anyone except Mēnodotus.

215

LUCILLIUS

The painter Eutychus had twenty sons,
And never once got one that looked like him.

216*

THE SAME

You know Cratippus: you have heard it all,
How he is 'into boys'. The latest news
Is shocking—really all that I can say
Is that the Nemeses are powerful.
Cratippus who is 'into boys' we find
To be pursuing very different game.
Would I have guessed it? I already did:
Cratippus, am I to pretend surprise
That you who told the world you were a wolf
Are suddenly revealed to be a kid?

221*

AMMIANUS

You put me off because you lick your pen;
Or not for *that*, but, when the pen is gone,
Because you keep on licking just the same.

222*

ANONYMOUS

CHILŌN and LICK ON—simple anagram,
But does it matter? Chilōn will lick on,
Regardless of the letters he contains.

223*

'MELEAGER'

You don't believe that Favorinus fucks.
Cease to be sceptical: it is confirmed:
He told me that he fucks with his own mouth.

225

STRATO

The bed contains two bottoms and two tops.
You make the total four, but they are three.
You wonder how? The middleman counts twice,
A wiggling interface for both his friends.

232

CALLIAS OF ARGOS

Polycritus, you were the golden boy;
You never slipped. But you are tipsy now,
And straight away become a ranting mess.
I must suppose that you were always bad.
Wine is the test and proof of character:
You have not suddenly turned gammon now;
Instead you have been suddenly found out.

235*

DEMODOCUS

Demodocus has this as well to say:
Chians are dreadful. They are all that way:

No 'He is bad; this other one will do';
Except for Procles—and he's Chian, too.

236

THE SAME

Cilicians are crooked to a man.
The only honest one is Cinyras,
And Cinyras is a Cilician.

257*

LUCILLIUS

When Diophantus slept and dreamed he saw
Doctor Hermogenes, he woke no more,
Despite the magic amulet he wore.

264

LUCILLIUS

Hermon the miser dreamed of money spent,
And was so mortified he hanged himself.

269*

ANONYMOUS

'The son of Zeus, victorious Heracles':
I am not Lucius, though they make me be.

291*

PALLADAS

How do you serve your city jotting lines,
Extorting fortunes by your calumnies,
And selling insults as a shop sells oil?

309

LUCILLIUS

Thrasymachus, a swindler robbed you blind;
Your life has come to nothing suddenly.
Poor man: you always saved for rainy days;
You lent your money out at interest,
Then lent as well the interest you received;
Drank water, often did not even eat,
And all so you might own a little more.
Still, reckon up your hunger then and now:
You own no less, than felt you owned before.

310*

THE SAME

You purchased hair, rouge, honey, beeswax, teeth:
For that amount you might have bought a face.

312

THE SAME

This tomb contains no body, wayfarer:
Marcus the poet built it as a place
To carve his one-line epitaph, to wit:
'*Weep: Maximus, twelve years, from Ephesus.*'
I saw no 'Maximus', but, passer-by,
Behold my poet. He should make you cry.

328*

NICARCHUS

Hermogenes, Cleobulus, and I
Once went all-in on Aristodice.
The share I drew was 'her grey sea to dwell'—
We split her parts between us, do you see,
And did not each enjoy all equally.
Hermogenes got 'hateful, gusting hall':

He drew the last, and down he went below,
Into the darkness of the haunted shore,
Where figs are tumbled in the noisy gale.
Imagine Cleobulus as our Zeus,
Ascending to 'the heavens' high above,
Taking his share with thunderbolt in hand.
'The earth remained in common to us all',
For there we spread our mat and took our share.

340

PALLADAS

Ten thousand times I swore to write no more:
My poems made so many enemies,
Idiots all. But when I see his face—
Pantagathus, that Paphlagonian—
I cannot help but catch the bug again.

341

THE SAME

'To praise is best, and disrespectful talk
Engenders hatred'—then again, how sweet,
Like Attic honey, is to vilify.

381*

PALLADAS

A woman, any woman, is a pain,
But has two moments when her worth is sure:
The one, her wedding night; the other, death.

384*

THE SAME

Why are they many, if we call them 'monks'?
If they are many, are they 'mono' still?
This mass of monks belies *mon*-astic life.

405

LUCIAN

Nicon the big-nose has a nose for wine,
The best of noses, but he cannot tell
Its quality unless he takes his time:
He takes three summer hours to catch its smell,
His nose being two hundred cubits long.
Prodigious hooter! When he crosses streams,
It often nets him lots of little fish.

418*

THE EMPEROR TRAJAN

Point your nose sunward, open your mouth wide,
And tell the hours to every passer-by.

END

BOOK 12
STRATO'S BOYISH MUSE

STRATO

'Let us begin from Zeus', Aratus said;
Muses, I shall not bother you today.
If I love boys and keep their company,
What is it to the maids of Helicon?

2*

THE SAME

No Priam at the altars on my page,
Woes of Medea or of Niobe;
No dozing Itys and no nightingales
Among my leaves, so do not seek them here.
Poets of old penned *them* exhaustively;
Instead find sweet Desire with pleasant Grace,
And Bacchus. They do not deserve a frown.

4*

THE SAME

For me the peak of pleasure is a boy
Of twelve years old; though if he is thirteen,
I find him more desirable by far;
Twice seven brings a sweeter bloom of Love;
Thrice five, he is more charming than before;
Year sixteen, they are gods; at seventeen,
They are not mine to chase, but are for Zeus.
The man who lusts for lads of later years
No longer plays with boys, but now begins
To seek 'And then the hero answered back'.

5

THE SAME

I like them pale; I love them honey-skinned,
And tanned—but then, I also like them black.
Nor do I spurn a boy with golden eyes;
More than all others, though, I love the boys
Whose eyes are dark, mysterious, radiant.

7

THE SAME

A girl has no real arse, no unfeigned kiss,
No artless scent of health upon her skin,
None of that sweet and sexy pillow-talk,
No guileless glance—and if she has been schooled,
That makes her worse. Their bums are always cold,
And you will find a problem graver still:
No destination for your wandering hand.

8

THE SAME

Passing just now the garland-seller's place,
I saw a lad who wove a clustered wreath;
Nor did I pass unwounded. As I paused,
I whispered to him, 'Is that wreath for sale?
What will you take for it?' The young man's blush
Was redder than his roses; he leaned in
And said, 'Be off, in case my father sees.'
I bought some wreaths, maintaining the pretence,
And back at home I garlanded the gods,
Praying to them the boy might soon be mine.

12

FLACCUS

His beard has started. When they called him fair,
Lado rejected lovers cruelly.
He loves a boy now. Nemesis is quick.

21*

STRATO

How long shall we steal kisses, nod and wink
Our secret messages with wary eyes?
How long shall we make small talk to no end,
Redoubling frustration and delay?
We shall anticipate till we have spent
The point of it. Before the jealous come,
Dear Phidon, let our words be joined by deeds.

23

MELEAGER

I have been netted, who in time gone by
Did often laugh at lovesick serenades.
Winged Love has hung me at your outer door,
Myiscus, and has fixed a caption there:
'The spoils of war, taken from chastity.'

32

THYMOCLES

You do remember, yes? You do recall
The time I told to you that golden line:
'*The moment is so fair, and yet so fleet.*'
The swiftest bird that flies cannot outpace
The passing instant of a young man's prime.
And now, behold: the flowers of your bloom
Are lying scattered all upon the ground.

38

RHIANUS

'The Hours and Graces poured their sweetened oil
Upon you, bottom, who disturb the sleep
Of old men, even. Tell me, Blessed One,
Whose are you, and which boy do you adorn?'
The bottom answered: 'I'm for Menecles.'

43*

CALLIMACHUS

I hate a poem that goes round and round,
And I derive no pleasure from a road
That is a thoroughfare for multitudes.
I am disgusted when I see a boy
Who passes from one lover to the next,
Nor do I drink my water from the well;
I am repelled by all things popular.
Lysanias, fair indeed you are, so fair;
But when I say it, Echo intervenes:
She tells me, 'He is with another man.'

44*

GLAUCUS

There was a time, a long, long time ago,
When simple gifts—a quail, a leather ball,
Some knucklebones—would let you have your way
With boys who were susceptible to bribes.
They want fine dining now, and cash in hand.
The toys of old no longer hold their sway;
Lovers of boys must seek new sweeteners.

46

ASCLEPIADES

Not twenty-two, and yet I tire of life:
You Loves, what now? Why burn me in your flame?
If I should die, how will you spend your time?
I see it clearly: you are stupid boys,
Who will play knucklebones just as before.

48

MELEAGER

I have been thrown: so, monster, set your foot
Upon my neck. I know you, yes indeed,
Your crushing burden and your darts of flame;

But if you hurl your firebrands in my heart,
Nothing will burn. It is already ash.

50

ASCLEPIADES

Drink up, Asclepiades. Why shed these tears?
What has upset you? You are not alone:
Cypris is cruel and a kidnapper;
Love is a wicked boy, whose darts and bow
Were sharpened up for other men besides.
You are not dead; why lie there in the dust?
Come, let us drink of Bacchus' heady brew:
Our human day is but a finger's-breadth.
Or shall we wait to see again the lamp
That leads to bed? Drink up, you lovesick man:
Sad you may be, but little time remains
Before we slumber in enduring night.

59*

MELEAGER

Tyre breeds them delicate, by Love it does;
Myiscus, though—he is the shining sun
Whose blaze extinguishes the other stars.

61

ANONYMOUS

Take heed; do not, Aribazus, consume
The whole of Cnidus in oblivion.
The very stone is crumbling away.

62

ANONYMOUS

You Persian mothers, you bear children fair;
Truly you do, but fairer than the fair
Is Aribazus in my reckoning.

72

MELEAGER

Sweet cockcrow now, and sleepless at the door
Young Damis shivers out what breath remains,
Pining for Heraclitus whom he saw:
He stood beneath the radiance of his eyes
As beeswax thrown upon a burning coal.
But rouse yourself, unhappiest of men:
I also carry Love's enduring wound;
Damis, upon your tears I shed my own.

81

THE SAME

You luckless lovers, self-deceived in soul,
All you who know the fire of loving boys,
You who have tasted of its bitter-sweet—
Bring icy draught of freshly melted snow
And pour it instantly about my heart:
I dared to look on Dionysius.
Brothers in servitude, put out the flame
Before it can attack my very core.

94

MELEAGER

To be with Diodorus is delight,
And Heraclitus catches every eye;
Dio speaks sweetly; Ulianus' loins . . .
But, Philocles, just touch this soft-skinned boy,
And look at him, and talk, and—all the rest.
Thus you will know envy is not my style.
Still, should you ever cast a lusting eye
Myiscus' way, I'll wish you beauty-blind.

99

ANONYMOUS

Netted by Love. I never even dreamt—
I never nursed a flame of manly heat
Within my heart. But netted, nonetheless.
And yet it was no lust for sinful deeds
That burned me all to ash, but guileless glance,
Close kin to honour and to sense of shame.
Long labour of the Muses, pine away:
My spirit has been tossed upon the fire;
It bears a burden of sweet agony.

108*

DIONYSIUS

If you return my love, Acratus, may you age
Like Chian wine; sweeter than Chian, too.
But if you choose another over me—
May gnats buzz round you, reeling in your fug
As though you were a pot of vinegar.

109

MELEAGER

Lush Diodorus sets the lads on fire,
But now another has him in his net—
Timarion, the boy with wanton eyes.
He bears the dart of bitter-sweet Desire.
What I see now is new and marvellous:
Fire is on fire, enflamed by fire's touch.

117

MELEAGER

Let die be cast, light torches, I shall go!
Well, look at you, so confident. So drunk.
What could go wrong? I shall go serenade.

'Go serenade'? Go where, you silly man?
Love does not care for details; light them now!
To think you were a logic student once.
Away with tiresome exercise of mind!
I have forgotten everything but this:
Love even stole the wits of steadfast Zeus.

118

CALLIMACHUS

If willingly, Archinus, to your door
I came in serenade, then portion blame,
Ten-thousandfold: but if I had no choice,
Take care you do not judge too hastily.
Strong wine and Love compelled: one hauled by force,
The other overruled my self-control;
And still I did not bellow as I came
My name and parentage, but only kissed
Your doorpost. If this act has done you wrong,
Then I am wrong: condemn your criminal.

123

ANONYMOUS

When Menecharmus, son of Anticles,
Was named the victor in his boxing-match,
I crowned him with ten ribbons of soft wool,
And three times kissed the blood that streamed his face:
To me it was more honey-sweet than myrrh.

125*

MELEAGER

Love sent to me at night a lovely dream:
A softly laughing boy of eighteen years,
Still in his chlamys, snug beneath my cloak:
I hugged his tender body to my breast
And harvested my empty fantasies.
The ache of recollection warms me still:

My eyes retain a remnant of the sleep
That snagged the fleeting phantom in its net.
My foolish, lovesick soul, cease finally
To burn yourself on empty images,
Including those that come to you in dreams.

132A

THE SAME

Long-suffering soul, just now you caught on fire;
Just now you fled the flame and had revived:
You caught a breathing space. Why do you cry?
The stony Love you nurtured in your breast—
Did you not know you weaned it for your doom?
You did not know? You must now realize
The pay your careful nursing has accrued,
Attacked by fire but also icy snow.
You chose this fate yourself, and must endure:
Your deeds have justified your suffering,
Scalded by honey heated till it seethes.

140

ANONYMOUS

I saw the fair Archestratus, and swore
By Hermes that he was not, *was* not fair;
Nor did he seem so very fair to me.
I swore—and Nemesis caught hold of me,
And I was laid forthwith into the fire;
The boy, a Zeus, smote me with thunderbolt.
Shall I entreat the goddess, or the boy?
Mightier than goddess is that boy to me:
Let Nemesis go glad upon her way.

154

MELEAGER

Sweet is the boy, and sweet to me his name:
Lovely *Myiscus*. How could I not love?

For he is fair, by Cypris, wholly fair;
And if he vexes, it is Eros' way
To blend some bitter in its honey-sweet.

159

THE SAME

The cables of my life are moored in you,
Myiscus, with what breath my soul retains:
Fair youth, I swear it by your very eyes,
That speak sweet nothings even to the deaf,
And by your shining brow: that if your gaze
Falls on me clouded, then I fear the storm;
Look kindly, and sweet spring is into bloom.

167

MELEAGER

A winter wind, yet Love the sweet-of-tears
Is bearing me, Myiscus, to your shore:
I have been swept away by revelling.
Desire blows hard and drives me in her storm:
But let me enter in your anchorage,
A mariner on Cypris' open sea.

168*

POSIDIPPUS

Of *Nanno* and of *Lyde* one apiece,
And pour a measure of the lover's friend,
Mimnermus, and of wise Antimachus;
Mix in the fifth from me, and for the sixth,
'From whosoever happened once to love'—
That, Heliodorus, is what you should say.
Call Hesiod's the seventh, Homer, eighth;
The ninth is for the Muses, obviously;
The tenth and last is for Mnēmosyne.
Cypris, I drink a cup that overbrims;

And for the rest, the Loves . . .

Sober or tipsy, far from lacking grace.

175*

STRATO

Either refrain from jealousy at friends
When they show interest in your boyish slaves,
Or else do not lay on such androgynes
To bear our cups. What man is obdurate
Against desire, or never yields to wine,
Or does not see a lovely boy, and stare?
These are the actions of all living men:
But, Diophōn, depart if you so care
To where no man indulges love or wine,
And host a party for Tiresias,
and Tantalus—the one to see no boys,
The other just to see and nothing more.

177

THE SAME

Moeris at evening, as we said goodnight—
He took me in his arms? I cannot say
If it was real, or only in a dream.
Already I recall what went before,
In every detail: all the things he said,
All of the questions that he asked of me;
But did he kiss me, too? I can but guess.
If it is true, how can it be the case
That I am walking, feet upon the ground?
For last night surely I became a god.

178

THE SAME

I kindled when Theudis radiant shone
Among the other boys, as if the sun

Had risen and extinguished all the stars.
I burn for him still now, when on his cheek
Appears the down that ushers in the night:
Though he is setting, still he is the sun.

179

THE SAME

I swore to Zeus that I would never tell,
Not even tell myself, what Theudis said
That I might take; and yet my traitor soul
Has flown into the heavens glorying,
And cannot keep its happiness untold:
So I shall speak it. May the god forgive:
He let me have him. Father Zeus, pray tell,
What pleasure lies in hidden victory?

185*

THE SAME

Those puffed-up boys in purple-bordered gowns,
The ones we cannot get at, Diphilus—
Like juicy figs high up on rocky crags.
The vultures and the ravens feast on them.

188

THE SAME

If kissing you offends, if to your mind
I overstep the mark and do you wrong,
Then kiss me back, and take revenge in kind.

189

THE SAME

Who crowned your head with roses all around?
If it was lover, he is fortunate;
If it was father—well, he too has eyes.

192

THE SAME

Long hair and piled-up ringlets do not please,
Schooled not by Nature, but by crafty art;
Instead the crusted dirt upon a boy
Who has come freshly from the wrestling ground;
A healthy frame, and oil upon his skin.
Desire for me is sweet when unadorned;
A conjured comeliness reveals the hand
Of softer and more girlish Paphian.

200*

THE SAME

I hate the kisses that are hard to snatch,
The protestations of antipathy,
The vehement rebuff and upraised hand;
Yet somehow too, I am not wholly fond
Of one who, when I take him in my arms,
Is willing to give in without delay,
And lets me have him each and every way.
The boy I want, must in between them lie,
And know how to resist—and to comply.

202*

THE SAME

Winged Love conveyed me, Damis, through the air,
When I received your letter and it told
That you had come here. Light and swift we flew,
Smyrna to Sardis. Had it been a race,
Both Zētes and Calaïs were outpaced.

203

THE SAME

I am not in the mood, and so you kiss;
I kiss you, and you are not in the mood.

I pull away, you are amenable;
I make a move, you are intractable.

205

THE SAME

My neighbour's boy, so delicate and sweet—
He leads me on, and more than casually.
His laughter says he knows his way around,
And tells me he is willing. But his age—
He is no more than twelve. They do not guard
The grapes that hang unripened on the vine;
The watchmen and the palisade will come
When he is luscious with maturity.

208*

THE SAME

You little book, you are so fortunate!
I am not really jealous, but some boy
Will, as he reads you, press you to his chin,
Or wind you tight and roll you round his lips,
Or cosset you between his dewy thighs:
You are so very lucky. Many times
You shall go wandering beneath his gown,
Or, tossed upon his chair, shall daringly
Caress those parts, and not engender fear;
And you will talk and win his confidence,
And take your time, and have your privacy.
Papyrus scrap, I beg, speak well of me:
Say something nice, and say it frequently.

209*

THE SAME

Lie not so very sullen at my side;
Diphilus, do not sulk and look away.
Forget about your gang of little friends,

And put some sexiness into your kiss.
Spice up the games that come before the act—
The touches, scratches, glances, pillow talk.

211

THE SAME

If you were uninitiated in
The consummation I beseech of you,
You would have grounds to fear, suspect perhaps
That it was something strange and terrible.
But if your master's bed has made of you
A skilled technician, why begrudge to give
What you yourself received? He summons you
To service him, and sends you then away,
And falls asleep, your lord, without a word;
But dalliance here will be quite otherwise:
You will be equal in the games we play,
You will converse as partner face to face,
And I will ask for more, but not compel.

213

THE SAME

You lean that splendid flank against the wall.
Cyrus, why tease? The stone is impotent.

224

THE SAME

We walked together in a righteous path,
From the beginning. Think then, Diphilus,
How we may seal it lasting for all time.
Each of us two has drawn a fate that flies:
Beauty resides in you; in me, Desire;
Both have their season, and the seasons change.
Now for a time they run in unison,
But if they tarry inattentively,
They will take wing and vanish all away.

228

THE SAME

If a young lad who comes up short in years
Should sully his impressionable age,
The greater share of ignominy rests
Upon the friend who won him to his will.
Conversely, when a youth gone past his prime
Admits an older lover, the disgrace
That he endures is twice the older man's,
Because he has submitted willingly.
And yet, dear Moeris, still there is a place
Between those borders of unseemliness,
Between 'not yet' and 'never more again';
And that is where we happen both to be.

230

CALLIMACHUS

If pretty, dark Theocritus hates me,
Please hate him fourfold. If he loves me, love.
Indeed, by fair-haired Ganymede I swear,
You, heavenly Zeus, you too were once in love . . .
But I shall say no more on that account.

232

SCYTHINUS

Now you stand tall—I will not speak your name;
Erect, unflagging, poking proudly forth
As if you will endure forever more.
When Nemesenus curled right up to me
And said I could have everything I want,
Then you just hung there like a condemned man.
Jut out, and burst, and weep, for all I care:
You will receive no mercy from my hand.

234

STRATO

Boasting about your beauty? Realize:
The rose blooms too, but when its bloom is gone,
They throw it on the dung heap right away.
Flower and beauty draw an equal share,
And jealous Time will wither both the same.

237

THE SAME

Be off with you, pretended Puritan,
You mediocre boy, who just now swore
You would no longer give yourself to me.
Swear me no more; I see right through you now.
I have it all: I know the where, the how,
And with what man, and how much was your fee.

242*

THE SAME

Your cock was rosy-fingered yesterday;
You flaunted it, dear Alcimus; but now
You're rosy-fisted to the elbow-joint.

245

THE SAME

Every dumb creature fucks—and only fucks;
But we are marked by rationality,
And have advanced beyond our fellow beasts
Through the discovery of buggery.
Those men who let their women rule their lives
Are level with dumb creatures all the same.

248

THE SAME

What man can reckon that the boy he loves
Has passed his peak of beauty, if he spends
His every moment in his company,
And never parts? What boy can fail to please,
Who pleased us yesterday? How could he change
To please us less tomorrow than today?

254*

THE SAME

Are they emerging from some holy shrine?
What is their source, this army of Desires
That shed bright beams on everything around?
Their brightness clouds my vision, gentlemen:
Which one is slave, which free? I cannot say.
A mortal man, their lord? It cannot be;
Or if a mortal, greater man by far
Than Zeus, who owned a single Ganymede,
Though mighty god. How many such has *he*?

256*

MELEAGER

Cypris, for you this garland Love did weave,
Containing every blossom that he plucked;
A wreath of boys to cozen every heart.
Therein he plaited Diodorus sweet,
A lily, and therein Asclepiades,
A lovely wallflower; Heraclitus too
He wove atop them, rose amid the thorn,
And Diōn, like the bloom upon the vine;
Thērōn as well, a boy who flowered gold,
Saffron his hair; a sprig of Uliades,
The tufted thyme; Myiscus' tender leaves,
A shoot of olive that is evergreen;
And clipped the lovely boughs of Aretas.

The happiest of isles is holy Tyre,
That owns the scented grove where grow the blooms
Of boys that Aphrodite breathes upon.

257*

THE SAME

I am THE END, and tell the waiting crowd
That now the race is at the final turn,
Most trusty guardian of the scripted scroll.
I say that he who gleaned from all the bards
And span their work together in this roll
Is *Meleager*: he completed it,
And wove this flower-wreath of minstrelsy
For Diocles, in lasting memory.
My whole lies wound here like a serpent coil;
I am enthroned beside his learning's end.

258*

STRATO

One day, perhaps, a reader will look back
At these my playthings, reckoning these toils
Of love were all my own. It is not so:
Incessantly I jot assorted lines
For every sort of man in love with boys,
Since some god gave me this capacity.

THE END

BOOK 13
EPIGRAMS IN ASSORTED METRES

I
PHILIP

Pentameter only

> Greetings, our Paphian goddess! To your power,
> Your deathless charm and lovely majesty,
> All mortal creatures of the fleeting day
> Pay homage by each noble word and deed:
> For you make manifest your dignity
> To every mortal, and in every way.

3
THEOCRITUS

Limping trimeter

> HIPPONAX lies within, maker of songs.
> If you are bad, do not approach this tomb;
> But if you are a good and earnest soul,
> And come of worthy parents, take some cheer:
> Sit down, and if you fancy, sleep a while.

7*
CALLIMACHUS

Comic tetrameter

> Lyctian Menoetas here hung up his bow,
> And said these words: 'Sarapis, take this horn,
> This quiver too; they are my gifts to you.
> The arrows, men of Hesperis now hold.'

9*

CALLIMACHUS

Bacchic pentameter: the epigram is not complete

> From wine-rich Chios many an amphora
> Cleaves the Aegean; many too that bear
> The choicest nectar of the Lesbian vine.

11*

SIMONIDES

Pentameter for a pantomimic song

> Who raised this statue? *It was Dorieus,*
> *From Thurii.* He was not Rhodian?
> *He was, until he fled his fatherland,*
> *Where he had wrought so many forceful deeds,*
> *Inspiring terror by his mighty hand.*

16*

ANONYMOUS

Three hexameters followed by a pentameter

> My fathers and my brothers: Spartan kings.
> My team of fleet-foot horses won their race,
> And I, Cynisca, set this statue here.
> I say I am the only one to take this crown
> Of all the women in the whole of Greece.

19*

SIMONIDES

Hexameter followed by a line of nine syllables

> The man who raised this statue won his race
> On foot at Delphi in the sacred games:
> he was Nicoladas, Corinthian.
> He also took Panathenaic crowns—

Five jars of oil, from races back to back.
At holy Isthmus did the Sea-lord's shore
Behold him take three prizes in a row;
Three times he conquered at Nemea too,
Four times as well at Pellana besides;
Twice on Lycaeus and at Tegea,
In Aegina and Epidaurus grand,
At Thebes, and in the land of Megara;
At Phlius in the stadium he won
Each one of the pentathlon's five events,
And brought his mighty Corinth happiness.

END

BOOK 14
ARITHMETICAL PROBLEMS,
RIDDLES, AND ORACLES

1*
'SOCRATES'

Polycrates:
Pythagoras the blest of Helicon,
You scion of the Muses, answer me:
Within your halls how many champions
Contend in the pursuit of cleverness?

Pythagoras:
Well, let me reckon them, Polycrates:
The half of them are busying themselves
With philosophic study, while a fourth
Labour to understand Divinity;
A seventh part pursue the silent path,
The inner voice of counsel for all time;
And three are women, of whom Theano
Is head and shoulders over all the rest.
Thus many of the Muses' exegetes
Have I assembled and am guiding here.

5*

Pale is my father; I, his child, am dark;
I am a bird that flies without a wing
Until I touch the clouds of upper sky;
When pupils meet me, then I make them cry,
Though they have none to mourn; and straight away
When I am born I vanish into air.

8*

Six-one, five-two, three-four: so runs the die.

9*

My husband's father did my husband slay;
My husband also slew my husband's sire;
My husband's brother slew my husband's sire;
My husband's father did my father slay.

13*

The pair of us are twenty minae's mass,
I, Zethus, and my brother. If you take
One-third of me, one-fourth of Amphion,
You will get six, which was our mother's weight.

14*

One wind; two ships; ten sailors ply the oars;
A single helmsman steers the course of both.

17

Hunting is school for war: it teaches us
To lie in ambush, meet the charge, give chase.

30*

My parents were a tortoise and a ram;
And at my birth I slew the pair of them.

38*

I kill my brother, he in turn kills me;
We die because our father wished it so,
And as we die, we kill our mother too.

56*

You look upon me, and I look at you,
Though you have eyes to see, and I have none.
And (you could say) I speak without a voice;
My speech is yours; I part my lips in vain.

65*

An oracle given to Homer

> The isle of Ios is your mother's home,
> And she will be your refuge when you die;
> Only beware the riddle of the boys.

67*

The oracle given to Laius of Thebes

> Laius, the son of Labdacus, you pray
> That I should grant you ample progeny.
> And I will give a son to call your own:
> But you are foreordained to leave the light
> At your son's hands: for so I have decreed.

69*

An oracle given to Lycurgus

> You come, Lycurgus, to my wealthy shrine,
> Favourite of Zeus and all Olympians.
> I wonder—shall I call you god, or man?
> I tend toward the former augury.

73

An oracle given to the Megarians

> Of lands, Pelasgian Argos is the best;
> Of horses, best are the Thessalian;
> Of women, Spartan; and of men, are they
> Who drink of Arethusa's lovely spring.
> No: better still than these, those who reside
> Twixt Tiryns and Arcadia rich in flocks,
> The linen-armoured Argives, fierce in war.
> But you—Megarians—are not even third;
> You do not even come in fourth, or twelfth:
> Never were in the running, sad to say.

78*

A Pythian oracle

> Upon the flatland of Arcadia,
> There is a place, Tegea, where winds blow,
> A pair of them, compelled by mighty power.
> It is a place of strike and counter-strike,
> Of misery piled high on misery.
> There does the fruitful earth conceal your prize,
> The son of Agamemnon. Bring him back,
> And you shall be the master of Tegea.

79*

Another

> Lydian Croesus, you rule many tribes,
> But you are a great fool. Do not desire
> To hear the cry for which you often prayed:
> Your son, articulate within your halls.
> Better for you by far to be apart,
> For his first speech shall mark a day of doom.

83*

Another

> Battus, you came to ask me for your voice:
> But Lord Apollo Phoebus points your way
> To found a town in sheep-rich Libya.

84

Another

> You have not been to sheep-rich Libya;
> I have, and if you know it more than I,
> I am astounded at your cleverness.

85

Another

Whatever man comes late to Libya,
That lovely land, once it is portioned out,
I say he will be sorry in the end.

93*

Another

Pallas cannot assuage Olympian Zeus,
Though she beseech him with a lengthy speech
And cunning counsel. So again I tell
This message that I make like adamant:
For when all else is conquered, all that lies
Within the pale of Cecrops and the fold
Of blest Cithaeron, then far-seeing Zeus
Gives to the Triton-born a wooden wall
That shall alone remain unbreached by foes,
To your and to your children's benefit.
Do not delay and face the cavalry,
The continental army that comes on
Afoot and mighty—no, you must give way,
Must turn your back: be sure a time shall come
When it shall be far otherwise for you.
And holy Salamis shall surely slay
The sons of women, when the grain is sown
Or when the corn is gathered in again.

101*

A riddle of Cleobulus

One father and twelve children; to each child
Are two times thirty children of its own,
Of two quite different looks: some white, some black;
And though they live forever, all must die.

102*

From the Pythia to the Emperor Hadrian

You ask what no man knows, the line and land
Of that immortal Siren among men.
The seat of Homer was one Ithaca;
Telemachus his sire; and Nestor's child
His mother, Polycaste. Him she bore
To be by far the cleverest of men.

115*

Constantine, coming near to Troy, had in mind to found a royal city; and when he received this oracle he withdrew and founded Constantinople

It is not right to plant a new-named Rome
On Troy's foundation, hewn so long ago;
Rejoice and go to that Megarian town
Beside Propontis, where the fish and deer
Graze one and the same meadow, side by side.

126*

ARITHMETICAL EPIGRAM BY METRODORUS

This tomb holds Diophantus. Be amazed!
It also tells the measure of his life,
By science. To his boyhood, God assigned
A sixth share of his span; a further twelfth
When granting that his cheeks should show their bloom;
And with one-seventh, lit the marriage-flame,
And in the fifth year after he was wed
Granted him progeny. That darling boy!
Alas, the chilly grave took that poor child
When his life's measure was but half his sire's.
Thereafter Diophantus soothed his grief
With this numeric craft for four years more,
Before he passed the limit of his span.

132*

Another

A Cyclops, Polyphemus, made of bronze.
How carefully has someone fitted here
An eye, a mouth, a hand, all joined with pipes:
His wound appears as if it bleeds for real,
And still he seems to dribble from his mouth.
Each of the spouts emits a steady flow.
That in the palm will fill the reservoir
In just three days; the eyeball, one; the mouth,
Two-fifths of one full day. What man can tell
How long it takes, when all three run at once?

147*

*Homer to Hesiod, when he asked how numerous was the Greek force that
campaigned against Troy*

There numbered seven pits of blazing fire,
And each held fifty spits, and on each spit
Were fifty joints of meat, and round each joint
Were thrice three hundred of Achaean men.

148*

*Oracle given to Julian the Apostate, when he celebrated his birthday by
holding horse-races at Ctesiphon*

Zeus the all-wise destroyed upon a time
The earth-born race, most hateful to the gods
Who hold Olympus' halls. The Roman king,
Our godlike Julian, assailed in war
The cities and long walls of Persian arms,
And sacked them utterly with fire and sword;
Remorselessly as well he overcame
So many other nations. Straightway too
In unremitting battle he subdued
The Alamannic land of western men;
Laid waste and ravaged all their fatherland.

END

BOOK 15
MISCELLANEOUS EPIGRAMS

3

On the tomb of St Nicander

> A boy of seventeen, pure, undefiled;
> God made me faithful martyr: *Nicander*.

4*

Epitaph at Nicaea, near the lake, on the obelisk

> Boast, O Nicaea, of this lofty tomb
> That stretches to the skies; this pyramid
> That borders on the sun. Here lies in rest,
> Interred within this vasty monument,
> The hierophant most famous among men.
> This mighty tumulus for Sacerdos
> Is also monument to Severa,
> Neighbour to heaven, not the world below.

7*

On the same

> My country was Nicaea, and my sire
> The hierophant of heaven; I in turn
> Inherited his sacred mysteries.
> I am, besides, the man who saved from hell
> My city when the earthquake shivered it,
> By seeking gifts from the Ausonian Zeus.
> I died a long way from Ascania,
> And in the Attic land from which I sprang
> I mounted on the pyre. My own dear son
> Who bears his grandsire's name designed for me
> This monument that catches every eye,
> And Excellence looks upon both of them.

9*

CYRUS THE POET

Encomium to the Emperor Theodosius

You match all of Achilles' famous deeds,
Except his furtive love; you shoot a bow
As Teucer did, without his bastardy;
And you have Agamemnon's splendid look,
Though wine does not unseat your native wit.
In intellect I rate you utterly
The wise Odysseus' equal, but aloof
From wicked scheming; and your words, my King,
Drip honey-sweet like that old Pylian's,
Though you have not yet looked as Time lays hand
Upon the third instalment of your line.

15*

CONSTANTINE OF RHODES

On the Cross he erected at Lindos

The son of John and of Eudocia
Wrought me here famous: he was Constantine,
Whom vaunting Lindos bore, the foremost man
Of all the generation that has gone,
And sceptred Leo's trusty adjutant.
His brother, Alexander, and his son,
Also a Constantine, both carried forth
The kingdom's sceptres warranted by God.

17

THE SAME

On the icon of Mary, Mother of God

To limn your portrait, Virgin, one would need
Not paint, so much as stars, O Gate of Light,
That you might be portrayed in radiance;
But stars do not submit to words of men.

What nature offers, then, and art affords—
By these you are among us sought and shown.

19*

On a doctor called Asclepiades

Asclepiades, a doctor, stole a girl:
He ruined her in union coerced,
And then invited to attend the feast
Of his despotic marriage a ménage
Of dancing men and women profligate.
The house fell down that evening. All went down
Into the halls of Hades; corpses lay
Mingled with corpses everywhere they fell.
The holy bridechamber, all twined with rose,
Dripped scarlet blood from bloodshed it had seen.

30

IGNATIUS

On Paul, a monk

His body, not his virtue, this tomb hides:
He is the famous Paul, whose shining words
Flash out as splendidly as does the sun.
The labours of his virtue own great praise.
He lasted here for twenty years and three,
Lived in accordance with the holy Word,
And peacefully received a worthy end.

32*

ARETHAS THE DEACON

Who also became Archbishop of Caesarea in Cappadocia

On his own sister

Although swift fate has snuffed my lamp of life
And doused my torchlight, still my destiny

Indulged the frenzy of its wickedness
By making my whole life insufferable:
It widowed me just as my bosom swelled;
Nor did I see my pretty child at play,
A lovely jewel for parents to enfold.
Therefore did grief unbearable oppress
And waste me with the firebrand of decline.
When I had come to three and twenty years
This tomb possessed me, that greets all our line:
Here did my aged parents weave a dirge
For all of us, and tore their grizzled hair;
And Anna's noble brothers in a band
Thought fondly on her loveliness, and sighed.

37*

COMETAS

On the poetry of Homer that he corrected

Your books, great-hearted Homer, Cometas
Found mouldering with age, and rendered them
More youthful: he stripped off the slough of time,
And showed them off all brilliant to the wise,
Those mortals in whose heart dwells intellect.

EPIGRAMS IN THE HIPPODROME
AT CONSTANTINOPLE

42

On the statue of Constantine the charioteer

Ever since Constantine went down below
And entered Hades' hall, with him has gone
All of the glory of the charioteers.

43

Another

Honours of gold befitted Constantine
In recognition of his excellence,
Because his art did never see his like:
When he was but a youth, he overcame
The drivers famed in song; and in old age
He taught the young that they were not his match.
People and monarch stood in awe of him,
Even when he was dead, and set him here
By precept that shall live in memory.

48*

On Uranius the charioteer

The equal of Faustinus' famous son
And Faustinus himself: *Uranius.*
Our ruler set his image beside both.
In homage to his countless victories
The people dubbed him Pelops most divine.
'Thus ever does a god lead like to like':
Who sees these three can speak so and be true.

END

'BOOK 16'
⟨THE PLANUDEAN APPENDIX⟩

12*

ANONYMOUS

Come sit beneath my pine, that honey-sweet
Sings as it leans in Zephyr's gentle breeze.
Behold as well the honey-dripping stream,
Where piping on my solitary reeds
I usher in a sweet and pleasant sleep.

23

SIMONIDES

Who are you, of what father and what land?
In what event were you victorious?
Casmylus I, son of Euagoras,
Of Rhodes, in boxing, at the Pythians.

24*

THE SAME

Milo's this statue, handsome as is he,
Who outside Pisa seven times was crowned,
And never once was wrestled to his knees.

26*

SIMONIDES

Beneath the glen of Dirphys we were slain;
Near Euripus they raised our barrow high,
By order of the people. Justly so:
We sacrificed the loveliness of youth
To face the savage cloud of battling.

38*

JOHN BARBOCALLUS

On a portrait of Synesius Scholasticus, set up at Berytus to mark his victory in battle

> Not only by Eurotas warlike men,
> Nor by Ilissus mindful of the law:
> As on a Spartan, or a citizen
> Of Athens even, Triumph and the Right
> Looked on Synesius in wonderment.

47

ANONYMOUS

> The great in war, undaunted general:
> Nicetas, for his excellence, the Greens.

55

TROILUS GRAMMATICUS

> Statue, who set you up? for what? for whom?
> 'Lyro, his city, for his wrestling.'

57

PAUL THE SILENTIARY

On a Bacchant at Byzantium

> It was not Nature turned the Bacchant's mind,
> But Art, that blended madness into stone.

60

SIMONIDES

> Who is this girl? *A Bacchant.* By whose hand?
> *Scopas'.* But which one robbed her of her mind?
> Bacchus, or Scopas? *Scopas, certainly.*

61*

CRINAGORAS

The East and West mark out the cosmos' span,
And Nero's exploits reached to both those ends.
The rising sun beheld Armenia
And as it set saw Germany the same,
Defeated at his hands. Let it be sung,
His double triumph: Araxes and Rhine
Know that the tribes that drink of them are slaves.

68

ASCLEPIADES, OR SOME SAY POSIDIPPUS

This statue is of Cypris; let us check
It is not Berenice. Who can say
To which of them it is the more alike?

79*

'SYNESIUS THE PHILOSOPHER'

'On his own sister'

This statue is of Cypris all in gold,
Or else of Stratonice, golden too.

80*

AGATHIAS SCHOLASTICUS

I was a slut amid Byzantine Rome,
Indulging all in fondness for a fee;
I am that great technician of her trade,
Callirhoe, whom, maddened by love's sting,
The painter Thomas set in portrait here.
It shows the depth of passion in his soul:
The wax of it is melted, like his heart.

81

PHILIP

On the statue of Zeus at Olympia

The god came down to have his portrait took
From highest heaven, Phidias; or else,
You went up there yourself to visit him.

82*

'SIMONIDES'

The Rhodian Colossus, eight times ten
In cubits, Chares made, the Lindian.

100*

ANONYMOUS

On a portrait of King Lysimachus

The flowing locks, the club, the fearless stare;
The shaggy brow: see these upon the man
And search his statue for a lion's skin.
If you should find one, he is Heracles;
If not, the portrait is Lysimachus'.

103*

GEMINUS

On a statue of Heracles

Where is your mighty cudgel, Heracles,
Nemean cloak, and quiver full of darts?
Where is your boasting and your haughtiness?
Why did Lysippus mould you thus downcast,
And mingle grief into the living bronze?
You are in sorrow, stripped of weaponry:
Who has laid waste to you? The boy with wings:
Truly a grievous Labour is Desire.

107*

JULIAN

On an Icarus in bronze, set up in a bathhouse

Wax killed you, Icarus; but now with wax
The bronzesmith has restored you to your form.
But do not beat your wings upon the air,
Lest you should once more plummet from the sky
And make these baths as well 'Icarian'.

120*

ARCHELAUS, OR SOME SAY ASCLEPIADES

On a statue of Alexander of Macedon

All Alexander's hardy recklessness
Lysippus moulded; all his human form.
This bronze of his, what power does it hold?
The brazen hero dares to look on Zeus,
And seems to say, 'I have subdued the Earth;
Zeus, you may keep Olympus as your share.'

135*

ANONYMOUS

On the picture of Medea in Rome

Timomachus has skilfully combined
Medea's mother-love and jealousy
As she drags off her children to their doom.
One part of her resolves upon the sword,
Another part recoils; she longs to save,
But also slay, the infants in her care.

150*

'POLLIANUS'

This *Polyxena*, Polyclitus wrought:
No other hand was laid upon its form.
It is a wondrous painting, and the twin

Of his own *Hera*. See her sundered gown,
And how she hides her naked modesty
So chastely with her hand. Poor girl, she begs
That they may spare her life; and in her eyes
Resides the sum of all the Trojan War.

151*

ANONYMOUS

On a painting of Dido

Stranger, you see the portrait true to life
Of famous Dido. See how it shines bright
With godlike beauty. Such indeed was I,
But had no character such as you hear:
I rose to fame by pious reverence.
For never once Aeneas I beheld,
Nor did I come to Libya that time
When Troy was burning; rather, to escape
Iarbas' threat to marry me by force
I drove a two-edged sword into my heart.
Why did you Muses give chaste Virgil arms
To use against me, helping him tell lies
That so besmirched my modest temperance?

152*

GAURADAS

Echo, my dear, grant me my wish in something.—*something*.
I love a maiden; but she does not love me.—*love me*.
The moment never lets me take advantage.—*vantage*.
So you go tell it to her, that I love her.—*love her*.
To prove it, here are coins that you can pay her.—*pay her*.
Echo, what else remains, but to get lucky?—*lucky*.

153

SATYRUS

Across the shepherds' meadow, tongueless Echo
Reverberates a canon of the birdsong.

161*

'PLATO'

On the statue of Aphrodite at Cnidus

> Neither Praxiteles nor chisel made you;
> You stand thus as you once did, for the judging.

168

ANONYMOUS

On the same

> Paris, Anchises, and Adonis: three,
> And three alone, have witnessed me unclothed.
> I know it—so wherefore Praxiteles?

172

ALEXANDER OF AETOLIA

> Pallas herself perhaps thus faithfully
> Rendered the Cyprian, choosing to forget
> The judgement in which Paris slighted her.

178*

ANTIPATER OF SIDON

On the Aphrodite rising from the sea

> See her ascending newborn from the sea,
> Cypris, the labour of Apelles' pen:
> See how she grips her water-sodden hair
> And wrings her dampened locks to shed the foam.
> Athena now and Hera both shall say:
> 'No more in beauty do we now contend.'

184*

ANTIPATER ⟨OF THESSALONICA⟩

On a statue of Dionysus

> Italian Piso's shield-companion,
> I, Dionysus, here a watchman stand

To guard his halls and bring prosperity.
Worthy, O Dionysus, is the home
That you have entered. Each is fit to each:
The hall to Bacchus; Bacchus to the hall.

188*

NICIAS

On a statue of Hermes

Cyllene's craggy mount with shivering leaves:
There is my home, but here instead I stand
As guardian of this fine gymnasium,
I, Hermes, on whose brow the lovely boys
Often set marjoram and hyacinth,
And garlands made of blooming violets.

206*

LEONIDAS ⟨OF TARENTUM⟩

One god alone the Thespians reverence:
Desire, the son of the Cytherean;
And him when rendered from no other stamp,
But only as Praxiteles perceived,
Who saw the goddess wearing Phryne's form
And paid the ransom for his longing heart.

210

'PLATO'

We reached the bosky grove, and found within it
The apple-cheeked young boy of Aphrodite.
He held not bow, nor quiver full of arrows,
But on the leafy trees we found them hanging;
While he himself lay bound among the roses,
Asleep and smiling. Tawny bees above him
On his sweet lips were pouring wax-formed honey.

213*

MELEAGER, OR SOME SAY STRATO

The wings upon your back carry you swiftly;
The arrows of your Scythian bow, unerring;
Yet still, Desire, beneath the earth I'll flee you.
And then? Not even Hades the all-conquering
Was able to escape your mighty power.

214

SECUNDUS

On statues of Erōtes

See these Desires, exulting in their spoils;
See how these little boys delight to bear
On strapping shoulders weapons of the gods—
The drum and thyrsus of Dionysus,
The thunderbolt of Zeus, the war-god's shield
And crested helm, Apollo's quiver full,
The Sea-lord's trident and the knotted club
That graced the mighty hands of Heracles.
What hope for mortal men, when highest heaven
Has fallen to Desire, and Cypris now
Has emptied the immortals' armoury?

217*

ANONYMOUS

On a statue of Calliope

Calliope am I, who gave my breast
To Cyrus, at which godlike Homer nursed;
The breast from which sweet Orpheus once drank.

222*

PARMENION

On the Nemesis of the Athenians

The Medes expected that my stone would be
The making of their trophy, but I changed,

And took the timely form of Nemesis,
A goddess justly placed on Rhamnous' shores
To witness Attic victory and skill.

227

ANONYMOUS

Wayfarer, lay yourself on this green meadow;
Unwind, and rest your limbs from heavy labour
Here where the zephyr-ruffled pine shall soothe you,
And listen to the song of the cicadas.
The shepherd on the hills at noon is piping
Beside the spring, beneath the shaggy pine-tree.
Escape the burning heat of dog-day autumn;
You'll cross the hill in time. Do Hermes' bidding.

232*

SIMONIDES

Goat-footed Pan, Arcadian, am I;
Foe to the Persians, the Athenians' friend;
It was Miltiades that set me here.

235

APOLLONIDES OF SMYRNA

I am the god of country folk. Why pour me
Italian vintages from golden vessels,
Or bend the necks of bulls upon my altar?
Spare your expense; these offerings do not please me.
I am the mountain Pan, carved from a tree-trunk:
Mutton I eat, drink simple wine from beakers.

236*

LEONIDAS ⟨OF TARENTUM⟩

Here on the drystone wall, Dinomenes
Set me the sleepless watchman of his greens.

I am Priapus: look upon me, thief;
See how I strain and jut. All this, you say,
For a few lettuce' sake? A few, indeed.

240*

PHILIP

I see the figs are ready to be picked;
You will forgive me if I take a few.
Don't touch them! Why so angry, Priapus?
Ask all you like. Your visit is in vain!
I'm really begging. *I demand my fee;*
You're not the only one with appetites.
Go on. What do I have, that you could need?
I hear there is a custom: 'quid pro quo'.
You are a god. You can't be wanting coin?
It's something else I want. What can it be?
Eat all my figs you want, and cheerfully
Give up the fig you carry at your rear.

256

ANONYMOUS

I occupy a hilly, desert place,
Good traveller, but I am not to blame;
It was Archelochus that set me here.
Hermes I am, and take no joy in hills,
Nor range upon the peaks, and much prefer
The open highway; yet Archelochus,
A solitary man, thus settled me
To keep him company, O wayfarer,
In lieu of any human neighbourhood.

267*

SYNESIUS SCHOLASTICUS

On a portrait of Hippocrates

Whence came your artist? *From Byzantium.*
And he was called—*Eusebius.* And you?

Hippocrates, the Coan. Tell me why
He painted you. *It was his Histories,*
For which his city granted in return
The honour of delineating me.
And why not paint a likeness of himself?
By giving me the honour in his stead,
He raised his reputation all the more.

269*

ANONYMOUS

On a portrait of Hippocrates

Hippocrates of Cos, who pioneered
The hidden pathways of the healing art:
Behold the Paeon of all humankind.

274*

ANONYMOUS

On ⟨a portrait of⟩ Oribasius, the doctor

Here is the godly Oribasius,
Physician to the Emperor Julian,
A genius who deserves to be revered:
His learned intellect was like a bee
That gathered nectar, flitting to and fro
Between the blooms of doctors gone before.

278*

PAUL THE SILENTIARY

On a picture of Maria the guitarist and singer

She holds the plectra both of lyre and longing;
With them she plucks the guitar, and the heartstrings.
Those she rejects are wretched, but the favoured
Is an Anchises, or a new Adonis.
And, stranger, if you wish to hear her country
And famous name—Maria, from the Pharos.

283

LEONTIUS SCHOLASTICUS

On a picture of a dancing-girl

> Tenth Muse, fourth Grace, and the delight of men,
> The glory of our city: Rhodoclea.
> Her eyes and feet are rapid as the wind;
> Her fingers, cleverer than Muse or Grace.

297

ANONYMOUS

> For Homer's root do seven cities vie:
> Cyme and Smyrna, Chios, Colophon,
> Pylos and Argos, Athens last of all.

299

ANONYMOUS

> Were you a Chian? *No.* From Smyrna, then?
> *Not I.* So was it Cyme? Colophon?
> Which did you come from, Homer? *Neither one.*
> Was Salamis your town? *Again, untrue.*
> So tell me where you came from, man to man.
> *I will not tell.* Why not? *I realize*
> *That if I tell the truth, I will incur*
> *The lasting hatred of the other towns.*

311*

ANONYMOUS

On Oppian's Halieutica

> In his papyrus columns, Oppian
> Has gathered up the tribes that swim the sea,
> And placed before the young an endless feast.

324*

ANONYMOUS

I am a pencil. Coming from the fire
I was of silver, but within your hands
I become gold, graceful Leontion:
So well Athena gifted you with skill,
And Cypris with the utmost loveliness.

331

AGATHIAS SCHOLASTICUS

On a portrait of Plutarch

The mighty sons of Italy here placed
Your famous portrait, man of Chaeronea,
Because your *Lives* combined in parallel
Greek heroes and the warlike sons of Rome;
And yet you never found another *Life*
To parallel your own unequalled tale.

EPIGRAMS ON THE STELAE OF
ATHLETES IN THE HIPPODROME
AT CONSTANTINOPLE

335*

On Porphyrius

The Emperor and populace erect
The son of Calchas, our Porphyrius,
Laden with garlands for his noble toil,
The youngest of the drivers and the best
By measure of his many victories.
He should have had a statue made of gold,
And not this brass, like all the rest here placed.

345

On the same

> You stand in company with Victory
> And kingly Alexander, you who plucked
> The honours that distinguish both of them.

383

On Faustinus, of the Green faction

> Behold Faustinus, charioteer of old,
> Who, once he found the faction of the Greens,
> Knew nothing of defeat upon the track.
> You see him as he was, an older man,
> But in his strength he was a stripling still,
> And never once was beaten in a race.

386

On JULIAN, charioteer of the Reds

> The hand has skill to birth the ancient dead
> A second time: for here is Julian
> In all the strength he showed in former age,
> And hauling to and fro the reins of Red.
> He stands now imaged high upon his car;
> His hand awaits the signal to begin:
> He only needs to see the turning-post.

388

JULIAN, PREFECT OF EGYPT

> As I wove once a garland,
> I found among the roses
> Desire; him I pinioned
> And plunged into the wine-bowl.
> I took him up and drank him;
> And now he sings inside me,
> And tickles with his feathers.

EXPLANATORY NOTES

ABBREVIATIONS

AP	*Anthologia Palatina*
Cameron	*The Greek Anthology from Meleager to Planudes* (Oxford: Clarendon Press, 1993).
Gow and Page (1965)	Gow, A. S. F., and Page, D. L., *The Greek Anthology: Hellenistic Epigrams* (Cambridge: Cambridge University Press, 1965).
Gow and Page (1968)	Gow, A. S. F., and Page, D. L., *The Greek Anthology: The Garland of Philip and Some Contemporary Epigrams* (Cambridge: Cambridge University Press, 1968).
Paton	*The Greek Anthology*, 5 vols (London: William Heinemann; New York: G. P. Putnam's Sons, 1916–18).

Other works in the Select Bibliography are referred to by author and short title.

All translations of ancient works are my own unless otherwise stated. All epigrams referred to in these notes appear in this selection unless otherwise stated.

BOOK 1

1.2 The Panagia or Theotokos (Church of St Mary) in this suburb of Byzantium housed some of Byzantium's most powerful relics. Justin I and his nephew Justinian I restored it in the early sixth century and an imperial palace grew up around it, eventually replacing the Great Palace as the main seat of the imperial court.

1.4 The rods are the fasces, the traditional emblem of a Roman magistrate's authority.

1.5 Amantius was eunuch chamberlain to Anastasius I in the early sixth century.

1.6 The church was built by Sphoracius in the reigns of Arcadius and Theodosius and contained the head of St Theodore 'the Recruit', a martyr of the early years of the fourth century (the head is now in Gaeta, Italy). Theodore was martyred by fire, making him an appropriate dedicatee for Sphoracius' thank-offering. The festival of Theodore, decreed in the closing years of his century, is still celebrated by Greek Orthodoxy during Lent.

1.10 Polyeuctus was a third-century martyr. The church that replaced Eudocia's original and housed the saint's skull was built in the early sixth century by her great-granddaughter, the fourth generation after Eudocia counting inclusively. The new church was Constantinople's largest; with the epigram, it restated the family's claim to imperial glory (from which they had been sidelined) and may thereby have provoked the building of Hagia Sophia. The two long inscriptions preserved as *AP* 1.10 are the main sources of information on Juliana's church, and were inscribed within it; fragments of the text were found in excavations in the 1960s.

1.11 Justinian I was an aggressive and successful conqueror, but an outbreak of bubonic plague devastated Byzantium during his reign. The Anargyri, 'Unmercenary Physicians', were Sts Cosmas and Damian, two brothers martyred in Cilicia in the late third century. They won many converts by charging no fee for their services. Their story was too good to use just once: tradition attests the martyrdom near Rome a couple of years earlier of a separate Cosmas and Damian, who were also brothers and Unmercenary Physicians.

1.12 Eudoxia was the oldest child of Eudocia (*AP* 1.10) and Theodosius II.

1.34 Platē ('Flat Island', the modern Turkish Yassiada) was a tiny island in the Sea of Marmara. In the ninth century it gained a monastery, and there must already have been a church by Agathias' day, but its main importance was as a place of political exile.

1.35 The Sosthenium was a church at the mouth of the Bosporus, dedicated by Constantine to the Archangel Michael, but (legend said) first founded by Jason's Argonauts after they witnessed a vision of a winged man prophesying their victory over Amycus, King of the Bebryces.

1.36 The Magistrus (Latin *magister officiorum*) was a rare senior appointment. Proconsuls were provincial governors of the highest rank.

1.62 The crossing of the Jordan by the Israelites, carrying the Ark, is told in the third chapter of the Book of Joshua.

1.80 The ruins of the Basilica of St John, believed to stand over the Apostle's burial site, can still be seen in Ephesus. No consistent distinction was drawn between John the Apostle, John the Evangelist, and the 'John' of Revelation.

1.88 This is not St Dionysius 'the Great', third-century Coptic Pope of Alexandria, but the first-century Dionysius the Areopagite. In the late fifth or early sixth century, an anonymous author ('Pseudo-Dionysius') forged a series of mystical texts under his name. The Byzantines revered them, and in the late Middle Ages they inspired European mystics such as Meister Eckhardt and Julian of Norwich.

1.98 Melite or Melita was the Byzantine capital of Malta. Almost none of its ruins survive. Gregory was writing two centuries earlier than Agathias, so his Theodorus is not the Theodorus of 1.36; the name ('Gift of God') was common.

1.103 Momus was the personification of censure and reproach. His earliest appearance is in Hesiod's epic *Theogony* (214), where Night gives birth to Momus and a sister, 'painful Woe'. Paton suggests Momus is here synonymous with Satan.

1.106 Like 1.1, this epigram celebrates a restoration of images after a period of iconoclasm. It hinges on the similarity between 'Chryso-' (of gold), and 'Christo-' (of Christ). The Chrysotriclinium was the throne room of the Great Palace, built three centuries earlier; it is known only through literary descriptions such as this one. The 'watchmen' form a frieze around the interior circuit of either the throne room, or the dome that capped it. It is clear from the companion epigram 1.107 that 'Michael' is Michael III, who ended the 'Second Iconoclasm' of the early ninth century. The title rendered as 'Bishop' here, Proedros, later came to mean President of the Senate; the context of the poem suggests the Archbishop of Constantinople and Patriarch of the Orthodox Church (cf. 1.120).

1.109 This is the Church of the Theotokos (Mother of God) at Blachernae, built near a fountain of holy water by Pulcheria and Marcian in the fifth century. I have not been able to identify the three restorers. 'Leo' cannot be Leo I, whose additions (a fountain enclosure and reliquary) were only twenty years after the church was built.

1.112 The Church of the Transfiguration on Mount Tabor in the Holy Land marked the accepted site of the Gospel episode in which Christ spoke with Moses and Elijah, confirming his identity as Son of God to his disciples.

1.113 The Presentation of the child Jesus in the Temple in Jerusalem is one of the great festivals of Orthodoxy; Western Christians celebrate it as Candlemas.

1.119 This hexameter poem of twenty-eight lines summarizes a longer poem written by a fourth-century Christian bishop, 'Patricius', and described as a 'cento': that is to say, a poem composed entirely by selecting and rearranging lines from a canonical source, in this case the works of Homer. The Empress Eudocia considered Patrick's poem incomplete, and undertook to revise and expand it; hers is the version that survives.

1.120 When Constantinople was besieged by the Avars and Persians in 626, the Emperor's son Constantine (later briefly Constantine III) processed along the city walls bearing the icon of the Virgin Mary from her church at Blachernae; the siege was lifted. Spared by the invaders, the church was then enclosed within a new section of city wall, creating the suburb of Blachernae and forming the hub of a new imperial palace (1.2).

BOOK 3

3.1 The thyrsus, an ivy-wound stalk of giant fennel, was the symbol of Dionysus, god of wine and the release that it brings, and of the satyrs and maenads who followed him. Dionysus was believed to have come to Greece from the East but his mother was from Thebes, whose king, Pentheus, denied the power of the new god; his dreadful punishment is the subject of Euripides' *Bacchae*. Rescued by her son from Hades, Semele became a goddess herself, and took the name Thyone.

3.2 Teuthrania was a city and region in what is now north-western Turkey. Its founding hero, Teuthras, took in Auge and her infant son after her father Aleus expelled them from Tegea in Arcadia. Telephus' father was Heracles, and as a grown man he duelled with Achilles. Aeschylus, Sophocles, and Euripides all wrote tragedies about Auge and Telephus, but only titles and a few fragments survive.

3.3 In this version of the story, Amyntor's mistress lied to him that Phoenix had slept with her; in others the accusation was true. In either case, Chiron the centaur cured Phoenix's blindness, and he went on to become Achilles' foster-father and join him on the expedition against Troy.

3.4 Rather like Amyntor in the preceding poem, Phineus was famous for blinding his sons from his first marriage on the basis of a woman's lies, in this case his second wife—but this poem presents a quite different version of the tale, in which the sons triumph over her. An older Phineus appears as a blind seer in the second book of Apollonius' *Argonautica*, translated by Richard Hunter for Oxford World's Classics under the title *Jason and the Golden Fleece*. The final line of this epigram turns on a double sense: the verb *damazō* (to tame an animal, or break it to the yoke) is used interchangeably of a woman being taken as a bride, and of lethal violence. Phineus' new wife is 'tamed', but not in the way she and her new husband expect.

3.6 The story of Apollo's overthrow of Python at Delphi is known in several versions; even so, this variant is unusual. The modern genus of snake is named after the chthonic monster. Apollo's priestess at Delphi was called the Pythia.

3.7 This episode from the Theban mythic cycle takes place two generations before, and shares some elements with, the Oedipus story. Zeus raped Antiope, who gave birth to twin sons, Amphiōn and Zethus, on Mount Cithaeron and left them to be raised by herdsmen. She returned or was forcibly brought back to Thebes, where Dirce treated her as a slave. Eventually she escaped and was reunited with her boys, who killed Dirce by tying her to the horns of a bull (hence 'double cord', one for each horn). The twins then became rulers of Thebes. Zethus and Amphion are the subject of a riddle at 14.13.

3.10 When the Argonauts stopped at Lemnos on their way to recover the golden fleece, Jason enjoyed a sexual relationship with the queen, Hypsipyle, but then abandoned her. The other women of Lemnos drove her out; she was enslaved by pirates and sold to Lycurgus, King of Nemea, who put her in charge of his infant son, Archemorus. While in her care, the boy was bitten by a snake and died. Asopis was a spring on Aegina; no 'girl' is known in association with it, or with the story of Hypsipyle's sons, and this part of line 5 is generally thought to be corrupt, like the nonsense-word 'aphouthar' that currently ends line 3.

3.13 Rhadamanthus was a wise king of Crete who became one of the judges of the dead, alongside Aeacus (7.343) and Minos (11.23). Homer's *Odyssey* places him in the paradisiacal Elysian Fields. In the more usual version he marries Alcmēne while they are both still alive.

3.14 The 'he' of the final line is Apollo; his sister Artemis shared in the deed but the figurative scenes and their accompanying epigrams emphasize the role of dutiful sons.

3.15 Uniquely in Book 3, this episode has a son saving his father, and not his mother. The 'Aleian plain' of Cilicia is where Bellerophon wanders blind in the sixth book of Homer's *Iliad* (6.201): its name means 'plain of wandering'. Bellerophon had performed a series of dangerous tasks for King Iobates of Lycia, including killing the Chimaera. Eventually Iobates let him marry his daughter, but Zeus punished the hero's excessive pride by sending a gadfly to sting Pegasus: Bellerophon was thrown into a thorn-bush and was blinded. This is the scene for the otherwise unknown mythological elaboration described in the epigram. Proteus was the King of Tiryns who had sent Bellerophon to Iobates to be killed; it is unclear what his son is doing so far from home, a generation later. It does not help that lines 2–4 of the text are badly mangled.

3.16 Desmontes, angered at Melanippe's pregnancy, exposed the boys on Mount Pelion and imprisoned and blinded her; when her sons grew up they rescued her, and Poseidon restored her sight. Desmontes is not usually Melanippe's father; as told here, her story is a variant on Tyro's (3.9) and serves as a bridge to Servilia's at the climax of the book (3.19). Boeotus was the eponymous hero of the Boeotians.

3.17 This episode is supposed to have occurred in Catana during an eruption of Etna in the fifth century BC. The brothers received local cult and were shown on the city's coinage. The city was rebuilt; the epigram cannot be.

3.19 According to the myth, Numitor, King of Alba Longa and descendant of Aeneas, was the maternal grandfather of Romulus and Remus. His brother Amulius seized the throne and killed his sons; the grandsons grew up and restored him to power in 752 BC, the year after founding Rome. Their mother's name was Rhea Silvia; it has been misremembered by the caption's author or misheard by a later copyist.

BOOK 5

5.3 In myth, Eos, goddess of Dawn, took the Trojan prince Tithonus as her mortal lover. She asked Zeus to make him immortal, but forgot to stipulate that he should stay forever young. He thus lives forever, getting older and older. The last poem in our selection from Book 5, 5.197, returns to the gossip of young men in their peer group.

5.6 This traditional but obscure saying about the Megarians is found again in an oracle at 14.73.

5.15 Praxiteles' cult image of Aphrodite at Cnidus was world-famous: see note on 16.206. Polyclitus pioneered the use of contrapposto in sculpture and was best known for his figures of male nude figures, such as the *Diadumenus*.

5.17 The watcher is Priapus, protector of fishermen and other seafarers; compare, for instance, 6.33.

5.19 Mount Erymanthus in the highlands of Arcadia was where Heracles undertook his fourth Labour, the killing of the Erymanthian Boar. Discus and rattle were toys for boys and girls respectively; Paton suspected a sexual double entendre but could not identify it, muttering only in the decent obscurity of Latin, '*sed latet spurci aliquid*'.

5.21 The roads outside ancient cities were lined with the tombs of their dead. The epitaphs of Book 7 are written as if for inscription on such tombs, and address the passing traveller, just as real epitaphs often did.

5.35 Compare Lucian 6.17, and Nicarchus' Homeric parody at 11.328. The closing reference is to Paris, who legendarily adjudicated the beauty contest of Hera, Athena, and (the winner) Aphrodite, thereby dooming his city, Troy. This poem and its sequel were judged too naughty for translation into English in Paton's Loeb, which rendered the lines describing the arses (1. 35) and pussies (1. 36) into Latin instead.

5.42 Martial writes similar epigrams, including 5.83 and a cycle in Book 4 (4.38, 71, and 81). Since Rufinus' date is uncertain, the reader is free to speculate which way the influence, if any, ran.

5.49 C. Cornelius Gallus began the tradition of Roman erotic elegy. He was condemned and his Latin poems were lost, but in 1978 archaeologists recovered nine lines from the ruins of an ancient legionary fortress in Egypt. Like his close friend Virgil, Gallus knew Greek well, and there is no reason to suppose this epigram is not by him. On the *Lyde* of the Hellenistic poet Antimachus, see note on 12.168.

5.55 We now know that Dioscorides borrowed 'white seed' from a poem by the seventh-century iambic poet Archilochus. This was lost for the better part of 2,000 years, before being rediscovered on papyrus (the 'Cologne Archilochus') and published to much scholarly excitement in 1974.

5.59 This must be the Archias whose Roman citizenship rights Cicero successfully defended, in the speech named after him (see Introduction, p. xv).

5.74 Lilies (for Anyte and Moero), roses (for Sappho), and narcissi (for Simonides and the lost Melanippides) are the first three flower-types named by Meleager in the poetic preface he wrote for his *Garland*, preserved in Book 4 of the Anthology.

5.131 This epigram was the model for Catullus' famous poem 85, *Odi et amo*. Philodemus (*c.*100–*c.*30 BC) spent much of his life in Italy, and he and Catullus (*c.*84–*c.*54 BC) could well have known each other.

5.139 The *plēktris* was a stringed instrument from Lydia; the player plucked it with the fingers, rather than using a plectrum as with the Greek lyre. Sappho was said to have introduced it to the Greeks.

5.179 'Rue': Meleager says Eros' laughter will soon be *sardanios*, which gives us our 'sardonic'. The word comes from a plant, Sardinian crowfoot, the bitterness of which made people who tasted it screw up their faces. The 'Pyrrhic' victory is 'Cadmean' in the Greek, from Cadmus, who legendarily founded Thebes but got all his companions killed in the process. The lynx among the herd of goats must have been proverbial, like our 'fox in the henhouse'.

5.189 The opening couplet echoes famous lines from Sappho (168B Voigt): 'The moon has set, and the Pleiades, and it is the middle of the night, and the time is going by, and I am lying alone.'

5.197 Ilias' name, 'Iliad', identifies her as a hetaera; like Homer's Troy, she has been the ruin of many young men.

5.198 There is something missing in the Greek after 'quiver', probably just an adjective describing it.

5.202 This epigram and its sequel in the *Anthology*, 5.203, make an obvious thematic pair. Philaenis is a hetaera's working name, and 'Philaenis' was credited as the author of a comprehensive sex manual; a fragment of its introduction survives on papyrus. Ovid must have consulted it when writing his *Art of Love*. A fictional epitaph, in which Philaenis indignantly denies authorship, is included later in the selection (7.345). 'Had their blood up': the Greek verb *phruassomai* is used both of horses whinnying and prancing before a race begins, and of men getting turned on.

5.205 Larissa was the main city of Thessaly, a region famous for black magic; see, for instance, Thelyphron's story in the second book of Apuleius' *Metamorphoses* or *Golden Ass*.

5.232 This homoerotic epigram should really be in Book 12, but the tail end of Book 5 (5.216–end) is full of poems by Paul and his fellow Byzantines, particularly Agathias and Macedonius. It clearly came to the Anthology as a single chunk, from Agathias' *Cycle*.

BOOK 6

6.9 Promachus is retiring from a career as a mercenary, and readers might well imagine him hanging up the tools of his trade at the temple of Apollo patron of mercenaries, 'Apollo Epicurius', at Bassae in Arcadia. Mnasalcas may take his inspiration from a poem in a different metre by Callimachus, 13.7, also in this selection.

6.17 This is a smutty parody of the epigrams on 'three brothers', represented in this selection by the pair that comes before it (the full Anthology has at least a dozen more), and to which we might compare the three sisters at 6.39.

6.18 Laïs of Corinth (fifth century BC) was antiquity's most famous courtesan; compare, for instance, the celebrity epitaph at 7.219.

6.21 'The sluice': the Greek is plural; this humble farmer has worked in an elaborately irrigated landscape, like that of Oxyrhynchus in Egypt (see Introduction, pp. xviii–xix).

6.33 Twelve epigrams by Quintus Maecius or Maccius come to the Anthology through the *Garland* of Philip; 6.89 is another of his. Philip made his selection from recent and contemporary poets in the first century AD, when the introduction of glass-blowing was beginning to speed up production and make glass affordable to ordinary people.

6.45 Greeks and Romans believed that hedgehogs would steal apples, figs, or grapes by rolling through the harvested fruit, then store it to feed their young through the winter. In the Middle Ages, the fruit-gathering hedgehog became an allegory of hard work and forethought. Hedgehogs in fact do no such thing, but farmers had a further incentive for trapping them: they could make good money selling the skins to fullers, who used them to comb cloth. This is why the hedgehog is hung up alive and uninjured, by its foot, and left to die: the fullers do not want damaged skins.

6.49 In book 23 of Homer's *Iliad*, Achilles presides over the funeral of Patroclus and awards prizes at games in his honour. The first contest is a chariot-race, and Diomedes wins it: his prizes (23.263–4) are a female slave skilled in crafts, and a great tripod. Every boy who went to school learned at least some Homer, typically from the early books of the *Iliad*; the epigram anticipates a reader who studied harder and can remember book 23 in detail.

6.50 The inscription celebrates the combined Greek armies' victory at Plataea (479 BC). Their commander, Pausanias, set up an individual memorial with its own Simonidean epigram: see 6.197.

6.51 Rhea was 'Mother of the Gods'. She was frequently identified with the Phrygian mother-goddess Cybele, whom the Romans called the 'Great Mother' (*Magna Mater*) and who was often represented in a chariot drawn by lions. Alexis is a former *gallus*, one of the priests of Cybele who castrated themselves in religious ecstasy (compare the Attis of Catullus, poem 63). There are more *galli* at 6.217 and 220.

6.58 Isidorus' place of origin is not quite clear. In myth, handsome Endymion was the mortal lover of Selene, the Moon; but the Endymion of myth never aged.

6.62 Used with the ruler, the rotating lead disc drew a straight vertical margin. As it did so, it marked the papyrus or vellum with the regularly spaced intervals for the horizontal line guides (as in the following epigram in this selection, 6.66). Scribes used pumice to smooth the surface prior to writing (cf. Catullus, poem 1), and cut their pens from reeds; they could erase mistakes before the ink was dry by wiping with a sponge. Epigram 6.66 by Paul 'the Usher' is one of a half-dozen imitations written by contemporaries of Agathias in sixth-century Byzantium, five hundred years after Philip.

6.73 Macedonius may call his shepherd Daphnis to evoke the young romantic hero of Longus' pastoral novel, *Daphnis and Chloe*. Compare 6.78.

6.76 Anchises was one of Aphrodite's mortal lovers; their son was Aeneas, one of Troy's leading warriors in Homer's *Iliad* and the protagonist of Virgil's *Aeneid*.

6.96 Virgil calls Corydon and Thyrsis *Arcades ambo*, 'Arcadians both', at *Eclogue* 7.4. Erycius was Virgil's approximate contemporary, and Ewen Bowie has suggested that they were both alluding to a lost original by Philetas, the Hellenistic founder of pastoral poetry. Nowhere else do we find 'Cyllenian' as a title for Pan; it belongs to Hermes, who was born on Mount Cyllene in Arcadia. Like Virgil in the *Eclogues* (notably *Eclogue* 4), Erycius is consciously amplifying Pan's Arcadian connections; this too might have its origin in Philetas.

6.114 The son of Amphitryo was Heracles. Orbelus was the name given to a range of mountains on the border between Macedon and Thrace. 'Emathia' was only one part of the historic kingdom of Macedonia, but its name goes back to Homer; accordingly, writers in the Roman era applied it to Macedonia as a whole: compare 6.335. The Philip of the poem is generally agreed to be Philip V (238–179 BC), initially an enemy and later an ally of Rome.

6.129 Athena had a sanctuary at Coryphasium (Pylos). Hagnon's victory was in southern Italy, close to Leonidas' own home city of Tarentum. If we take him to be a fellow citizen of Leonidas, it makes sense that he travels to Spartan territory in the Peloponnese to dedicate his trophies: Tarentum was a colony of Sparta. If this poem is really by Leonidas it must have been written before, or at least in reference to the period before, 272 BC, the year Lucania was conquered by Rome.

6.146 In epigram at least, the name 'Lycaenis' typically identifies the bearer as a hetaera. It means 'She-wolf', which must have been meant to connote sexual openness; Romans called prostitutes 'she-wolves' (*lupae*), too.

6.161 M. Claudius Marcellus (42–23 BC) was the nephew and intended heir of Augustus. Crinagoras was an Augustan court poet (see Introduction, p. xvi), and this epigram commemorates Marcellus' return to Rome in 25 BC from Spain, where he and his cousin, the future emperor Tiberius, had served as military tribunes in Augustus' Cantabrian Wars. Two years later he was dead of fever. In the sixth book of his *Aeneid*, Virgil makes Marcellus the bitter-sweet culmination of Aeneas' vision of Rome's future heroes. Hair cut from the head was a common offering to thank a god for keeping a traveller safe, but a short haircut also marked the transition into manhood. Crinagoras had a steady trade in welcoming home Julio-Claudian heroes: compare 16.61, on Tiberius' return in 13 BC.

6.164   Lucillius is a sceptic poet whose epigrams are mostly found in Book 11, and this dedication comes with a characteristic humorous twist. The sea-gods to whom he dedicates his hair include Poseidon (son of Cronos; his brothers are Zeus and Hades); Nereus, the Old Man of the Sea and father of the Nereids; and the Cabeiri, divine protectors of sailors worshipped on Samothrace and Lemnos. The misattribution to Lucian is a copyist's error, of a kind that is easily made: ΛΟΥΚΙΛΛΙΟΥ and ΛΟΥΚΙΑΝΟΥ look very similar. What makes it really careless is that Lucillius includes his own name in the poem.

6.190   Gaetulicus takes on the voice of Leonidas of Tarentum, one of whose epigrams (6.300, not included in the selection) he imitates here. The sickness from which Aphrodite previously cured Leonidas might be love (we have two of his erotic epigrams), but compare the similar poem by Philip, 6.231, in which a man praying to Isis for relief from poverty adduces her past favour in saving him from a very real death by drowning. In the Hellenistic period, Isis was assimilated to Aphrodite; she had an important role in state cult, but ordinary people also invoked her as mother-goddess to cure their illnesses. Perhaps we can find a trace of this syncretism here.

6.197   Pausanias of Sparta, nephew of Leonidas, led the allied Greek forces that defeated Xerxes at the Battle of Plataea. He was later found guilty of conspiring with Xerxes.

6.199   Hecate, goddess of crossroads, was the protector of travellers.

6.200   Ilythyia or Eileithyia, also called Eleutho, was the Greek goddess of childbirth.

6.214   Gelo, tyrant of Syracuse, and his brothers dedicated this tripod at Delphi to commemorate their victory over the Carthaginians at the Battle of Himera—coincidentally fought the same year as Salamis (480 BC; see the epigram which immediately follows, 6.215). Damarete was Gelo's wife, and she is credited with striking a valuable coin in connection with the victory: the Damareteion, worth ten Athenian drachmae (Diodorus Siculus 11.26). It was always rare, and only a few examples survive. The Sicilian *litra* was small change, but modern scholars gauge the Attic talent to have massed about twenty-six kilograms. According to Simonides, then, the tripod was over a ton of solid gold—and this was only a hundredth of the wealth the brothers had taken as spoils and ransom.

6.217   This epigram inaugurates a Meleagrian sequence of epigrams on the same topic, by Hellenistic authors, and it has long been recognized that the attribution to 'Simonides' is spurious.

6.220   Atys castrated himself to become a priest of Cybele; his *thalamē* is the ritual container in which he carries his severed parts. His journey is taking him about 400 kilometres west from the traditional centre of the cult, Pessinus on the river Sangarias (Sakarya), to the great city of which Cybele was patron: Sardis, at this time capital of the Seleucid Empire.

6.223 This imaginary giant sea-centipede, 'vast' and 'thousand-footed' (Theodoridas, *AP* 6.222), lends its name to a whole genus of venomous creepy-crawlies. Aelian, a rhetorician of the early third century AD, leaves us a full description (*On the Nature of Animals* 13.23). The following translation is A. F. Scholfield's, for the Loeb Classical Library (1958):

> Now in the course of examining and investigating these subjects and what bears upon them, to the utmost limit, with all the zeal that I could command, I have ascertained that the Scolopendra is a sea-monster, and of sea-monsters it is the biggest, and if cast up on the shore no one would have the courage to look at it. And those who are expert in marine matters say that they have seen them floating and that they extend the whole of their head above the sea, exposing hairs of immense length protruding from their nostrils, and that the tail is flat and resembles that of a crayfish. And at times the rest of their body is to be seen floating on the surface, and its bulk is comparable to a full-sized trireme. And they swim with numerous feet in line on either side as though they were rowing themselves (though the expression is somewhat harsh) with thole-pins hung alongside. So those who have experience in these matters say that the surge responds with a gentle murmur, and their statement convinces me.

6.225 Nicaenetus' description of the 'Libyan Heroines' resembles a scene in the *Argonautica* of his approximate contemporary Apollonius of Rhodes (third century BC). In its fourth book, Jason and his companions are sailing back to Greece when they are driven into the feared coastal shoals of Libya, the Syrtes. They despair for their lives, but three goddesses comfort Jason and tell him how to escape the shallows. They call themselves 'the shepherd goddesses of the land, endowed with human voice, the heroines, guardians, and daughters of Libya'; when he relates the visitation to his crew he describes them as 'three goddesses . . . dressed in goatskins from the top of their necks around their backs and waists, just like young girls'. The translation is Richard Hunter's, for Oxford World's Classics.

6.231 Damo's prayer is addressed to Isis; compare Gaetulicus at 6.190 to Aphrodite, noted above. Gilding the horns of an animal intended for sacrifice is a practice attested in inscriptions as well as literary sources.

6.235 The identity of the Emperor addressed as 'Caesar' is not certain. Alan Cameron makes a strong case for Claudius, step-grandson of the long-lived and revered Augustus, noting that Claudius became emperor in middle age and with chancy health.

6.236 Augustus took rams as trophies from the defeated fleet of Mark Antony and Cleopatra at the Battle of Actium (31 BC) to decorate the *Rostra ad*

Diui Iuli, a speaker's platform he built at the front of his temple to Julius Caesar in the Roman Forum (29 BC). By Philip's time the rams had hung there for the better part of a century. Compare 6.251, another Actium poem by Philip.

6.244 'Antonia' must be Antonia the Younger, daughter of Mark Antony and Augustus' sister Octavia. She married Livia's son Drusus and gave him three children: a daughter, Livilla; Germanicus, who would have succeeded Tiberius if he had not died young; and the future Emperor Claudius. Hēpione was the wife of Aesculapius, semi-divine patron of physicians; their daughter was Hygieia, the personification of health, from whose name we get 'hygiene'.

6.251 The humble gifts are offered in extravagantly rare terms: the lamp's poor flame is *brakhupheggitos*, the lamp's mouth is *hēmimethēs*, the oil-flask is *biopheidēs*. Apollo had a cult sanctuary on the clifftops of Leucas or Leucadia, the modern Lefkada (it was from these same cliffs, incidentally, that Sappho supposedly threw herself for unrequited love of Phaon). As John Miller has noted (*Apollo, Augustus, and the Poets* (New York: Cambridge, 2009)), coins struck by Octavian at Nicopolis, the 'Victory City' he founded near Actium to celebrate his defeat of Antony and Cleopatra, bore the image of Leucadian Apollo; Apollo is also given credit for the outcome in an epigram written when the city was newly dedicated, 9.553. The sailors of Philip's poem are probably meant to be thought of as merchantmen setting out for Nicopolis.

6.269 The 'tireless voice' is the poem itself, inscribed by Arista on the base of her votive statue. Leto's daughter was Artemis; her cult 'Artemis Aethiopia' is tenuously attested.

6.277 Berenice II, wife of Ptolemy III Euergetes, famously dedicated a lock of hair that vanished only to reappear in the heavens as a new constellation, the *Coma Berenices*; the Arsinoe of the poem is probably her daughter ('Arsinoe III'). Berenice's offering was to Aphrodite, goddess of marriage; for her unmarried daughter, a virgin goddess is the appropriate dedicatee.

6.281 Mountainous central Phrygia was named 'Burnt Phrygia', *Phrygia Kekaumenē* or *Katakekaumenē* (Latin *Phrygia Combusta*), for its volcanic activity; Mount Dindymus or Dindyma was in Phrygia's east. Leonidas never went to Phrygia: he gives it 'headlands', but it is landlocked. 'The tossing of the hair, so different from conventional behaviour ⟨of an unmarried girl⟩, constitutes a service to the goddess, a proof of devotion that Cybele should gratefully reciprocate' (Marco Fantuzzi, in Kanellou, Petrovic, and Carey (eds), *Greek Epigram*).

6.307 A parody of the dedicatory epigram form: this barber does not dedicate his tools to a patron god at the end of a successful career, but throws them away because he is so bored of his trade. He tries to start over as a philosopher, only to fall back on barbering when he runs out of money. Like the humble offerings of Philip's sailors at 6.251, the barber's tools are extravagantly described in new-coined words: the sheet is *philetheiros* (hair-loving), the felt scrap is *hupoxurios* (rubbed-on by razors), the knives and scissors are *lipokoptoi* (abandoning cutting), the probe is *sulonux* (nail-paring). The mocking description of Eugathes as a 'Gardener' is inventive, too: Epicurus, founder of Epicurean philosophy, taught in a garden at Athens.

6.321 This birthday poem to Nero from a Greek court poet addresses him as a living god. Its trick is irreproducible in English. The Greeks had essentially no numerical notation apart from their alphabet: alpha was one, beta was two, and so on, with a step up into tens at iota and hundreds at rho. Therefore, every Greek word could be thought of as being a number consisting of the values of all the letters it contains: for instance, the first word of this poem in Greek, *thuei*, is 9 (theta) + 400 (upsilon) + 5 (epsilon) + 10 (iota) = 424. The same went for lines of verse, or elegiac couplets. Leonidas specialized in 'isopsephy', writing epigrams in which each couplet had the same numerical value. Modern editors have a devil of a job making the sums work; as the text stands, I make the total from the first couplet 5,620, and from the second, 5,689. Leonidas' birthday poem to Nero's mother, 6.329, is also isopsephic.

6.329 This is the younger Agrippina, great-granddaughter of Augustus and mother of Nero.

6.332 Trajan had subjugated the Dacians (whom the Greeks called Getae) in AD 106; he climbed Casius to set up his Dacian trophy in the winter of 114/15, between campaign seasons in his war against Arsacid Parthia. His adoptive heir Hadrian, an accomplished writer of inscriptional epigrams, came with him and composed this poem to mark the occasion. When Trajan died two years later (117) with Parthia still unconquered (and probably unconquerable), Hadrian reversed his predecessor's policy and pulled Rome back to a defensible border at the west bank of the Euphrates. Casius, near the mouth of the Syrian river Orontes, had been a sacred mountain since time immemorial, and Hadrian as emperor climbed it again to see the sunrise and offer sacrifice, encountering a storm that killed the officiating priest (*Scriptores Historiae Augustae* 'Hadrian' 14.7). The aurochs was the wild ancestor of domestic cattle; it is now extinct, but lingered in the forests of Poland into the seventeenth century.

6.335 This poem is addressed to the poet's patron, L. Calpurnius Piso 'Pontifex', and marks a known occasion: in 11 BC the Senate sent Piso to Thrace to put down a revolt. Antipater's epigram begins with the Macedonians' own word for their characteristic broad-brimmed hat, the *kausiē*. The hat's Macedonian ('Emathian') origin is a good excuse for Antipater to wish Piso victories as great as those of Alexander. Piso's new hat did indeed bring him luck, as reported by Antipater in 16.184—he returned victorious, was awarded a triumph, and went on to a long career as a senior statesman, bringing Antipater along for the ride. The poet offers him another little birthday gift at 9.93, in this selection.

6.337 Theocritus addresses his eleventh *Idyll*, 'The Cyclops', to this same Nicias, who wrote poetry in addition to practising medicine. A few of Nicias' own epigrams survive, including 16.188, in this selection. In Homer, Paeon is the physician of the Olympian gods; his name became a title shared by Asclepius and Apollo, the gods of healing. The wood-carver Eëtion is otherwise unknown, though there are several characters by that name in myth.

6.340 Aphrodite was worshipped under Pandemic ('vulgar') and Uranian ('spiritual') aspects; the distinction is explained by Plato in his *Symposium* (180 D-E). In the late nineteenth century, this passage in Plato became a touchstone for the homosexual subculture that was beginning to emerge among classically educated men, who identified as 'Uranians'.

6.343 This inscriptional epigram comes to the Anthology from the *Histories* (5.77) of Herodotus, who saw it on the base of a statue of a four-horse chariot, set up just outside the Propylaea on the Athenian Acropolis. It celebrates a double victory—two battles fought and won on the same day, in 506 BC. According to Herodotus the Chalcidians were great breeders of horses and the Athenians took many as spoils of war. The tithe was from the ransoms received for the prisoners, whose fetters hung as a trophy nearby. See also 16.26.

BOOK 7

7.1 From the ancient *Life of Homer*: 'They say he starved himself to death on the island of Ios because he failed to solve the riddle posed to him by the fishermen.' This biographical tradition tells us that when Homer asked the fishermen what they had caught, they answered, 'Whatever we caught, we threw back; what we are carrying is not our catch.' The answer was 'lice'. Alcaeus' poem seems to attest a variant tale in which Homer did not starve, but drowned himself. The epigrammatist (third century BC) should not be confused with the more famous Alcaeus, a lyric poet and contemporary of Sappho. 'The clashes of the other heroes too' suggests that Alcaeus considered at least one additional poem from the Epic Cycle to be genuinely Homeric, beside the *Iliad* (the tale of Achilles, son of Thetis) and the *Odyssey*. He may have had in mind the *Little Iliad*, which began with the funeral-games of Achilles and ended with the fatal Trojan decision to bring the wooden horse inside their city.

7.9 Pindar (*Pythian* 4.4.315) called Orpheus 'father of song', and Damagetus here credits him with inventing hexameter, the metre of epic poetry. Orpheus famously descended to the Underworld and sang for Hades to win back his dead wife, Eurydice. The story did not end well.

7.11 Erinna's masterwork was her *Distaff*, praised also by the unknown poet of 9.190. It inspired the handful of epigrams by 'Erinna' in the Anthology, all of them exercises in ancient fan fiction.

7.15 Maeonides, 'son of Maeon', was a conventional title of Homer. It was not a straightforward patronymic, but reflected the biographical tradition that assigned his birth to the land of Lydia, which Homer himself had called Maeonia.

7.32 This epitaph too is for Anacreon, one of a dozen in this book of the Anthology (Homer is next most popular, with eight). He was one of the nine lyric poets of the Greek canon, so famous that Julian does not need to give his name. Hardly any of his work survives.

7.36 The ivy's connection to the stage is that ivy wreaths were the prize for the best dramatists at the dramatic festivals of Athens. Bees are 'ox-born' because it was believed that a new swarm of bees could be generated by killing an ox and leaving its body to rot; the final book of Virgil's *Georgics* (4.284 ff.) credits this ancient miracle of *bugonia* to Aristaeus, the divine mediator of agricultural knowledge to humankind. Virgil drew his information from the Hellenistic tradition of lore in which 'Erycias' participated alongside Meleager (compare 3.363), and which he found expressed on a grander scale in didactic epics such as the *Theriaca* and *Alexipharmaca* of Nicander of Colophon. Sophocles' 'slate' is the standard reusable notepad of antiquity, a tablet made of wood and filled with wax.

7.42 The Gates of Horn and Ivory, through which issue respectively true and false dreams, are familiar from Homer's *Odyssey* (19.560–9) and are ambiguously echoed in Virgil's *Aeneid* (6.893–8). The *Causes* are Callimachus' *Aetia*, his four-book epic explaining the origins of local cults.

7.53 This dedicatory epigram would be more at home in Book 6. The putative context is the apocryphal 'Contest of Homer and Hesiod', a sing-off between the two great epic poets. 'Heliconian Muses' are the first two words of Hesiod's own *Theogony*.

7.71 The ancient biographical tradition around Archilochus attests his grudge against the family of Lycambes, who agreed to let the poet marry one of his daughters but then changed his mind; the iambic poet responded with a series of sexual slanders that drove them to suicide (in 7.352, the daughters protest that he made it all up). Archilochus' reputation for bitter personal abuse is not consistently borne out by the surviving fragments of his work, but made him a figure of fascination to Roman authors, including the satirists. Very similar stories attached to his fellow iambicist Hipponax; see 7.536.

7.80 Heraclitus of Halicarnassus wrote 7.465. Callimachus' epitaph for him is best known in the famous nineteenth-century translation by William Johnson Cory: 'They told me, Heraclitus, they told me you were dead . . .'. The nightingale in Greek is a singer, *aēdōn*, and Penelope in the *Odyssey*

(19.517) compares her shifting moods to the bird's 'many-toned' laments. Nightingale became a poetic synonym for poets themselves; Callimachus now extends the analogy to include their works.

7.116 Cynicism, the austere philosophy propounded by Diogenes (see 7.63, and cf. 11.155), took its name from the Greek word for dog. Cynics 'barked' at society's pretensions, and Diogenes taught that humans should emulate dogs and live in accordance with their own animal nature, trusting their instincts. Various stories are told of Diogenes' death, including that he was bitten by a rabid dog: the ancient biographers loved a tidy moral.

7.153 This epigram is preserved in Plato's *Phaedrus* (264D), where Socrates notes that the epitaph is unusual in that its lines can be read in any order. The attribution to Homer is fanciful. If Cleobulus (sixth century BC and semi-legendary) really was the author, then the poem probably was genuinely inscribed on a grand funerary monument; whether that tomb held Midas is another matter.

7.155 If this is not a real epitaph, it is very like one: the motif of the performer who died many times on stage, but only once for real, is found in funerary inscriptions in both Latin and Greek.

7.179 The 'nook' in which Manes rests is in Greek a *kalubē*, which typically means a hut or cabin: in this instance, perhaps his ashes occupy a niche in the master's family columbarium.

7.214 Tethys was the sister and consort of Oceanus. She has no story of her own in myth; poets used her name to mean 'the sea'.

7.219 I see no reason why these lines should not be by Sextus Pompey, a rival to Octavian as his father had been to Caesar.

7.248 Herodotus (7.228) records that three monuments were set up to mark the battlefield at Thermopylae, where a massively outnumbered, Spartan-led force bought time for the allied defence (480 BC). This epitaph was on the monument to all the Greek dead, most of whom were Peloponnesian; the Spartans received their own, famous inscription (see 7.249); and Simonides added a third epitaph for his personal friend, Megistias the seer.

7.251 Simonides wrote separate epitaphs for the Spartan and Athenian dead at Plataea (479 BC), the battle in which the allied Greeks conclusively defeated the Persian land forces (Pausanias 9.2.5). This epigram is generally thought to be his epitaph for the Spartans; see 7.253 for the Athenians.

7.273 Hesiod's *Works and Days* (615) notes the setting of Orion in November as a sign for farmers to start ploughing, and as the end of the sailing season.

7.343 Aeacus in legend was a king of Aegina, Athens' closest island neighbour; his descendants, known by the patronymic 'Aeacids', included Achilles.

The 'four virtues' are *phronēsis* (prudence), *dikaiosunē* (justice), *sōphrosunē* (temperance), and *andreia* (courage).

7.345 On the sex manual attributed to 'Philaenis', see the note on 5.202.

7.352 Persephone, daughter of Demeter, is 'unnamable' because initiates of Demeter's Eleusinian Mysteries never divulged the secrets they had learned. The word for 'young girl' in line 7 of the Greek is *korē*, which was also a cult name of Persephone.

7.377 It is hard to square this polemical portrait of Parthenius of Nicaea, the scholar-poet who brought Callimachean poetics to Rome and taught Virgil his Greek, with what survives of his work. If Parthenius really did call the *Odyssey* 'mud', he will have had in mind the famous contrast drawn in Callimachus' *Hymn to Apollo* between the 'Ocean' that is Homer and the muddy 'Assyrian river' of Homer's imitators. The Cocytus was similarly unclean, a swampy tributary of the Acheron, the great river of Hades.

7.417 Gadara, the modern Umm Qais in northern Jordan, had been a Seleucid possession. It had no historic connection to Athens; Meleager calls it 'Attic' because it was a highly cultured town that produced men of learning. Philodemus was Meleager's contemporary and a fellow Gadarene; he too wrote love poems, several of which are included in the selection from Book 5.

7.419 Meleager, a proud citizen of the world (see 7.417), advertises his fluency across three of the great Eastern Mediterranean cultures. Merope was an ancient name for Cos.

7.442 This sub-Simonidean epitaph may refer to the battle of 369 BC in which Sparta defeated a Tegean–Argive alliance, but is a poor match to the outcome if so.

7.447 'Slog': the *dolikhos* was a long-distance foot-race. Hero of Alexandria, who used it as a scientific unit of measurement, defined the *dolikhos* as twelve stades, well in excess of a mile.

7.493 In 146 BC, a Roman army under L. Mummius destroyed Corinth, killing all its adult male inhabitants and taking the women and children as slaves. Scipio Aemilianus 'Africanus' did the same to Carthage that same year.

7.497 'Thymōdes too': 'Because there were other similar tombs close by' (Paton).

7.506 Michael Tueller (in Kanellou, Petrovic, and Carey (eds), *Greek Epigram*) connects this epigram with, among others, 9.14 as expressing Hellenistic epigrammatists' fascination with 'the unstable border between land and sea'.

7.525 Callimachus' epitaph for his father Battus says nothing about the man's own achievements and does not even name him; instead it celebrates the family reputation earned by the poet's grandfather (after whom

Callimachus was named) and enhanced by the poet himself. The Greek
city of Cyrene in Libya grew rich on its famous silphium trade; in the
early first century BC it became a Roman province, but Catullus (poem 7)
still celebrates it as 'silphium-bearing Cyrene'. Its founder, also called
Battus, was Callimachus' distant ancestor: the oracles he received at
Delphi ordering him to establish a new city in Libya, and telling him
off for dithering, are at 14.83–5 in this selection.

7.536 Compare 7.71 on Archilochus; and contrast the gentle growth on the
tomb of Sophocles (7.36) and Ibycus (7.714).

7.538 Manes is a Phrygian name. Greeks often assigned names to their slaves
based on where they came from, or took them from the slaves' cultures
of origin: slaves called 'Manes' appear in several plays by Aristophanes,
and there is one in 7.179.

7.542 The Hebrus (modern Maritza) was the great river of Thrace; its iciness
was proverbial for poets including Horace and Virgil, and it was indeed
known to freeze over. Flaccus uses 'Bistonian' merely as a poetic syno-
nym for 'Thracian'; the Bistones were a minor Thracian tribe who lived
nowhere near the Hebrus. Flaccus' poems were included in the *Garland
of Philip*, placing him before the middle of the first century AD; a few
decades later, Martial would produce a similarly themed epigram in
Latin (his 4.18) about a boy impaled by an icicle that fell from a Roman
aqueduct.

7.543 'Pliny (*NH* x.13) tells of ships being similarly sunk by flocks of quails
alighting on them at night' (Paton). Mind you, this is the same Pliny
the Elder who thought African pygmies were fighting a perpetual war
against cranes (*Natural History* 4.44).

7.564 This epigram from Agathias' *Cycle* is probably exactly what it purports
to be, a genuine inscription commissioned by a Roman official to com-
memorate his restoration of a 'Homeric' monument. Asia had a number
of proconsuls called Maximus, among whom T. Statilius Maximus
(157–8) and S. Quintilius Valerius Maximus (168–9) seem likely candi-
dates. Homer's Troy was a magnet for Roman tourists, who fancied
themselves Trojans through Aeneas. In Homer, Laodice is Priam's most
beautiful daughter and is married to the king's counsellor, Antenor.
When Troy fell, she prayed to the gods to keep her from being taken as
spoils of war; obligingly, the ground opened up and swallowed her.

7.565 The exceptional naturalism of portraiture in Roman Egypt of the early
centuries AD may be gauged from the many surviving instances in
encaustic or tempera, painted on wooden panels to attach to the mum-
mies of the recently deceased. Julian's epigram describes a portrait
made by Christian heirs to this tradition.

7.590 In this unusual dialogue, a traveller passing by a tomb reads aloud
details from a dead man's epitaph, but is repeatedly interrupted and
corrected—by a fellow traveller, or by the epitaph the deceased *ought*
to have had?

7.593 Eugenia was Agathias' sister, and by this poem's witness an author in her own right. Cutting off locks of hair as an offering to the dead was a classic gesture of mourning, and not just for women: his comrades cast locks of hair upon the fallen Patroclus in book 23 of Homer's *Iliad*. Themis, goddess of justice, mourns alongside the (unspecified) Muse and Aphrodite because Eugenia died young; her death was unfair.

7.595 Agathias included a pair of Julian's poems on this Theodorus, who 'recalled from oblivion back to life . . . the work of learned poets' in the 'countless pages of his books' (7.594). Since Theodorus is otherwise unknown it is for the reader to decide—was he a grammarian, writing commentaries on the classics? An anthologist, like Agathias himself? Or perhaps even both?

7.626 This epigram is very clearly not an epitaph, but praises the son of a living emperor for his success in collecting wild beasts for staged hunts in the arena. The obvious occasion would be the games organized by Titus, son of Vespasian, in AD 80 to inaugurate the Colosseum: the anonymous poet courts Titus' patronage by imagining that the applause will echo to the furthest corners of the world, which, furthermore, are now made safe for cultivation and pasturage by being stripped of the dangerous animals that once roamed there. The Latin poet Martial wrote a whole book of epigrams (his first, the *De Spectaculis*) in response to these same shows. The Nasamonians were a nomadic tribe of Libya; ancient readers would know of them from, for instance, Herodotus (2.32).

7.633 Crinagoras was an Augustan court poet who composed epigrams to mark political events (see Introduction, p. xvi). In associating the death of Cleopatra Selene, last of the Ptolemaic dynasty, with a celestial phenomenon he echoes Hellenistic royal propaganda such as Callimachus' *Lock of Berenice*, with the additional justification that his subject's name, Selene, means 'Moon'. Crinagoras had previously written a poem to celebrate her marriage to Juba of Numidia, 9.235, also in this selection.

7.733 The beginning of the first line of the Greek text, and the end of the sixth, are corrupt, but the sense of the poem is clear enough.

7.741 Crinagoras puts a brave face on the 'Varus Disaster', the battle in AD 9 in the Teutoburg Forest in which three legions under Quinctilius Varus were wiped out by an alliance of German tribes led by Arminius. All three eagle standards were taken by the enemy, though later campaigns recovered them. Othryades was the sole Spartan survivor of the 'Battle of the 300 Champions' (*c*.546 BC), fought by 300 men on each side to settle a dispute between Sparta and Argos. Two Argives survived, and went off to report that they had won by virtue of superior numbers; Othryades remained, and claimed victory for Sparta by virtue of possession of the battlefield. He committed suicide rather than return home as sole survivor. Cynegeirus or Cynaegeirus was the brother of the Athenian playwright Aeschylus, and died heroically achieving victory against the Persians at Marathon.

7.747 This epitaph for the Emperor Julian accords to him Helen's description of Agamemnon at *Iliad* 3.179, at the start of the episode (sometimes called the *teichoscopia*) in which she looks out from Troy's wall and identifies the principal Greek heroes to Priam. Julian 'the Apostate', the Empire's last pagan ruler, became emperor in 361: two years later he began a campaign against Sassanid Persia, but was defeated at the Battle of Samarra in Iraq and died of wounds, forcing his battered army to sue for peace. Roman strength in the east never recovered.

BOOK 8

8.1 The relics of St John Chrysostom, who had died in exile (d. 407), were brought back to Constantinople and interred in the Church of the Holy Apostles in 438. The church no longer exists but we know Theodosius I ('the Great', d. 395) was already buried there.

8.2 St Basil 'the Great' (d. 379) was Gregory's lifelong friend and a founding figure of the monastic tradition. The poet writes his signature into the poem to declare his authorship for all time: compare 8.98.

8.11 The Palatine manuscript preserves eleven of Gregory's sequence of a 'dozen' poems mourning Basil.

8.16 The poet commemorates his father, Gregory of Nazianzus 'the Elder', in a sequence of a dozen epigrams, the same number he dedicated to his best friend, Basil. This imaginary epitaph is spoken by the father (or is read out on his behalf by the visitor to his tomb), but expresses the pious sentiments of the son towards a model parent.

8.22 The epitaph takes a pastoral turn because, like the poet, Gregory the Elder was a shepherd of souls (he was Bishop of Nazianzus).

8.25 Over fifty poems by Gregory commemorate his mother, Nonna, who died while praying. It is clear from another epigram (8.33, not in this selection) that she was in a great deal of pain; whatever her ailment was, premodern medicine was helpless to diagnose or treat it.

8.112 Gregory commemorates Martinianus in a sequence of twelve poems, as he had Basil (including 8.2 and 11) and his own father (including 8.16 and 22). Martinianus' tomb is threatened by or actively being desecrated by robbers in all twelve. In this epitaph, the dead man declares that he was an *oneiar* to the living; the word evokes Homer (Hector is so called in the *Iliad*), Hesiod, and the Homeric Hymns.

8.123 The Greek verb *petomai* (fly) is used metaphorically of avid intellectual pursuits. Paton's translation rather beautifully imagines the Muses as flowers and Euphemius as an industrious bee, flitting between them and 'gathering the honey of both the Greek and Latin muse'. The plural Muses stand in for the range of genres within the two literary traditions—epic, tragedy, history, and so on.

8.134 Gregory's other epitaphs for Amphilochus establish that he was a forensic orator who died of old age (presumably at Constantinople) far from his small city of origin. His Diocaesarea ('God's Caesarea') was probably the one in Cilicia, southern Turkey; there was another in Galilee where Mary, mother of Christ, was thought to have been born.

8.170 'And ⟨Abraham⟩ looked toward Sodom and Gomorrah, and toward all the land of the plain, and beheld, and, lo, the smoke of the country went up as the smoke of a furnace' (Genesis 19:28; King James Version). The last third of Gregory's collection consists entirely of poems lamenting violated tombs and calling down God's wrath on the perpetrators: 8.221 and 237 are examples.

BOOK 9

9.19 The Pisa of this poem is not the Italian city famous for its leaning tower, but the Greek town whose territory included Olympia, site of the ancient Olympics: compare 16.24. Eagle was victorious at all four of the great Panhellenic athletic festivals, the other three being the Isthmian Games at Corinth, the Pythian Games at Delphi, and the Nemean Games. Some said these last had been founded by Heracles himself after the first of his Twelve Labours, the killing of the Nemean Lion.

9.28 This 'Pompey, or some say Marcus the Younger' and 7.219's 'Pompey the Younger' are sometimes merged so as to attribute both poems to a 'Pompeius Macer', supposed to have been close to Ovid; in an article of 1992 for *Classical Quarterly* Peter White dismissed him as a phantom.

9.59 A prayer for the safety and success of Gaius Caesar (20 BC–AD 4), the young nephew of Augustus, as he sets off in 1 BC on an official mission to Syria. Augustus had adopted Gaius and his younger brother Lucius to replace the dead Marcellus as his heirs. He sent Gaius east as his personal representative to settle provincial unrest and deal with Parthia, having first arranged the boy's marriage to his cousin Livilla. In AD 2 Gaius was badly wounded by Armenian rebels who had invited him to parley; he never recovered and died two years later. Lucius had already died of illness. Compare (in this selection) Crinagoras at 6.131, praising Marcellus, and Thallus at 6.235, a birthday poem for a serving Emperor. We know Antipater as a poet patronized by members of the imperial household and by L. Calpurnius Piso: see 6.335; 9.92–3; and 16.184.

9.63 An epitaph for the woman who inspired Antimachus' *Lyde*. This scholarly elegiac poem in two books (on which, see also 12.168) influenced Callimachus, though he called it 'a bloated composition that lacks clarity' (fr. 398 Pf.). Callimachus was not in the habit of holding back: compare 9.507. Codrus was the last of the half-mythical kings of Athens.

9.69   Given the chronology of epigram's development it is highly unlikely that the author was the famous Parmenion (Latinized as Parmenio) of Macedon, trusted general of Philip and Alexander.

9.106   Critics generally overrule the Anthology's author-heading and assign this poem to the other, Egyptian Leonidas, whose trademark was isopsephy (see note on 6.321). '*Isopsephia* is so easily created (by making a few changes to the text) that he may be preferred with fair confidence', declares Page in *Further Greek Epigram* (p. 511), raising the question of whether Leonidean isopsephy is being rediscovered or invented here—though to be fair, it is hard to see what the point of the poem would be without it.

9.155   In suggesting to tourists at Troy that later ages may not fairly judge a city's greatness from the ruins left behind, Agathias invites his readers to recall the famous analysis of Sparta in the preamble to Thucydides' *History of the Peloponnesian War* (1.10): 'For example, if the city of Sparta were to become deserted, with only the temples and the foundations of buildings left to the view, I imagine that with the passage of time future generations would find it very hard to credit its reputed power. And yet the Spartans occupy two-fifths of the Peloponnese.' By Agathias' time, Thucydides' thought-experiment had come true: Sparta dwindled into a quaint tourist attraction under Rome, was sacked by Alaric's Visigoths in AD 396, and never recovered.

9.190   This epigram is written as if to preface a copy of Erinna's one famous work, the *Distaff*, a favourite of the Hellenistic poets for its evocation of women's experiences and emotions. A substantial fragment rediscovered on papyrus by Italian excavators at Oxyrhynchus in the 1920s and now in Florence (BML inv. 18106) confirms that it was in hexameters, just as the anonymous epigrammatist said.

9.203   Achilles Tatius' *Leucippe and Clitophon* is a romantic novel written in the early second century AD; Tim Whitmarsh has translated it for Oxford World's Classics. The heroine's three apparent deaths (all of them illusory) are by drowning, human sacrifice, and decapitation. Whether Photius (ninth century) or Leo wrote this epigram, *Leucippe and Clitophon* was clearly a popular read in early medieval Byzantium.

9.205   Artemidorus of Tarsus, a grammarian of the first century BC, made the first anthology of pastoral poetry. His collection is lost, but its introductory epigram was copied into some manuscripts of Theocritus, and that is where Cephalas will have seen it.

9.210   Urbicius dedicated a short military treatise to Anastasius I around the end of the fifth century; it still survives. He opens with a precis of part of Arrian's *Ars Tactica* (AD 136/7). The elderly Hadrian could indeed have read Arrian, though too late to put his suggestions into practice; he died the year after its publication. The Isaurians were Turkish mountain bandits who backed a rival claimant to the imperial throne;

Anastasius wore them down in the 490s and fought Sassanid Persia to
a stand-off in the 510s, so maybe the manual worked.

9.220 Pausanias attests sacred groves of planes at Lerna and Olympia, and
the trees were especially associated with the cult of Helen of Sparta.
Their cooling shade and philosophical associations (notably their role
in Plato's *Phaedrus*) made them favourite trees for parks and gardens:
compare 9.669.

9.235 The marriage of Cleopatra, daughter of Cleopatra and Mark Antony, to
Juba II of Numidia was stage-managed by Augustus. He put them in
charge of sorting out Mauretania, where they did well. Another epigram
by Crinagoras, 7.633, marks Cleopatra Selene's passing at an unknown
later date.

9.239 Gow and Page (1960) suggest that the addressee is Antonia Minor,
daughter of Mark Antony and Octavia, noting that Plutarch in his
Life of Antony (87) praises her in very similar terms. Because line 3
of the Greek does not scan, Crinagoras' authorship of that couplet has
been doubted; the Loeb edition omits it without comment. The lines
are probably more or less authentic; if so (or indeed if inserted by
a competently informed forger), they give us the length of the standard
Hellenistic edition of Anacreon, information we have from no other
source.

9.241 'Apollo became a herd⟨sman⟩ for the sake of Admetus, Poseidon
a horse for that of Demeter, Zeus a swan for Leda, Ammon a snake
to lie with Olympias and beget Alexander' (Paton). Euagoras, though,
does not need to transform himself into anything: he is rich.

9.285 The wise elephant submitting to imperial authority is echoed at Martial,
Book of Shows 17. 'Caesar' could be any emperor, but Philip calls his
Caesar *ouranios*, a dweller in heaven among the gods; the usual reading
is that the elephant is pulling a chariot containing a statue of the deified
Augustus, in a ceremonial procession organized by one of his Julio-
Claudian successors.

9.332 Nossis was from Locri in the toe of Italy, and her epigrams describing
dedications at its temple of Aphrodite (compare 9.605) are sometimes
read alongside late antique sources that attest a practice of sacred pros-
titution there.

9.342 Parmenion's 'marathon' is the mile-plus *dolikhos*: see note on 7.447.

9.363 On 'ox-born bees', see note on 7.36.

9.366 The Seven Sages of Greek tradition were famous statesmen and thinkers
of the sixth century BC. Thales' advice to avoid *egguē*, meaning
a down-payment given or received, is the origin of 'Neither a borrower
nor a lender be', one of the bits and pieces of timeworn advice given
by Polonius to his departing son in Act 1, Scene 3 of Shakespeare's
Hamlet. The most famous of the sayings, 'Know yourself' (Polonius'
'to thine own self be true'), was inscribed at the entrance to the Temple

of Apollo at Delphi; its authorship was contested between all the Seven Sages and other authorities besides.

9.369 Cyrillus' original is two lines long.

9.383 The Egyptian year began in our September–October with *Thoth*, the first month of the regular and sediment-rich inundation that made fertile Egypt a great power and, later, Rome's bread-basket. Rome inducted its new consuls on 1 January, during *Choiac*, but the news cannot have reached Egypt until after *Tybi* had begun (9 January). *Mesori* was the final month of low water, with the floods imminent.

9.395 Cheesecake is Paton's heroic guess for *ekkhuton*, an unknown dish that is formed by pouring, and is then cooked; perhaps something like a flan or quiche.

9.400 Hypatia was a Neoplatonist mathematician and astronomer at the Museum of Alexandria. She was lynched by a Christian mob in AD 415, long after Palladas' time. The constellation Virgo suits Hypatia well, and not just because she was a virgin: Aratus' *Phaenomena* (115–34) tells that Virgo was formerly Justice, who walked among men telling them unwelcome truths, but eventually gave up on them to assume her place among the stars. By implication Hypatia, a pagan martyr to objective truth, is with her now. Virgo is one of the twelve zodiacal Houses; fast-moving Mercury, her ruling planet, passes into her fairly often. The conjunction of Mercury with Virgo epitomizes Hypatia's specialness: Mercury was the god who taught astronomy to mankind. I thank Saffi Grey for explaining all this to me.

9.425 Poseidon is the god of earthquakes as well as the sea; Hephaestus is god of fire. Formerly the Phoenician *Biruta* and Seleucid *Laodicea in Phoenicia*, Berytus was the principal city of Roman Phoenicia and a byword for the study of law. The earthquake of AD 551 all but destroyed it: when the Arabs conquered in 635 they found only a village. That village grew into a city again, and keeps its ancient name: Beirut. The same poet wrote 16.38, before the city's fall.

9.451 The unknown poet says 'of *Greek* speech', which is to say, civilized. Greeks thought the languages of other cultures were unintelligible babble, 'bar-bar-bar', hence barbarian. Clearly short poems on 'What X might say' formed their own distinct tradition; the examples in Book 9 stand out from the rest of its epigrams by being composed in hexameters.

9.460 This and the following epigrams are rooted in an ancient schoolroom exercise in which students internalized the rules of rhetoric by composing imaginary speeches to, or soliloquies by, notable figures from myth and history. The Roman name for this exercise was *suasoria*, but it was already a fixture of Hellenistic secondary education.

9.471 The epigram plays on readers' memory of lines from the beginning of Homer's *Odyssey* (1.3–5): 'Many were those whose cities he viewed and whose minds he came to know, many the troubles that vexed his heart as he sailed the seas, labouring to save himself and to bring his comrades home.'

9.483 The Greek and Roman name for a peach was 'Persian apple', and learned authorities attested that the hero Perseus had introduced them to Egypt: thus Pliny the Elder (*Natural History* 15.13). According to popular belief they were deadly poisonous, but Pliny declares them perfectly safe, blaming the error on a mix-up of plants with similar names. Actually the popular belief contained a grain of truth: peach stones contain a compound that breaks down into cyanide if ingested, though in such small quantities that even a child would be in little danger (cherry stones are a better bet). Garbled recall of this epigram induced Dr Thomas Moffett or Muffet, author of *Health's Improvement* (1655, posthumous), to warn his fellow Elizabethans of the fruit's dangers: 'Peaches must be sparingly eaten, for many are dangerous, and killed *Theognostus* that fine Scholer, so much lamented in the Greek Epigrams.' Perhaps Moffett imagines this poem's Theognostus to be the Alexandrian theologian of the first century AD, or the ninth-century grammarian; more likely he has no idea, and really, neither do we.

9.490 This epigram is one of two in this book that began life in an ancient novel, Heliodorus' *Aethiopica*. 'Fear-all' (*pantarbē*) is the name of a precious stone, perhaps the ruby; the novel's heroine, Chariclea, owns one set in a ring that she believes will protect her from fire (8.11.8).

9.502 *Conditum* is Roman spiced wine. The cookbook of Apicius opens with a recipe for an 'extraordinary' version (*conditum paradoxum*) with honey, pepper, bay, saffron, dates, and mastic; it is delicious. Apicius also gives a simpler, 'travelling' version.

9.516 Ligurians had a reputation as good fighters, but not to be trusted. Crinagoras passed through the Alps in company with Augustus in 26/5 BC, on the way to Spain, and Gow and Page (1960) accordingly take his statement at face value, 'presumably from personal observation . . . It would be interesting to know what animal's fat it was that was found to cancel the odour of the human body.'

9.528 Bronze statues were always at risk of being melted down for coinage or scrap, even before Christians started calling them idols; elsewhere (9.773, not in this selection) Palladas notes an Eros melted down to make a frying pan.

9.572 Lucillius is the principal scoptic or satirical poet of Book 11. This epigram, written as an ironic introduction to his second book of epigrams, suggests that his influence on Martial may have extended to the latter's decision to issue his books as a numbered series. Nero's handout was small: the 'coin' is copper.

9.606 Inclusion in a book of epideictic epigrams implies that this is a rhetorical exercise, but baths were a viable context for various kinds of inscription. We may imagine the swimming Aphrodite represented in mosaic, like the Graces in the examples that follow; both were staples of the mosaicist's repertoire. Various stories were told of how Tiresias lost his sight; Callimachus tells this one. This is a men's bath; the poems that follow are composed as if for women's facilities.

9.609A Like a customer's graffito beneath the management's signage, 609A sends up the cliché of 609.

9.631 'Danaan' is one of Homer's regular terms for the Greeks besieging Troy; Podalirius and his brother Machon, the sons of Asclepius, were the army's surgeons. As noted by Paton, the thermal baths of Agamemnon at Smyrna are 'still existing and so called'; they attract health-conscious tourists to this day.

9.641 The Sangarius is a river of Turkey flowing north into the Black Sea, and still bears its ancient name ('Sakarya'). A military road crossed it running east, towards the threat of Sassanid Persia, on a pontoon bridge that had been swept away many times. In the 550s/560s Justinian built a permanent replacement in limestone, over 400 metres long. Most of it still stands, though no longer over the Sangarius; the river has shifted course.

9.648 Cibyra was a city in south-west Turkey. A companion epigram, 9.649 (not included in this selection), reveals that Macedonius had built the inn himself as an investment. Perhaps the epigram was painted on its wall to greet customers.

9.669 'Magic dell': like the water that runs of its own volition (*autorrutos*), the hillside park tends itself (*autophutos*), with no need for a gardener.

9.713 Here begins a sequence of thirty-one poems on the Cow, a bronze statue of the fifth century BC by the Athenian sculptor Myron, of Discobolus fame. There are six more later in the book as well, by Julian, Prefect of Egypt (9.793–8). The statue was a Roman favourite. Apparently it looked very much like a cow.

9.746 The 'Milan Posidippus' papyrus (see Introduction, p. x) gives us many new examples to which to compare the Anthology's handful of epigrams on carved gemstones. The 'golden pale' is the setting that attaches it to the ring, surrounding the carved face of the stone as a fence encircles a fold. Diana Spencer points out to me that jasper is often green, which would give the cows an appropriate pasture. Assuming the attribution to be genuine, the author is either Polemon I, a Roman client-king of Pontus, or his grandson, Polemon II, who descended from Mark Antony on his mother's side; Gow and Page (1960) assign the poem to this second Polemon because history otherwise gives him less to do. Perhaps Polemon is describing the signet ring with which he himself sealed and authenticated his documents of state, pressing the image of the seven cows into a disc of heated wax as his personal imprimatur.

9.767 In another poem on gaming with dice, 9.769, Agathias declares: 'To men of easy-going mind it's just a game, but for those who lack self-control it is outrage and offence and exhaustion—they cannot help themselves.'

9.810 'The Persian war, which, after all, was not very successful' (Paton), to
       put it mildly. Justin II launched his war against Sassanid Persia in 572;
       he was a disastrous commander-in-chief and the campaign quickly fell
       apart. He is reputed to have lost his mind, and abdicated not long after.
       The war dragged on another twenty years, ending in stalemate.

BOOK 10

10.2   Bromius ('Roaring') was an epithet of Dionysus.

10.18 The name Gobrys is not otherwise found, 'but Gōbryas was a well-
       known Persian name' (Gow, *Further Greek Epigrams*).

10.19 Gow and Page (1960) reckon it a fair bet that 'Lucius' is the
       L. Calpurnius Piso who patronized Crinagoras and Antipater (see
       e.g. 10.25).

10.20 There is absolutely a double entendre in 'business'.

10.25 The occasion is probably Piso's voyage east as Augustus' new governor
       of Pamphylia in Asia Minor in 13 BC.

10.43 Greek letters were also numbers (see note on 6.321), and 7, 8, 9, and 10
       are respectively zeta, eta, theta, and iota. Read as a word, the numbers
       of those hours spell out ZĒTHI—'live!'. The time for after-work
       enjoyment is the evening, so the poem's 'six hours' cannot be the first
       six hours of the Roman day; they would only bring us to noon (see note
       on 11.44).

10.44 Here begins a long sequence by Palladas, whose poems dominate the
       remainder of the book. The poet is making a bilingual pun on the Latin
       honorific *Domine* ('Lord') and the Greek *domenai*, 'to give'.

10.55 The quoted line is from Homer, and is spoken by the disguised
       Odysseus to his wife, Penelope, when first they meet again after twenty
       years apart; she does not yet know who he is.

10.64 The unnamed addressee is male; perhaps a disgraced politician?

10.82 *Hellēn*, 'Greek', was by the fourth century a synonym for 'pagan'.

BOOK 11

11.19 Greeks held that only barbarians drank wine with no water in it, but
       Strato is calling for his to be mixed very strong; it can be watered down
       further once he is dead. Deucalion is the Greek Noah; forewarned by
       his father Prometheus that Zeus would drown mankind, he built an ark
       in which he and his wife Pyrrha saw out the flood. After the waters
       receded, the pair threw stones—the 'bones' of the earth—over their
       shoulders to repopulate the world with a new race of humans.

11.23 After his death, King Minos of Crete (he of the Labyrinth and Minotaur)
       became one of the three judges of the dead, alongside Aeacus and
       Rhadamanthus.

11.29   Compare Scythinus at 12.232.

11.39   Macedonius tells his slaves to get rid of yesterday's cups because the girl is rumoured to perform oral sex, which was believed to contaminate the mouth. The theme is common in Martial. Compare 11.155.

11.41   Philodemus calls his thirty-seven years *selides*, columns of writing in a papyrus book-roll. When a reader finished an ancient book they rewound it to the beginning, ready to be read again; but at the end of the book of a person's life, there is nothing left to rewind. Philodemus asks the Muses to write Xanthippe into his life story as the *korōnis* to his youthful passions. A *korōnis* was a symbol inserted in the left-hand margin of a text to mark its end, or (as here) the end of a major section. Compare Meleager at 12.257.

11.43   Prometheus moulded humans out of earth and water.

11.44   Philodemus invites his wealthy patron to attend a feast that is none the worse for being humble, while frankly hinting that he would not mind being in a position to entertain more lavishly. Epicureans celebrated the birthday of their founder, Epicurus, not just on the twentieth day of his birth month (February) but every month. Romans divided day and night into twelve hours each, with sunrise and sunset as the termini; the hours of daylight were therefore longer in summer (compare 11.405) than in winter. By inviting Piso to turn up after 'nine', Philodemus is telling him to come when the day has moved three-quarters of its way towards sunset. This was a conventional time to be settling in for dinner: 'the ninth [hour] commands us to hit the dining-couches piled with cushions', writes Martial (4.8). Sows' udders were a delicacy: the Roman cookbook of Apicius gives a recipe (7.1.251, also good for wombs) and suggests making *patina*, a kind of lasagne, with the leftovers (4.2.129–30). Phaeacia is the blessed land that hosted Homer's Odysseus before the last leg of his voyage home to Ithaca.

11.70   Twelve was the minimum age for a girl to marry under Roman law; for boys it was fourteen. To marry so young was rare, though.

11.80   Statues of athletes normally bore inscriptions celebrating their subjects' victories over their rivals, but Apis' statue is erected *by* his fellow boxers, who are delighted to be matched against so feeble an opponent.

11.84   In the punchline the useless pentathlete declares himself *pentatri-azomenos*, 'five times threed'. An ancient wrestler won his match by forcing his opponent to the floor three times. In time, the technical term acquired wider metaphorical use to mean beating an opponent more generally.

11.102 The hyperbolically thin *leptos* is a standard figure of fun in Lucillian scoptic epigram. Compare Martial 3.98: 'Want to know how skinny your arse is, Sabellus? It's so skinny you can fuck people in the arse with it.'

11.121   All the epigrams from 11.112 to 126 are on lethally incompetent doctors. Falling ill was often a death sentence, so patients were right to worry. Compare 11.257.

11.133   The instruments Eutychides ('Son of Good Fortune') ordered burned upon his pyre are citharas, seven-stringed instruments usually translated as 'lyres'. The word is the same as our 'guitar'.

11.134   Lucillius warns Heliodorus that he cannot beat him at literary trivia. The line he quotes is from Homer, *Iliad* 6.143, spoken by Diomedes to Glaucus.

11.135   The 'Marcus' of this poem could be a dig at Lucillius' younger contemporary M. Valerius Martialis, i.e. Martial, who leaves us several literary epitaphs for dead boys (e.g. 3.19; 6.29; 7.38 and 96). Martial wrote in Latin, and 11.312 quotes a line from 'Marcus' in Greek, but the make-believe dead boy of that poem bears a Roman name as well, Maximus.

11.139   Zēnonis' programme of study is full of double entendres: 'figures' (*schēmata*) are figures of speech, such as metaphor and hyperbole, but also sexual positions. Martial enjoys a broadly similar play on words at 11.19: 'You ask why I don't want to marry you, Galla? You're so well spoken; and my cock so often conjugates improperly.'

11.141   Lucillius' lawyer has a simple case to argue but cannot help grandstanding with famous rhetorical examples from Greek history. Othryades was the sole Spartan survivor of the Battle of the 300 Champions; see note on 7.741. Martial wrote a superior Latin imitation of this epigram (6.19) that has the lawyer declaiming similarly irrelevant anecdotes from early Roman history: 'but you're holding forth on Carrhae and the Mithridatic War and the treacherous Punic Menace . . . Postumus, can we get to the bit about my three little goats?'

11.155   Cynic philosophers were ascetics who publicly denounced their society's vices; this one is a hypocrite who hides his own guilty secret, that he enjoys performing oral sex. Compare 11.39 and (for instance) Martial 3.80.

11.216   Lucillius shames Cratippus as a *cinaedus* (also called *pathicus*). Ancient male sexuality was meant to be active and penetrative; it was fine for a man to chase after boys romantically and sexually within proper limits, but unacceptable for him to submit sexually to another male. There is little to no space within this ideology for what we would term gay relationships between consenting adults. See, for instance, Martial 2.51, 4.48, and 12.42; and compare his 12.35, which ups the ante on this very epigram.

11.221   This epigram and the two that follow (11.222–3) denounce men who perform oral sex, an act seen as passive and degrading. Compare, for instance, Martial 1.77; 2.89; 3.28, 80, and 83; 9.4 and 67; 11.45 and 66; 12.35.

11.222 The Greek anagram is exact: the personal name *Kheilon* has the same
       letters as *leikhōn*, 'licking'. The fictional target of this poem is given
       a comically inappropriate name: Chilon of Sparta was one of the Seven
       Sages (see note on 9.366), famous for stern morality and good sense.
       As in 11.39 and 155, and in this poem's immediate neighbours, 11.221
       and 223, performing oral sex is represented as a shameful perversion.

11.223 The target of this poem must be the famous sophist Favorinus of
       Arles (second century AD), a friend of Plutarch and Herodes Atticus.
       According to Philostratus' *Lives of the Sophists* he was born a eunuch.

11.235 Richard Porson had Demodocus' paradoxes in mind when he wrote his
       epigram of 1836: 'The Germans in Greek | Are badly to seek; | Not
       five in five-score, | But ninety-five more,— | All, save only Hermann,
       | And Hermann's a German.'

11.257 Martial 6.53 is a version of this: 'In his dreams, he caught sight of
       Dr Hermocrates.' The names are apt ones for professional healers,
       of whom Hermes was the divine patron. Amulets were frequently worn
       to ward off the evil eye that brought disease and misfortune.

11.269 A mock-inscription on the Colossus of the Sun from which the adjacent
       Flavian Amphitheatre later acquired the name by which it is popularly
       known, 'Colosseum'. The Emperor Commodus (whose *praenomen* was
       Lucius) had ordered that it be modified into a portrait of himself as the
       reincarnation of Hercules, complete with club, and bearing a statement
       of his own gladiatorial victories (Cassius Dio 73.22).

11.291 Palladas perhaps has in mind Martial's condemnation of a cheap
       slanderer at 10.3 and 10.5.

11.310 Beeswax and honey had cosmetic uses. Greek rouge was orchil,
       extracted from a coastal lichen.

11.328 A squalid sexual parody of the tripartition of the cosmos by Zeus,
       Hades, and Poseidon at *Iliad* 15. 187–93. The sea, Hades, and Olympus
       stand here for vaginal, anal, and oral penetration respectively. A copy
       of the poem found on papyrus at Oxyrhynchus gives 'Didymarchus'
       instead of Cleobulus; perhaps a real-life Didymarchus altered the text
       to write himself into the fantasy.

11.381 Palladas' original plays feebly on the similarity of the words for bridal
       chamber (*thalamos*) and death (*thanatos*).

11.384 Monk, *monachos*, does indeed begin by meaning 'single' or 'solitary'.

11.418 The addressee's nose is so big it will make a good gnomon, throwing its
       shadow on the dial of his teeth to mark the time of day.

BOOK 12

12.2 In making his case for erotic epigram Strato echoes, or is echoed
      by, poems by Martial that reject themes of mythological violence
      (e.g. 4.49, '*my* Muse doesn't swell and strut in the trailing robe of

Tragedy'; 10.4, 'my page smells human'); and that give fair warning of racy content (e.g. 1.4, 'lay aside that stern look'). Itys' mother Procne killed him to punish his father Tereus for raping her sister, Philomela. The gods turned Procne and her sisters into birds so that they could escape Tereus; Procne became a nightingale.

12.4 The closing words are *ton d'apameibomenos*, 'And in reply to him', a frequent formula in Homer. A boy of twelve catches Strato's eye, by his account deliberately, in 12.205.

12.21 'The jealous': 'hairs' (Paton).

12.43 Callimachus' punchline plays on the similarity of the words for 'fair' and 'another': he calls Lysanias *kalos, kalos*, but is interrupted by his own echo telling him *allos*.

12.44 Quails, like cocks, were prized as fighting birds.

12.59 At 12.178, Strato develops Meleager's motif.

12.108 'Acratus': 'The name means "unwatered wine"' (Paton). Compare Strato at 11.19. The lovers of the *Boyish Muse* are intoxicated with boys.

12.125 The *chlamys*, a short wool cloak, was the characteristic garb of ephebes, young men of eighteen to twenty years in age. Grown men wore a heavier cloak, the *chlaina* or *himation*.

12.168 The final pentameter does not connect with what it follows; perhaps two lines are missing. *Nanno* and *Lyde* were works by Mimnermus (seventh century BC) and Antimachus (fourth to third century BC) respectively, named after the women they loved; Mimnermus is 'the lover's friend' because he was held to have invented erotic elegy. Mnēmosyne was the goddess of memory.

12.175 Tiresias, the famous seer, was blind (see note on 9.606); Tantalus' punishment in Tartarus, the portion of the Underworld reserved for the worst criminals, was forever to be unable to eat and drink the delicious fruit and cool waters that were just beyond his reach. This is the origin of our word 'tantalize'.

12.185 Strato and Diphilus cannot touch boys who wear the *toga praetexta*, white with a purple border: it signifies that they are junior Roman citizens. Any attempt to seduce them will be harshly punished.

12.200 Martial's epigrams about his sexual tastes are consciously in dialogue with Strato's, whether addressing boys—'I only want struggling kisses; kisses I've seized' (5.46), 'What if you gave me all ⟨your kisses⟩, without holding back?' (3.65)—or girls: 'Galla, tell me "No"; love stales unless its joys bring pain. But, Galla, don't say "No" for very long' (4.38). Compare Strato at 12.203.

12.202 Zētes and Calaïs were the flying sons of Boreas, the North Wind, and shipmates of Jason on his quest for the Golden Fleece.

12.208 Strato calls his book a *biblidion*, the diminutive form of *biblos*, just as Martial calls his own books *libelli*, 'little books'.

12.209 In line 2 of the Greek, Strato entreats the boy not to be a *paidion* (a little boy) out of an *agelē*, a 'herd' of boys who go around together. In Sparta of old, the *agelai* had been the military-style units in which boys were raised and trained: see Plutarch, *Life of Lycurgus* 16.

12.242 A dirty joke based around Homer's habitual epithet for Dawn, 'rosy-fingered' (*rhododactulos*). As so often in Book 12, the point is how quickly late adolescence steals a boy's charms. Just the other day (*prōēn*) Alcimus' penis was small, which Greek men considered cute and sexy; but now it is huge (*rhodopēchus*, 'rosy-forearmed'), which ends his attractiveness as boyfriend material and turns him into a figure of mockery. It helps to know that the 'finger' (*dactulos*), which in practice meant the finger-joint, was the smallest Greek unit of measurement; twenty-four dactyls made a cubit (*pēchus*), the length from fingertip to elbow.

12.254 Martial frequently flatters Domitian as a living god, and admires his good taste and ample resource in collecting beautiful young men: his Jupiter (9.36) notes to Ganymede that 'our Caesar has a thousand cupbearers who look like you. His whole vast palace teems with gorgeous hunks.' I am confident that Strato too is courting Domitian's patronage.

12.256 The poems that come down to us as *AP* 12.256–7 were Meleager's conclusion to his *Garland*. He opened his *Garland* with a verse preface (now found in the fourth book of the Anthology) that listed the poets whose epigrams he had woven into it alongside his own; he now begins to close it with a complementary list, of the boys whose attractiveness inspired the poems he himself contributed. Myiscus was especially inspirational—see in this selection 12.23, 59, 94, 154, 159, and 167; for Diodorus, see 12.94 and 109.

12.257 The end of a work of literature was marked by a marginal flourish, a *korōnis* (compare Philodemus 11.41); this poem gives it voice.

12.258 This was Strato's *korōnis*, riffing on the one Meleager had written a century or so earlier, see 12.257.

BOOK 13

13.7 Lyctus was a city of Crete, but Sarapis or Serapis was a syncretic Graeco-Egyptian deity promoted by the Ptolemies; presumably Menoetas is celebrating the end of a successful career as a mercenary in that dynasty's service. Hesperis was an ancient Cyrenean foundation on the coast of Libya; it is now Benghazi.

13.9 Chian and Lesbian wines aged well and were prized by Greek and Roman connoisseurs.

13.11 Dorieus was exiled from Rhodes in the early years of the Peloponnesian War along with other members of his aristocratic family; we find him commanding Thurian ships on the Spartan side at Thucydides 8.35.

We know from Thucydides and Pausanias (6.7.1) that he was several times Olympic champion in the *pankration*, a mixed martial art in which practically any form of attack was allowed.

13.16 Cynisca (her name means 'Puppy'), sister of King Agesilaus, sponsored the chariot team that won at Olympia in 396 BC and again in 392. Pausanias (3.8.1) tells us 'she was exceedingly ambitious to succeed at the Olympic games . . . After Cynisca other women, especially women of Lacedaemon, have won Olympic victories, but none of them was more distinguished for their victories than she' (trans. W. H. S. Jones, Loeb Classical Library, 1918). The marble statue-base from which an unknown Hellenistic scholar copied this inscription can still be seen at Olympia.

13.19 Nicoladas was victorious at most of the famous Panhellenic festivals (Pythian, Isthmian, Panathenaic, and Nemean) and at more minor and local events as well. At Pellana or Pellēne in Achaea, the prizes for victory were woollen cloaks; 'Lycaeus' is Mount Lycaeus in Arcadia, the setting for the Lycaean Games dedicated to Zeus and Pan; and Tegea's games, the Alaiea, honoured the local goddess Alea. The Delphinian Games on Aegina were held in their month of Delphinius, in honour of Apollo. The Megarian Games featured a kissing contest, mentioned in Theocritus (*Idyll* 12).

BOOK 14

14.1 '*Solution:* 28 (14+7+4+3)' (Paton). The puzzle is sometimes attributed to Metrodorus, a grammarian and mathematician of late antiquity. Theano of Croton is, depending on one's source, the student, wife, or daughter of Pythagoras.

14.5 '*Answer:* Smoke' (Paton). The Greek *korē*, 'girl', was also the word for the pupil of the eye.

14.8 Modern dice carry the same distribution of spots as ancient ones: the face with six spots is opposite to that with one spot, and so on.

14.9 '*Answer:* Andromache. Achilles, father of her second husband, Pyrrhus, killed [her first husband] Hector, Pyrrhus killed [Hector's father] Priam, Paris killed Achilles, and Achilles killed her father Eetion' (Paton, and thank heavens for him).

14.13 '*Solution:* Zethus weighed twelve minae, Amphion eight' (Paton). Another puzzle devised or collected by Metrodorus. For Zethus and Amphion, see note on 3.7. The mina is a very ancient unit of weight, going back to the Sumerians; the Athenian definition was 100 drachmae, each drachma being about 4.5 grams, making one mina less than half a kilogram. The weight of the mina crept upwards in the Hellenistic and Roman periods but Zethus and Amphion still declare themselves to be unrealistically light.

14.14 '*Answer:* The double flute. The sailors are the fingers' (Paton), and the ships are the hands; the musician is the helmsman.

14.30 The answer is the lyre, called the *chelys* (tortoise) because Hermes made the first lyre by hollowing out a tortoise and fitting its shell with strings and two ram's horns. The strings ended at a wooden bridge fitted between the protruding horns.

14.38 '*Answer:* Eteocles and Polynices, the sons of Oedipus' (Paton) and brothers of Antigone and Ismene. The mother is probably Euryganeia, the second wife attributed to Oedipus in variants of his myth in which the incestuous nature of his marriage to Jocasta was discovered quickly, before they could have children together. As famously told in the epic Theban Cycle and in Aeschylus' *Seven Against Thebes*, Eteocles and Polynices led rival armies against each other in a terrible war for the throne vacated by Oedipus, culminating in a duel in which each brother killed the other. The implication of this poem is that Euryganeia committed suicide on hearing the news.

14.56 The answer is a mirror.

14.65 On the riddle posed by the boys, see the note on 7.1.

14.67 The Delphic Oracle told Laius, King of Thebes, that his newborn son would grow up to kill him and marry his wife, so he abandoned the baby to die on Mount Cithaeron; but a shepherd saved it, and the boy grew up to fulfil the prophecy unknowingly. He was Oedipus.

14.69 Lycurgus was the half-legendary lawgiver who gave Sparta its 'mixed' constitution, combining what the Spartans considered the best elements of monarchy and oligarchy with a radical social equality more usually associated with democracy.

14.78 Part of a long sequence in Book 14 of oracles from Herodotus' *Histories*. This is from his account (1.67) of the wars between Sparta and Tegea. The Spartans, who kept losing battles, 'sent emissaries to Delphi to ask which god they should propitiate to start winning the Tegean War, and the Pythia replied that they had to bring the bones of Orestes the son of Agamemnon back home. They could not discover Orestes' grave, however, so they sent emissaries again, this time to ask the god to tell them where Orestes was buried' (trans. Robin Waterfield for Oxford World's Classics). This epigram was the Pythia's reply. It baffled them, but a clever Spartan called Lichas, visiting Tegea, happened to visit a blacksmith who told him he had found a coffin of prodigious size. Lichas realized the 'winds' were the blacksmith's bellows, the 'strike and counter-strike' were his hammering upon the anvil, and the 'misery' was the suffering that iron weapons bring to the world.

14.79 This too is from the first book of the *Histories* (1.85). The son was mute from infancy, and Croesus sent to the oracle to ask whether his condition might be treated. The son finally cried out when Cyrus captured Croesus' capital of Sardis and Croesus himself came under attack in his palace.

14.83 This and the following are from *Histories* 4.155–9. Battus came to the Pythia seeking a cure for his stammer, and was instead sent to found

Cyrene. His first colony was on an island off the coast; when it ran into difficulties and he approached the oracle again he was sternly reminded of Apollo's orders, see 14.84–5. The poet Callimachus claimed descent from Battus: see 7.525 and note.

14.93   The Athenians sought advice from the Delphic oracle in the aftermath of Thermopylae (480 BC; epitaphs for the dead in that battle are at 7.248 and 249). This oracle, as famously interpreted by Themistocles (at Herodotus 7.141), persuaded the Athenians to trust the 'wooden wall' of their warships. The result was the allied Greeks' victory over Xerxes' fleet at Salamis, after which Xerxes withdrew to Persia, leaving the conduct of his campaign to a subordinate. The following year (479), a Spartan-led force conclusively defeated the remaining Persian land forces at Plataea (7.251 and 253, in this selection). In myth, Pallas was the daughter of Triton, son of Poseidon. As she was fighting a mock-battle with Athena, Zeus distracted her, causing her death; Athena took the title 'Pallas' in her memory.

14.101 '*Answer:* The year, months, days, and nights' (Paton).

14.102 Enquiring after Homer's origins was a familiar pastime among keen readers such as Hadrian; compare, for instance, 16.299.

14.115 Constantine established his New Rome at Byzantium, founded on the western shore of the Hellespont by Byzas of Megara in 657 BC.

14.126 '*Solution:* He was a boy for 14 years, a youth for 7, at 33 he married, at 38 he had a son born to him who died at the age of 42. The father survived him for 4 years, dying at the age of 84' (Paton). Book 14 has several sequences of arithmetical epigrams written or compiled by one Metrodorus (see note on 14.1); the last and longest runs from 14.116 to 146.

14.132 '*Answer:* 6/23 of a day' (Paton). They eyeball gushes and the mouth drools because Odysseus and his crew escaped Polyphemus' cave by plying him with wine and then blinding him.

14.147 Paton reckons the answer at 315,000 (7 × 50 × 900), but I take the Greek to mean that each spit carried fifty joints of meat, not that they carried one each; this makes for 15,750,000 Achaeans.

14.148 This so-called oracle neither predicts the future nor advises a course of action; it merely praises its subject. Mortal 'earth-born' peoples included the Thebans, who sprang from the dragon's teeth sown by Cadmus, but the meaning here must be the Giants, born of Gaia. Greek art often depicted the battle in which the Olympians defeated them, called the Gigantomachy. The Alemanni were a German tribal confederation who broke through the Roman frontier in AD 213 and settled around the Rhine. Julian was deputy ('Caesar') to the Western Emperor Constantius II ('Augustus') when he defeated the Alemanni in battle at Strasbourg (AD 357), following up with aggressive raiding that compelled them to sue for peace and offer tribute (AD 358). On his Persian campaign, see note on 7.747. Ctesiphon was the capital city of the

enemy, and Julian passed his thirtieth birthday besieging it; he was
dead within the month.

BOOK 15

15.4 The 'obelisk' of the manuscript's caption must be the pyramid-tomb
described in this poem, and in the four that follow it (15.5–8). The lake
is Lake Ascania (modern Lake Iznik), on which Nicaea lay. Ewen Bowie
identifies the tomb's owner as C. Cassius Sacerdos, a hereditary priest
of the imperial cult in the early first century AD, and member of an
eminent local family that would later produce the historian Cassius
Dio. Severa was his wife; in the poem that closes the sequence (15.8),
she boasts that her 'husband, son, character, and beauty will make me
more sung-of than Penelope of old'.

15.7 Ausonia is Italy, and the 'Ausonian Zeus' is the Emperor. Hadrian visited
Nicaea in AD 123, not long after the earthquake, and sponsored its
rebuilding; Sacerdos claims credit. Hadrian cannot have needed much
persuading: he did the same for Nicomedia around this time, and was
an indefatigable restorer of cities and monuments generally. None of
the epigrams gives the name shared by Sacerdos' father and son, but
Bowie ('Doing Doric') finds in 'Excellence' a clue that they were both
called Cassius Chrestus ('Worthy', 'Trusty'), a name well attested in
local inscriptions. The poetic gesture of holding back the name evokes
Callimachus' famous epitaph for his father, 7.525 in this selection.

15.9 Theodosius possesses all the individual excellences of the Homeric
heroes and avoids their defects. In some post-Homeric versions of the
Trojan War story, Polyxena is a daughter of Priam with whom Achilles,
the city's enemy, falls in love; Homer calls Teucer, half-brother of Ajax
and a great archer, illegitimate (*Iliad* 8.284); Achilles angrily denounces
Agamemnon as 'heavy with wine' (1.225). Pylos was the home of Nestor,
the wise old counsellor. Scholars follow Alan Cameron in taking the
author of these lines to be the Egyptian-born Flavius Taurus Seleucus
Cyrus, who was urban and praetorian prefect (AD 439) and then consul
(AD 441) at Byzantium under Theodosius; his popularity threatened
the Emperor and he was relegated to a provincial bishopric. Cameron
believes this epigram to be merely a fragment of a larger hexameter
poem praising Theodosius, written before Theodosius' daughter Eudoxia
gave him grandchildren (438–40); Christopher Kelly (*Theodosius II:
Rethinking the Roman Empire in Late Antiquity* (New York: Cambridge
University Press, 2013)) adds that this would place the poem early in
Cyrus' career, and that 'it may have been instrumental in bringing him
to the emperor's attention'.

15.15 Cameron has argued strongly that Constantine of Rhodes oversaw
the production of the manuscript of the *Palatine Anthology* in the gen-
eration after Cephalas, and suggests that Book 15 was added by him.
Leo VI died in 912, and was succeeded by his brother Alexander

(Emperor 912–13) and his son, Constantine VII 'Porphyrogenitus', sired out of wedlock but 'born in the purple' of the imperial bedroom suite (913–59).

15.19 In Achilles Tatius' novel *Leucippe and Clitophon* (on which see 9.203), Callisthenes, who desires Leucippe, decides to kidnap and rape her; by his or the author's understanding at least, under 'Byzantine law' the only penalty he will face is to be required to marry her, which is what he wants anyway, regardless of her consent (2.13.3). Supernatural punishment was not just meted out to men who took wives by abduction: in a first-century AD epigram by Apollonides (9.422, not in this selection), a widower defies the dying wish of his first wife by quickly marrying a second time. The first wife has her vengeance from beyond the grave when the roof collapses and kills the newly-weds on their wedding night.

15.32 Arethas, a contemporary of Cephalas and a reader of his Anthology (as demonstrated by Cameron), leaves us two epitaphs for Anna (15.32–3) and a third for a nun (15.34). In this one, Anna relates her sad life-story to the passer-by in first-person inscription.

15.37 These lines probably introduced Cometas' recension of Homer, which is itself lost. The Greek word for old age, *gēras*, is also the name for the old skin shed by a snake as it grows.

15.48 Faustinus' son was Constantine, the charioteer celebrated in 15.42–3. Faustinus (on whom see also 16.383) drove for the Green faction, his son for the Whites. 'Thus ever . . .' is a line from the *Odyssey* (17.218), spoken spitefully by the goatherd Melanthius to taunt the disguised Odysseus. One may wonder if the Byzantine mob nicknamed Uranius 'Pelops' not so much for his 'countless victories' but because the Pelops of myth cheated in his famous race to win the hand of Hippodamia. Pelops won, and the Peloponnese ('Isle of Pelops') still bears his name, but he incurred a curse that brought two generations of his family (Atreus and Thyestes, Agamemnon and Aegisthus) to bloody ruin.

BOOK 16

16.12 Paton titles this poem 'On a Statue of Pan', which sounds about right.

16.24 Milo of Croton, a Greek city in Calabria, won his first Olympic victory while still a boy and was men's champion at least five times thereafter, making him undefeated champion for at least twenty-four years. In later life, he led his fellow citizens to victory in battle against their neighbours, the Sybarites. Simonides was his contemporary. On the Greek Pisa, see note on 9.19.

16.26 Dirphys (modern Dirfi) is a mountain in Euboea; the Euripus is the strait that separates Euboea from the mainland. Simonides' epitaph is for the Athenians who fell in the two battles celebrated in 6.343, which was inscribed at Athens; see the note that accompanies that poem.

16.38   Paton suggests that Synesius won his victory against the forces of the
Sassanid Khosrow I, known to the Greeks as Chosroes, who invaded
the Byzantine Empire in 540. Synesius was no career soldier but a lit-
erary scholar who perhaps owed his victory to reading military manuals
of the kind described at 9.210; the Anthology preserves one of his own
epigrams, 16.267, coincidentally also celebrating a painted portrait.
Berytus was to enjoy the fruits of Synesius' victory only for another
decade; in 551 the city was devastated by an earthquake. Barbocallus
wrote its epitaph, 9.425.

16.61   The Nero of this poem is not the unwarlike emperor of AD 41–68, but
his great-grand-uncle, Tiberius Claudius Nero, born in 42 BC into
a branch of the Claudian family in which Nero was a traditional *cognomen*.
Tiberius went East with Agrippa in 20 BC to face down the Parthians,
and raided into Armenia, which became a buffer state between the super-
powers (and continued to give trouble: see note on 9.59). Subsequently
he campaigned against tribes in the Alps and Transalpine Gaul, con-
quering what is now Switzerland, and then repeatedly and successfully
in Germany. A likely occasion for this poem is his return to Rome in
7 BC, and his mother Livia, Augustus' wife, probably had a hand in
commissioning it. When Tiberius was in his late forties (AD 4) Augustus
reluctantly adopted him as his heir, at which point he took the name
Tiberius Julius Caesar. He succeeded Augustus as emperor (AD 14–37)
but was unpopular.

16.79   Of interest because both the attribution and the descriptive caption are
clearly wrong; they belonged to a completely different poem which
we must presume to have been lost, probably an epitaph like that by
Agathias (7.593).

16.80   Thomas has taken Callirhoe's portrait using the encaustic method, in
which the artist mixes pigments into melted beeswax and 'paints' the hot
mixture directly onto a wooden board. Many of the mummy-portraits
from the Fayum (see 7.565 and note) are encaustic. 'Byzantine Rome',
like 'New Rome' (14.115), is Constantinople.

16.82   'This attribution ⟨to Simonides⟩ is of course wrong, as the Colossus
was erected long after his time' (Paton). Eighty cubits would make
it more than thirty-six metres tall; most ancient sources say seventy,
which is still roughly as big as the Statue of Liberty. Erected in 280 BC,
it collapsed a few decades later, in 226.

16.100 Lysimachus was one of the less successful Successors to Alexander; his
heirs were murdered not long after his own death in battle (281 BC).

16.103 As penalty for the accidental slaying of a fellow Argonaut, the Delphic
Oracle commanded Heracles to spend a year in servitude to Omphale,
queen of Lydia. In the popular story related in Lucian's *Dialogues of the
Gods* (15), she took his lion-skin and club for herself, dressed him in
women's clothing, and made him do housework. Omphale eventually
freed him and they married, producing at least one son.

16.107 The part of the Aegean between the Eastern Cyclades and the coast of Asia Minor was called the 'Icarian Sea' because it was believed that Icarus had fallen to his death there, after flying too close to the sun and melting the wax that held the feathers of his artificial wings. The statue has been made using the lost-wax process, in which the figure is worked in wax, around which a clay mould is then formed; the mould is then heated so that the wax melts and drains away, leaving it empty to receive the molten bronze.

16.120 Alexander made Lysippus his official portraitist. He created a tousled, upward-gazing portrait type of which various versions and copies survive. We still see and imagine the great conqueror as Lysippus, and his employer, wanted us to.

16.135 This painting inspired a number of epigrams now in the Planudean Appendix (16.135–41 and 143). According to Pliny the Elder (*Natural History* 35.136), Julius Caesar put Timomachus' *Medea* and *Ajax* on public display in front of his Temple of Venus Genetrix (dedicated 46 BC) in the new Forum of Caesar. Timomachus was a contemporary artist whose picture of Medea's agonized indecision was probably inspired by Euripides' famous play.

16.150 The *Polyxena* was by Polygnotus, and was famous (Pausanias 1.22.6); Polyclitus was a sculptor (who, to complicate things further, did carve a *Hera*). The epigram is probably the work of an unknown Byzantine rather than Pollianus, a sharp literary critic of the second century who would be unlikely to make such a silly mistake. Polyxena was the youngest daughter of Priam and Hecuba, and the Greeks did not spare her: Neoptolemus (also called Pyrrhus), son of Achilles, sacrificed her on his father's grave, as related in Euripides' *Hecuba* and *Trojan Women*.

16.151 Dido rebuts the version of her story told by Virgil in the fourth book of his *Aeneid*. She calls the Latin poet 'chaste' (*hagnos*) because he was remembered as uninterested in pursuing women; his reputationally damaging 'lies' thereby mirror the lies that Phaedra told to save *her* reputation after her similarly chaste stepson Hippolytus rejected her sexual advances (the subject of Euripides' tragedy, *Hippolytus*). Martial reports Virgil (8.55) as instead romantically attracted to boys.

16.152 Echo herself, of course, was legendarily unlucky in love; the story of her thwarted desire for Narcissus is told in the third book of Ovid's *Metamorphoses*.

16.161 This poem and 16.168, 172, and 178 evoke the mythical beauty contest in which Pallas Athena, Hera, and Aphrodite attempted to sway Paris' judgement with bribes. Paris chose Aphrodite, who granted him the world's most beautiful woman, Helen. Thus began the war that destroyed his city, Troy.

16.178 Apelles' *Aphrodite Anadyomene* (fourth century BC) was antiquity's most famous painting; Roman descriptions of it probably inspired Botticelli's *Birth of Venus*.

16.184 Antipater wrote an epic to celebrate Piso's victory over the Bessi of southern Thrace, prefacing it with a dedicatory epigram that survives (*AP* 9.428, not in this selection). On Piso's mission to Thrace, see note on 6.335. The Bessi were Dionysus-worshippers and Piso surely brought home this statue as spoils of war. The god of wine will have found himself quite at home: Gow and Page (1960) note that Piso was a heavy drinker.

16.188 Boys had their bloom, and blooms stood for boys. Meleager opens his *Garland* with a verse in which he equates marjoram and hyacinth to his fellow pederastic poets Rhianus and Alcaeus, and the violet to his own poems; and closes it (12.256) by crediting as inspiration 'the blooms of boys that Aphrodite breathes upon'. Hermes was born in a cave on Mount Cyllene in Arcadia, and is often called 'Cyllenian'.

16.206 Thespiae was a great centre of the cult of Eros, and Praxiteles' marble statue of him (fourth century BC) was world-famous: Pausanias (9.27.3) relates that it was carried off to Rome by Caligula, sent back by Claudius, and taken again by Nero. According to the second-century sophist Athenaeus (*Deipnosophists* 590–1), not only Praxiteles' *Aphrodite of Cnidus* but also Apelles' *Aphrodite Anadyomene* (see 16.178, above) were modelled on Phryne, the great fourth-century courtesan.

16.213 The short composite recurve bow was the weapon of the Scythian horse archer.

16.217 Cyrus of Panopolis (early fourth century AD) composed 15.9 in this selection, an epigram or epic fragment that favourably compares the Emperor Theodosius to the heroes of Homer. At 7.9, Damagetus credits Orpheus with the invention of epic poetry, of which his mother, Calliope, became the patron Muse.

16.222 According to Pausanias (1.33.2–3), Phidias carved the statue of Nemesis at Rhamnous from a block of Parian marble that the Medes had brought with them for the trophy of what they believed to be their own inevitable victory. Phidias was an Athenian himself, so the 'skill' attested by Nemesis includes his own talent as a sculptor as well as the tactical brilliance of Miltiades at Marathon (see 16.232). Pliny the Elder (*Natural History* 36.5.4) says the statue was made by one of Phidias' pupils, Agoracritus. If he is right, then probably Pausanias was misinformed by a local guide, but the inclusion of Parmenion's poem in the *Garland* of Philip (mid-first century AD) shows that the attribution to Phidias was already current in Pliny's lifetime.

16.232 Miltiades was the architect of the Athenian victory at Marathon in 490 BC. According to Herodotus (6.105–6), the runner Phidippides, who had been sent to seek military aid from Sparta, was on his way back to Athens empty-handed when he encountered Pan on Mount Parthenion; the god instructed that the Athenians should offer him cult, and suggested that he would make it worth their while. Miltiades' dedication on the Acropolis expresses his gratitude for Pan's help in achieving victory.

16.236 In addition to his role as guardian of fishermen (as e.g. at 6.33 and 89), Priapus was the protector of orchards and gardens (e.g. 6.21 and 102). His statues often held a menacing billhook, and he always had a jutting erection with which he might sexually punish thieves. In 16.240, he strikes a bargain with one would-be scrumper; the 'fig' of the punchline is a sexual euphemism (see note following).

16.240 The fig at the poem's close is a sexual double entendre for a boy's anus; compare Martial 12.33 and 12.96.

16.267 The multitalented 'Eusebius' of the poem is not the famous Eusebius who in the early fourth century was Bishop of Caesarea, and we cannot know what his writings were: the Greek *logoi* could indicate proverbs, fables, speeches, or (as guessed here) histories.

16.269 On Paeon, see note on 6.337.

16.274 Oribasius was personal physician and friend to Julian 'the Apostate' (Emperor 361–3), and compiled for him two anthologies of passages from Galen and other great medical writers of the past; a little survives.

16.278 Anchises and Adonis were Aphrodite's two mortal lovers (not at the same time).

16.311 Oppian, a poet of the second century AD, wrote Greek epics on how to hunt (the *Cynēgetica*), trap birds (*Ixeutica*), and fish (*Halieutica*); the fishing poem survives, as does a separate *Cynēgetica* by a later Oppian or pseudo-Oppian.

16.324 The Elder Pliny (*Natural History* 35.36) names a Leontion as the partner of the philosopher Epicurus; Diogenes Laertius in his hostile *Life of Epicurus* dismisses her as a 'courtesan'. Neither credits her with ability as an artist.

16.335 Beginning here, a run of more than fifty poems (16.335–87) commemorates Byzantium's greatest charioteers. The majority (16.335–62) concern just one man, the Libyan-born Porphyrius (fifth to sixth centuries AD), also called Calliopas. He is 'the youngest of the drivers' in this poem, but he carried on racing into his fifties or sixties, and was the most successful charioteer of all time. The epigrams were genuine inscriptions: several have been found, cut into the bases of two monuments that were erected in Porphyrius' honour on the central *spina* of the circus. Alan Cameron deduces from the text of the Anthology that Porphyrius was awarded seven such monuments over the course of his career, and that they stood alongside monuments to four other racers. 'The Emperor' of the poem will be Anastasius I (AD 491–518).

INDEX

Authors of epigrams included in this volume are identified with an asterisk (*).

The Oxford World's Classics Website

www.worldsclassics.co.uk

- Browse the full range of Oxford World's Classics online
- Sign up for our monthly e-alert to receive information on new titles
- Read extracts from the Introductions
- Listen to our editors and translators talk about the world's greatest literature with our Oxford World's Classics audio guides
- Join the conversation, follow us on Twitter at OWC_Oxford
- Teachers and lecturers can order inspection copies quickly and simply via our website

www.worldsclassics.co.uk

American Literature

British and Irish Literature

Children's Literature

Classics and Ancient Literature

Colonial Literature

Eastern Literature

European Literature

Gothic Literature

History

Medieval Literature

Oxford English Drama

Philosophy

Poetry

Politics

Religion

The Oxford Shakespeare

A complete list of Oxford World's Classics, including Authors in Context, Oxford English Drama, and the Oxford Shakespeare, is available in the UK from the Marketing Services Department, Oxford University Press, Great Clarendon Street, Oxford OX2 6DP, or visit the website at www.oup.com/uk/worldsclassics.

In the USA, visit www.oup.com/us/owc for a complete title list.

Oxford World's Classics are available from all good bookshops. In case of difficulty, customers in the UK should contact Oxford University Press Bookshop, 116 High Street, Oxford OX1 4BR.